Ho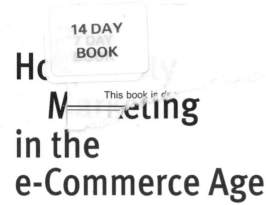 Marketing
in the
e-Commerce Age

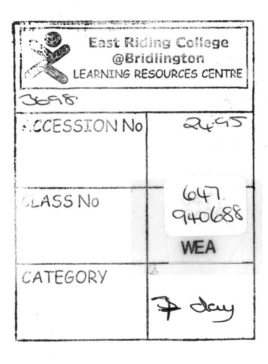

Cover images kindly supplied by, and reproduced with permission of, Crowne Plaza Hotel, Canberra ACT; Origin Pacific airline of New Zealand; Falls Farm of Tasmania; INDULA Safaris and Tours; David Sterling's IT Solutions

Hospitality Marketing in the

e-Commerce Age

SECOND EDITION

Neil Wearne and Kevin Baker

Pearson Education Australia
Unit 4, Level 2
14 Aquatic Drive
Frenchs Forest NSW 2086

www.pearsoned.com.au

Publisher: David Cunningham
Copy Editor: Ross Gilham, Ginross Editorial Services
Proofreader: Ross Gilham, Ginross Editorial Services
Cover, design, and typeset by: Lauren Statham, Alice Graphics

Printed in Malaysia

1 2 3 4 5 06 05 04 03 02

National Library of Australia
Cataloguing-in-Publication Data

Wearne, Neil.
    Hospitality marketing in the e-commerce age.

    New ed.
    Includes index.
    For tertiary students.
    ISBN 1 86250 511 X.

    1. Hospitality industry—Marketing. 2. Hotels—Marketing.
    3. Tourism—Marketing. 4. Restaurants—Marketing.
    5. Electronic commerce. I. Baker, Kevin, 1949– . II. Title.

647.940688

 An imprint of Pearson Education Australia

Contents

The Authors

The late Neil Wearne was the marketing specialist and lecturer at the Regency Hotel School in South Australia from 1989. In that time he developed marketing courses and lectured students in the Diploma of Business (Hospitality). He combined his extensive experience in marketing management with his flair for communication to write a number of texts for students of hospitality marketing. Neil's talents in the areas of human behaviour, communication, illustration, and writing produced a focus on the practical aspects of marketing which students understood. He maintained involvement with the hospitality industry and was able to inspire students with reference to current hospitality business practices. He maintained a dynamic marketing perspective, and is remembered by colleagues and students for his vital energy and innovative approaches to learning.

Dr Kevin Baker is professor of Hospitality Management at the International University of Applied Sciences, Bonn, Germany. Previously, he was senior lecturer at the Australian International Hotel School, Canberra. He has had appointments as visiting professor at universities in China and Indonesia, as well as a visiting fellowship at the Australian National University. Kevin was raised in his family's hotel, and has held senior executive positions in the hospitality industry, including six years as chief executive officer of assisted-accommodation properties. His PhD from the University of Sydney examined the role of the Royal Exchange as a market and meeting place of commerce. In addition to approximately twenty articles on issues affecting hospitality, he has also written *Project Evaluation and Feasibility Analysis* (2000, Hospitality Press) and *Internal Control and Fraud Prevention* (1999, Hospitality Press), as well as co-authoring *Hospitality Management—an Introduction* (2001, Hospitality Press) with Dr Jeremy Huyton.

Acknowledgments

Thanks to David Cunningham for his renewed faith in the authors' work, and also to Ross Gilham for his expertise in editing. Special thanks to Justin Wearne and the Wearne family for being prepared to allow Neil Wearne's work to be revised and added to. Also to Grahame Latham, Head, Regency Hotel School, who wrote the outline biography of Neil Wearne. Dr Baker also acknowledges the contribution and support of Jane, Paul, Mary, Kevin, Angeline, Jim, and Penny.

Introduction

This book is for students of hospitality—which means that it is primarily a textbook for people seeking a tertiary qualification in the subject of hospitality marketing. But it is also a book for those in business who want to add to their knowledge of marketing. It is entitled *Hospitality Marketing in the e-Commerce Age* because the emphasis is upon marketing hospitality, while recognising that the marketplace has been fundamentally changed in the twenty-first century by the advent of e-commerce and its marketing tools.

There are thirty chapters, each one covering a topic of marketing. This enables a course to be structured around this work by creating either two semesters of fifteen lessons (with a session of revision) or three semesters of ten lessons.

Every endeavour has been made to make it an easy book to read with a minimal requirement for referral to a lecturer or other sources of information. Operators and executives will discover that in many areas of marketing, especially with regard to e-commerce, fresh insights are put forward that will materially assist them in the management of their establishments.

The teaching approach taken in this book is to direct the decisions concerning marketing strategies towards what happens *to and for the customers*. The objective is to build a customer base by constantly improving the experiences of customers at the point of sale. This approach is fundamentally different from the operators of establishments who consider marketing as primarily concerned with *sales and advertising*. This book shifts the major emphasis of hospitality marketing onto building a business from the *inside*—by word-of-mouth (communicated through various means, including the Internet)—rather than relying mostly on the endeavours of *outside* promotion.

Marketing is not like mathematics. There are very few true absolutes. Whereas in mathematics a hundred people can add up the same set of numbers and should all arrive at the same answer, a hundred marketing people could be given a mass of data and arrive at a hundred different marketing plans. Each plan might appear to be as workable as another. In practice, however, the chances are that twenty will be successful, another thirty will provide a mediocre result, and the remaining fifty will fail (some more quickly than others). There is a limited certainty in the implementation of a marketing strategy because its success or otherwise is reliant upon the reactions of people, singly and in large numbers, who form a market. The unpredictability of human behaviour means no one can be sure what people will do in a given set of circumstances. You can assess only what is most likely to happen—based on how the market has reacted before. Upon this history of behaviour the theories of marketing are based.

Marketing is a series of decisions—a process—and a step-by-step disciplined process is the best way to capitalise on an opportunity or overcome a difficulty. Without this discipline, you can overlook, and thus fail to consider, some aspect of the process. The subject is learnt by an examination of common practice and a study of the theories that have evolved from the experiences of others over time. The use of e-commerce fits into this study of the theories and practices of marketing, because e-commerce is properly one more tool (although an extremely powerful one) that can be used by the marketer—rather than being an end in itself.

To assist the student and the practitioner of hospitality marketing, this book contains lists and procedures that can be referred to, or memorised, to help in deciding what to do when planning customer outcomes.

Throughout this book the subject of marketing is taught by stating the theory behind the topic (or defining its meaning), explaining how the theory is applied, giving examples, and providing lists of options for application of the theory.

Chapter 1

The Marketing Function

Aims of this chapter

The aims of this chapter are:
- to introduce the subject of marketing, its main functions, and its role in society;
- to explain marketing terms; and
- to introduce the first steps of the marketing planning process.

Putting marketing into perspective

Marketing should be an easy subject to understand. Everywhere we look there is evidence of marketing activity—media advertising, advertising signs, delivery vans, shops and retailers of all descriptions, factories, personal services and, of course, hotels and restaurants in profusion. These are all visible indications of people busily marketing their places and their products for money and profit.

Fundamentally, marketing is about attracting customers and selling products to them. The complexities of the subject arise in building or expanding a market, and from the necessity in an open market to compete against others for the available business. These complexities require the owner of a business to have merchandise that has maximum sales appeal, prices that offer value, and additional services (such as delivery and credit) that make it easier for customers to make their purchases.

For the operators of a hospitality establishment, marketing is the means by which they can turn the basics of food, beverages, and lodgings into desirable products by adding value through service and presentation. The product offered to consumers by the hospitality industry cannot be touched—it is *intangible*. And if the service is not used immediately it becomes available—it is instantly *perishable*. Once the night has passed, the hotel cannot sell accommodation to a guest; nor can a restaurant provide extra meals next day for the seats that were empty the night before.

Being a good marketer is arguably the most important skill to have in business. If there are no sales, there is no business. If there is no business, other skills become redundant.

Marketing can be defined as the process of creating, or making available, products and services that satisfy market needs and wants. The marketing process involves careful planning by management to allow for a large number of market variables. All of these market variables are caused by the separate requirements and preferences of people who, when grouped together, comprise a market.

The starting-point in marketing planning is always people and their needs and wants. Other variables that management must consider include the financial and human resources at its disposal, and the external influences that might not be within its ability to control—such as government actions and economic change.

Among the many important factors that have to be considered by management in the marketing process are the actions of competitors. Other establishments in a given market are constantly endeavouring to increase their shares of the available business. Financial loss or profit for a business owner depends on the success or otherwise of the moves and counter-moves made in a competitive marketing environment.

In many industries, and in the hospitality industry in particular, the term 'marketing' is often used to refer to selling and advertising. But marketing is not just selling and advertising. This is marketing in what we might call the 'minor sense'. These are important marketing activities, but they are only the communication components of marketing. Effective marketing in the 'major sense' requires planning from the initial conception of a product right through to its delivery to the customers, and thereafter to the retention of the customers. Although selling and advertising are the noticeable aspects of marketing, they are only part of a total planning process. In the *minor* sense, selling a second-hand piece of furniture involves a marketing function. In the *major* sense, marketing involves, for example, the distribution and after-sales service of a range of motor vehicles nationally and internationally through a distribution-and-dealership network.

An historical perspective

Marketing is as old as civilisation. It is the origin of business. It started with simple bartering and then evolved into the centralised exchange process of a town market. Before long, trade—the exchange of goods and services for money—between cities and countries began. This resulted in large numbers of merchants venturing to distant places and across oceans in search of new markets and opportunities for trade. Towns, roads, sea lanes, train lines, and air routes have arisen as a result of trade and its movement of goods to markets and buyers to markets.

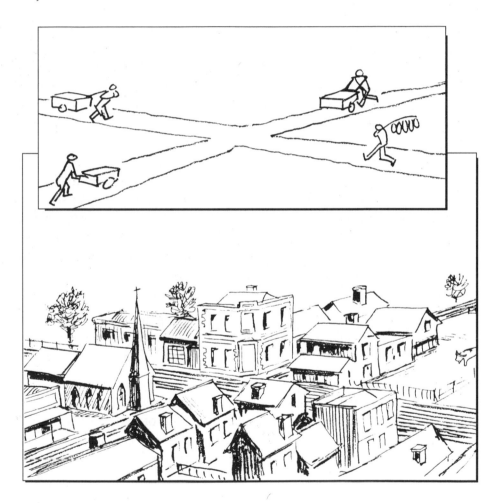

Figure 1.1 Many towns all over the world have arisen from trade, usually at the intersection of major roads. An hotel was often the first substantial building to be erected.

Authors' presentation

The growth of hospitality, arguably the oldest professional activity, has always been tied to the expansion of business, tourism, and travel. Providing travellers with a place to stay and eat is mentioned in the earliest writings of people, and the concept of an hotel (a 'public house' or inn) predates the writing of the Bible. The Egyptians, Greeks, and Romans built pleasure and tourist resorts that rivalled today's massive complexes in style and grandeur, if not in modern appliances.

In many ways, therefore, civilisation functions as a consequence of trade and marketing. The successors to the traders or merchants of the past—who searched for and found solutions to people's needs and wants—are now called 'marketers'. In the past 150 years, the process of developing goods and services that can be produced and sold for profit has become a sophisticated business practice referred to as 'marketing'. Most markets do not just happen—they are brought into being by those who understand how people think. Good marketers have an appreciation of the fact that most people want to improve their ways of life, and marketers respond to this by creating products and services to help them achieve their aspirations.

Essentially, 'hospitality' means kindness in welcoming strangers or guests. In earlier common usage, the word 'hospitality' had this sense—a far wider meaning than it tends to have in common usage today. It had a more definite sense of conveying the bestowal of friendship and trust. But this older sense of 'hospitality' has not been entirely lost. The *Concise Oxford Dictionary* maintains this sense when it defines 'hospitality' as 'the friendly and generous reception and entertainment of guests or strangers'.[1] Perhaps ironically, the word comes just after 'hospitalism' in the dictionary—which is 'the adverse effects of a prolonged stay in hospital'! One definition of hospitality is:[2]

> A commercial contract to enter into a service relationship that involves supplying the amenities, comforts, conveniences, social interactions, and experiences of shelter and entertainment that a guest or customer values.

These days, the services and products offered to the modern traveller by hospitality establishments cater for every human comfort. The hospitality business is a massive industry encompassing all forms of transport, tourism, accommodation, dining, drinking, entertainment, recreation, and games. The major proportions of the world's hospitality industries are in Europe (45%) and North America (30%). The Asia–Pacific region accounts for 13%, and Africa and Latin America contribute the remaining 12%.

The tourism and hospitality industry is an important industry for Australia. The industry directly employs approximately 700 000 people, and indirectly employs 350 000 more—approximately one-eighth of the labour force. The tourism industry makes up approximately 4.5% of gross domestic product

(GDP),[3] with a financial impact of AUS$58 billion according to the *Tourism Satellite Account* released in 2000, the first official study of how the industry relates to Australia's national accounts. International tourists made up 21% of the industry's contribution to GDP in 1997/98, and the balance (79%) was generated by domestic tourism. There are estimates that, by 2030, there will be twenty million visitors a year to Australia, the equivalent of the nation's present population.[4] The World Travel and Tourism Council expects that, by 2010, travel and tourism will generate more than 250 million jobs worldwide.

Impact of hospitality marketing on society

A new project—an industry initiative or a real estate development—can be a huge boost to the prosperity of a city or state. Such projects usually involve finance, the production of a huge range of materials, and the employment of a large number of people. As these wage-earners spend their earnings, the stimulus to economic activity extends to the increased sale of food, cars, appliances, and so on. This is called the 'multiplier effect'.

An increase in tourism has a similar multiplier effect. The industry provides employment and economic growth through consumption and investment in infrastructure (such as hotels and airports), and also produces foreign exchange (that is, currencies other than the local currency). Foreign exchange brought into a country by the tourism industry is of importance because it is gained by domestic production and offsets current account deficits (that is, the difference between imports and exports). The tourism and hospitality sector of the world economy makes up approximately 12% of the world's GDP, employs 8% of all employees, and accounts for approximately 11% of capital investment through-out the world.[5] This makes the global tourism and hospitality industry one of the largest in the world in terms of employment and economic activity.

There are several forces driving the growth in world tourism. These include the expansion of many world economies due to the spread of technology, and the parallel growth in international trade relations. In addition, travel is becoming more affordable, and more people can afford to travel. The World Tourism Organization and the World Travel and Tourism Council have produced optimistic growth forecasts for world tourism (of 4% per year) as development spreads throughout the world and as new tourist destinations are publicised.

The provision of tourist facilities and hospitality establishments for a city or region is called its 'infrastructure'. The market demand for hospitality in a city or state determines the extent of its infrastructure and therefore how many hotels, motels, tourist resorts, restaurants, caravan parks, and so on are required.

The demand for hospitality changes as a result of government action, weather, business 'booms and busts', tourism fashions, special events, festivals, and building projects, or simply as a result of increased availability of money. Economic, political, and environmental change can quickly affect this volatile industry. Sudden changes in undersupply or oversupply of facilities can occur. The challenge for marketers is to meet each development as it occurs, and to maintain a viable customer base despite these changes.

Opportunism is seldom a sustainable basis for growth of hospitality. For example, during the 'Gold Rush' period in Australia (the middle-to-late nineteenth century), the wealth mined from the ground led to many huge towns mushrooming around the mining centres. Hotels were foremost among the new building developments. In some towns, hundreds of hotels were spawned, ranging from basic drinking taverns to opulent palaces. When the ore ran out and the mines died, most of the population left, leaving the majority of these hotels as interesting relics of a colourful past.

In the suburbs and small towns of Australia, and at many crossroads, there remain numerous small hotels, many dating back to the early days of European settlement. These are typically run by owners, rely on the bar trade, and are commonly referred to as 'pubs'. The names also date from the nineteenth century. It seems that almost every small town has a 'Royal Hotel' or a 'Commercial Hotel', or an 'Imperial Hotel'.

There are also small accommodation properties, often referred to as 'bed & breakfast' ('B&B') enterprises, that have developed in response to a growing demand. These can be found in suburban settings in larger popular resorts, but can also be rural-based. Usually a B&B is run by a family–owner, as an extension of a private home, and can have as few as two or three rooms available for guests.[6]

The hospitality industry must be realistic about the sudden swings in demand that can occur. Hospitality is a very dynamic business and every decade witnesses a shift in market demand for various types of accommodation and products. New trends in travel, tourism, and accommodation requirements have emerged. As the changes continue, the study of the hospitality business, as always, has to be based on why people travel, why certain destinations are preferred, and why certain types of accommodation and hospitality are in demand.

The world's tourism remains skewed towards the wealthier countries, with approximately 60% of the world's tourism industry distributed in Europe and 12% in North America, although other destinations and markets (such as China, Thailand, and Australia) continue to gather market share. Reflecting this distribution, the people who travel are mainly from the United States, the United Kingdom, Germany, France, and Japan.[7]

'Markets', 'market demand', and other definitions

Some of the main terms used in marketing require definition.

A *market* is a place of trade, or a group of people who have common needs and wants. The *Oxford English Dictionary* defines a market as ' . . . the trading opportunities provided by a particular group of people'. It defines marketing as 'the part of a business which controls the way that goods and services are sold'.[8]

Needs are basic human requirements—such as food, shelter, transport, money, security, and sex. *Wants* are the ways in which individual people prefer to satisfy these needs. For example, someone might *need* a vehicle to get to work and use for recreation, but that person might prefer (or *want*) a particular type and brand of motor car. Other people might want a bicycle or a motor bike.

For a hospitality business, a market is a group of people requiring a place to stay, eat, or drink. Because not everyone *wants* the same solution to their *need* for a product, there are many *submarkets*, and products are developed to satisfy the requirements of these submarkets. These submarkets are termed 'market segments'.

The size of a market is measured by the number of people who want a particular type of product or service to satisfy their needs. This is called 'market demand'. A coffee shop in a small suburban shopping centre, for example, has a small *market* and therefore there is limited *demand* for its services.

The differences in the wants and needs of each market segment can be a result of where people live, their ages, how they live, the sizes of their families, how much money they have to spend, their lifestyle preferences, what they want to achieve in life, peer-group pressure, and their attitudes towards the way in which a product performs or functions. The understanding of these differences is part of the planning process called 'market analysis', and the process of measuring the differences is covered by *demographics* (the science of population statistics) and *psychodynamics* or *psychographics* (the study of mental processes and forces).

What is a 'product'? Services are products. Ideas are products. Countries and cities are products. Even people can be products. Anything that can be marketed is a product, even if there is no profit motive. An hotel refers to everything it markets as a 'product' (or an 'outlet'). These products include bars, dining-rooms, room service, or valet service.

How do they make their money?

The hospitality industry consists of many different types of businesses, and each has its own means of producing income. The main types of businesses in the hospitality industry are hotels, motels, tourist resorts, holiday homes, guest houses, taverns, restaurants, bars, cafés, bistros, and coffee shops. There are also specialised tourism and hospitality areas of business. These include eco-tourism (sometimes called 'nature tourism'), farm tourism, heritage tourism, pilgrimage tourism, and so on. These areas are of growing importance and significance to the industry. Ecotourism has become a major focus of Australia's national tourism marketing efforts since at least 1994.[9]

All these styles of establishment have certain things in common—they all add value to their business activity by providing a place and a service for guests, and they all receive a fee in exchange. The difference between what it costs the hospitality establishment to provide the place and the service, and the fee received in return, is called 'profit'.

Rooms, bars, restaurants, valet services, shops, holiday packages, and so on are called 'products' or 'outlets' by the industry. Each product or outlet is expected to contribute to the hotel's income. They are therefore referred to as 'profit-earning centres'.

A star-rated hotel, resort hotel, or motel receives most of its income from its main product—which is room hire or accommodation. This usually represents approximately 60–65% of its total revenue. This is why an hotel's *occupancy rate* (the number of customers occupying beds) is of continuing concern to the management of a property.

Most hotels endeavour to achieve a 70% occupancy rate. This means that, on average throughout the year, 70% of available rooms should be occupied. Obviously, during some months, the percentage will be lower than average, and at other times it will be higher than average. Most rooms are hired for business reasons. (See Chapter 6, 'Customer mix percentages', page 75, for more on this.) Therefore, fewer rooms are occupied on weekends than on working days. One of marketing tasks of management is to fill the 'down periods' with customers to maintain the desired 70% average. Management does this by offering special-value packages, weekend rates, and holiday package rates. Management might also seek accommodation business from conventions, seminars, conferences, and groups.

The occupancy rate is affected by many factors, and can vary widely among cities and countries. The 1999 Arthur Andersen Hotel Industry Benchmark Survey of fifteen capital cities in Asia reported that there was a wide variance in occupancy rates between one capital city and another. In only one city (Seoul) did the average occupancy rates reach 80%. In Jakarta, the average occupancy rate was only 29%.[10]

In the Australian hospitality market, the average occupancy in the year to June 1999 was 72% and the average rate was AUS$141. The largest player in the Australian hotel market is the Sydney area, where there is a strong demand due to the convention sector (among other sectors), although the impact of hotel construction to cope with the influx of visitors for the 2000 Olympic Games has resulted in an oversupply of rooms. Melbourne rates just behind Sydney in total number of rooms, but has the highest occupancy rate in Australia (79%). The Gold Coast and north Queensland continue to benefit from mainly Asian visitors. Adelaide had a 3% growth in yield (a function of occupancy and rooms rate) to June 1999, the highest result for any capital city in the country. Perth has shown some effects of oversupply, although the situation is improving.[11]

Providing rooms for guests requires a considerable investment by the owners of a property in the building, its facilities, and its fittings. This money is recovered over time by including a fixed amount (called 'capital recovery') into the price of every room offered for hire.

As well as providing a comfortable (often glamorous) property for guests to visit, the hotel has to employ staff for cleaning, maintenance, reception, guest services, and sales. In addition, it has to have people to manage and keep books of account. There are many sundry costs involved in the running of an hotel. These expenses, largely involving labour, are termed 'general overheads', and they are incorporated into the price charged for the hire of a room.

The amount that is charged for room hire, the end price to the guest, depends on three factors:

◆ the perceived value to guests provided by the hotel's property and services;
◆ the market demand for hotel facilities and services prevailing at the time; and
◆ the intensity of competition offered by other hotel operators.

After room hire and accommodation, the next-highest income earner for hotels is food & beverage sales—that is, income from restaurants, bars, cafés, room service, coffee shops, and the food and liquor required for banquets, parties, and catering. Industry figures indicate that food & beverage sales account for approximately 32% of most hotel incomes.

Telephone calls made by guests provide a further 2–4% of income. This is achieved by the hotel adding a 'labour-and-facility charge' to the normal telephone charge.

Rentals from shops owned by a property—such as a barber shop, florist, newsagent, dress shop, hairdresser, and so on—contribute approximately 2% of income. These businesses are often run by independent operators who gain customers from the hotel's guests.

The balance of an hotel's income, approximately 0.5–2%, is contributed by services paid by guests for such things as laundry, valet, and drycleaning. Also, many hotels charge for the use of recreation facilities—such as a swimming pool, gymnasium, golf course, tennis court, and so on—depending on the type of operation.

Apart from the establishments that provide accommodation, nearly every other type of hospitality business makes money from food & beverage sales. They buy raw materials—such as food produce, beverages, and liquor—and add value by using labour to turn these into some form of value-added product or service for sale to customers.

As a general rule for food & beverage types of outlets, the cost of the materials amounts to about one-third of the sale price; the labour required to make and serve the products amounts to another one-third; and the remaining one-third is gross profit. The gross profit has to allow for a percentage to cover either capital recovery (if the property is owned) or rent (if the premises are leased). An allowance also has to be made for general overheads. What is left is net profit before tax.

Most taxation jurisdictions regard the costs of materials, labour, overheads, interest paid on capital, and rent as tax-deductible expenses. These are also known as 'running costs'. Owners and managers of establishments endeavour to minimise running costs so that they can maximise the amount of profit. This requires a careful balance between what the customers are prepared to pay and how much it costs to provide the products. The marketing function has to take this balance into consideration. Its purpose is to find customers and meet their demands by providing products and services that have sufficient value to attract them to buy at the right price. If the marketing job is done well, the establishment will make money.

Marketing planning

Marketing is like a journey. You have to plan for it. This is called the 'marketing plan' and there are many factors to consider in marketing planning. The principles involved in marketing planning are universal and can be adapted to almost any business or organisational activity.

To continue with the analogy of marketing being like a journey, marketing requires a 'destination' and reasons for going there. The destination, and the reasons for it, are called the 'marketing objectives'. You have to prepare for the journey, and find out as much as possible about what can be seen and enjoyed at the ultimate destination. It is wise to be prepared for anything that might happen along the way. This is called 'market analysis'.

The means of getting there, the route to be taken, and how the problems of travel can be overcome, are called 'strategies'. Strategies are designed to achieve the previously defined objectives.

'Marketing planning' is the name given to a series of steps that makes use of procedures and disciplines to direct the marketer's thinking, so that all the available information is examined before making a decision on the best strategies to implement.

The acronym 'ORGANISATION' is an easy way of remembering the steps involved in the strategic planning process of marketing. Let us take the letters of this word one by one.

O: Orientation

What is the business about? What is its mission? A business needs a reason for existence (aside from the fundamental motive of making money). If it does not make money it will not survive, so 'making money' is simply another way of saying 'surviving'. A mission statement is more than this. A mission statement must describe the areas of activity in which a business intends to operate, which services or products it intends to provide, and which needs and wants of the market it proposes to satisfy. A mission statement should also express a sound philosophy upon which to base attitudes to customer service, management, and staff policies.

R: Research

Who needs or wants the business and its products? A marketer can never have enough information about the market in which the business intends to operate. A study of the people who comprise the market, and its segments, is mandatory.

G: Gather data

It is essential to know what is happening in the marketplace. Much of this information can be obtained from sales figures, market share, customer preferences, competition, and so on. The advent of electronic commerce has opened a plethora of new opportunities for gathering information from a variety of sources of data.

A: Analyse the data

Assess the market. When all the available information is sorted, possibly with the aid of computer analysis, a big picture of the market should emerge. Decisions can now be made.

N: Narrow the market

The next step is to narrow the total market into target markets, and to select the most viable ones.

I: Identify what is to be achieved

Set marketing objectives. The marketing objectives are the 'engine' or driving force for the entire marketing planning process.

S: Strategies

Decide the marketing-mix strategies—the methods to be employed to achieve the marketing objectives. The marketing-mix strategies can be remembered as six 'Ps'—people, product, positioning, price, place, and promotion. (The six 'Ps' are discussed in more detail in Chapter 3, 'The marketing-mix strategies', page 40.)

A: Arrange distribution

Decide where and how to sell the establishment and its products.

T: Tactics

Decide which tactics will be used to implement the strategies. Tactics are short-term strategies—the communication tools of marketing—which usually embrace the promotion functions of selling, advertising, sales promotion, direct mail, publicity, and so on.

I: Implement the plan

Inform the market through promotions or tactical communications.

O: Observe the results and gather feedback

What changed as a result of the plan? Perhaps the establishment gathered more customers, or a larger market share, or a greater awareness of its products and services.

N: Next

What changes, improvements or modifications to the plan are now necessary to make the marketing more effective?

These are the basics of marketing. Each of these steps will be explained in full in the forthcoming chapters. However, it should already be apparent that marketing is really *common sense*.

Questions for discussion or revision

1   Provide some examples of the 'multiplier effect' of recent changes to the economy as a result of government actions.

2   What would be the 'multiplier effect' of building a large new hotel in your area? Which people, products, or services would be involved or affected in some way?

3   What new technologies in the past twenty years have significantly changed the way in which we live? How have they been marketed?

4   We tend to think of a 'thing' when we use the term 'product'. Can you name some products that are not 'things'?

5   By applying the definition of 'marketing' (page 7) to an hotel, and associating that definition with the dictionary definition of 'hospitality' (page 4), what should be an hotel's main marketing concern?

Chapter 2

Hospitality and e-Commerce

Aims of this chapter

The aims of this chapter are:
- to explain environmental factors;
- to describe e-commerce and its importance in hospitality; and
- to outline some factors and issues of e-commerce.

Theory

An hotel does not produce a quality guest experience in a vacuum. The social, political, and economic environments in which an establishment operates greatly affects its marketing decisions. A small hotel has to fit as a whole entity into the physical and social ambience of a city or suburb. A large, four-star or five-star hotel has to meet the needs of a large clientele—interstate and international businesspeople and tourists, as well as the local market—but it still has to fit in with the environment of the region. Building a business, or changing it, requires an understanding of the environment in which the place is going to operate. Environmental factors are either internal (controllable) or external (uncontrollable).

The *external*, uncontrollable factors (also called macro-environmental factors) are market demographics, economics, competition, changing social needs and lifestyle values, new technology, and government and legal changes.

The *internal*, controllable factors (also called micro-environmental factors) include the information technology (IT) and financial capabilities of the establishment, its human resources, its location, its suppliers, and its agents or distributors. Taken together, these constitute its knowledge and ability to produce a product that matches the requirements of the market, and an image or position in the market that is competitive.

It can be argued that location is 'uncontrollable'—in that moving a property is not possible. However, the initial choice of location *was* controllable.

In the twenty-first century, every organisation's environment has become inextricably linked with, and shaped by, computer-based relationships and commerce. The word 'e-commerce' has come to be used for the business environment. It is possible to run a very small hospitality establishment without the aid of computerisation in any form, but the number of such establishments is declining daily. Even a four-bedroom bed & breakfast uses e-commerce—for example, whenever its mobile phone is used. The smallest restaurant uses e-commerce when the owner replaces a system based on a simple cashbox with a system involving the use of a cash register (possibly a point-of-sale register). In small hotels, computerised accounting and electronic communications are necessities. For larger hotels, extensive computer systems that shape functions as diverse as reservations and stock control are essential. Adapting to the e-commerce age is no longer an alternative for hotels. It has become a survival strategy.

Environmental factors

The aim of large hotels is to produce a quality guest experience. An hotel is a product in itself, but this basic product has many diversified subproducts. Taken together, they form a product mix. This might include accommodation, bars, telecommunications sales, dining-room, laundry, valet service, hair care, shops and, in many cases, a variety of recreational facilities (such as a swimming pool, golf course, tennis courts, and more). Which of these products should be offered to customers, and in what form? Whatever management decides, the reputation or image of the hotel will affect all of its products.

Each of the environmental factors is subject to change, and clever management has to be alert to both short-term and long-term changes, and make adjustments to the product mix and allocation of human and financial resources to cater for these changes. Adjustments to social change have become increasingly necessary in recent years. The preference for more relaxed dining, for example, has caused many hotels to change their restaurants to become less formal. The strong interest in fitness and aerobics has created gymnasiums, spas, and areas for aerobics classes. The surge in the number of backpackers has created a growth in places that offer simple, low-cost accommodation and meals. Many two-star and three-star operations have successfully made this type of transition.

Potential customers

A hospitality establishment has to be mindful of its total customer potential and the degree of competition it will meet in attracting custom. An hotel cannot position itself to appeal to everyone. It must decide which segment of the market it intends to capture, which requirements of that segment of the market it intends to satisfy, and whether it has the resources to do these things—clearly the use of IT for information-gathering and information analysis is crucial here.

A large hotel chain sets out to dominate a market with a tried and proven formula that has worked in other markets. Even so, within a chain, each individual hotel's product mix is adapted to the environment in which it operates. The chain's overall strategy is not an inflexible formula.

One sector of the industry in which small operators can compete effectively with larger properties is the backpacker sector. Backpackers, generally young and well-educated, are frequent users of the Internet for communications and

Figure 2.1 The social, political, and economic environments in which an establishment operates greatly affects its marketing operations.

Authors' presentation

information. This sector can therefore market its product among prospective clients at least as efficiently as can large properties.

The demographics of the potential customer base

Demography is the statistical study of human population and distribution. Every hospitality establishment needs to consider its customer potential in terms of number, age, gender, and income, and whether it will draw its custom from local, interstate, country, or international sources. Food & beverage outlets can be themed to suit a population demographic, and there can be a market advantage in developing what Hensdill has described as 'innovative, symbiotic relationships in hotel dining that help build incremental revenue and foster brand identity'.[1] For example, a theme restaurant that offers a country's regional food has limited potential for success in a small city if there are already several competitors offering the same type of fare. The size of the population does not justify another restaurant of the same type. The restaurant's only hope is to invest considerable time and effort in an attempt to take the available business away from the existing players.

Similarly, there is always a restaurateur who fondly believes that there is room for a 'really good restaurant' that is the pinnacle of gourmet food and immaculate service. In a depressed economy, and in an area that is mostly populated by middle-to-low income earners, it is unlikely that there will be sufficient potential customers to justify such an expectation. There are more financial casualties in the 'top end' of the eating market than there are in the far larger 'lower end' of the market—where price and value are the major considerations.

One of the continuing hospitality trends is what Dickey has called a 'boom in small, offbeat hotels where the interior design is cutting-edge or richly opulent'.[2] These are also termed 'boutique' hotels. They cater for a particular market segment—usually people who have the wealth and inclination to seek something different and exclusive. This is a case of seeking a particular market demographic.

The market's social needs and lifestyle values

In a small town, the community's needs for entertainment, celebrations, dining, and various meetings usually revolve around the local hotel or club, if these are marketed properly. The environment dictates the type of operation that the management needs to run.

A city establishment has a far greater market potential—certainly a more diverse market—but it has to decide which of the many social and lifestyle markets to target.

Cultural considerations

People's views of the world and the society in which they find themselves are conditioned by the country of their origin and the society that has shaped their beliefs and values. The hospitality industry is an industry that has to be multi-cultural in everything that it does. When choosing their menus for example, food & beverage managers are influenced by the wide variety of cultural preferences among their potential clientele. The devolution of the hotel industry now offers opportunities for specialisation in the products on offer, and thereby opportunities to attract specific markets to certain establishments.

The need to understand cross-cultural communication is not restricted to relationships *within* a hospitality operation. Hospitality corporations and chains exist within a network of external business contacts, and this is especially so in the Asia–Pacific region, where suppliers of hospitality services frequently operate within a set of Western cultural norms, whereas the tour wholesalers are operating with a background in Asian norms and values.

Cultural sensitivity is important in developing a multicultural awareness of the marketplace. When dealing with Asian cultures, multicultural awareness for European managers and staff must include an understanding of the concept of 'face' in relationships with Asian people. This includes an understanding of the importance of communicating through mediators, or communicating obliquely, to avoid placing an Asian colleague or guest in a situation where that person might 'lose face' and feel humiliated—even though the Westerner who caused this might be entirely unaware of the feelings of the offended person.

Multicultural awareness in relation to Arab cultures involves an understanding of how business and social relationships are intermingled, and how a person seeking to market in an Arab culture must take time to develop personal relationships with business partners.

The marketplaces of the tourism and hospitality industries have been affected by changing trends in consumer preferences and cultural considerations—the term 'trends' being used here to describe a sequence of events that have some momentum and durability.[3] Some identifiable consumer and cultural trends in international trade today include:

◆ the increasing speed of international transportation and communications;
◆ the growth of global communication;

- the dissemination of global lifestyles;
- the opening of new markets in Asia, eastern Europe, and the Arab countries;
- increasing product and service branding; and
- the globalisation of business and corporations.

Economic conditions prevailing

In times of recession, people seek greater value from their expenditure. The number of people travelling and wanting accommodation falls. The size of an operation affects the economies of scale necessary to meet times of boom, recession, and recovery, and these must be understood before they occur.

As economic conditions change, management should be aware of the possible need to seek different markets. Alternatively, some establishments remain committed to delivering a 'top-of-the-range' service for those guests who are less affected by adverse economic conditions.

Tourism and hospitality spending is largely *discretionary* for non-business travellers. The term 'discretionary' means that if people have less money to spend, or if concern about future conditions causes them to save rather than spend, they will choose to do without a product or service that they see as unnecessary.

Economic conditions can change rapidly, and changes can be a result of events in other national economies. High inflation and interest rates reduce the amount of money that people have to spend on items that involve discretionary spending (for example, resort holidays, which people can freely choose to purchase or not to purchase as they see fit) or on items that are very competitive (for example, a cheaper stay at a three-star hotel rather than a stay at a five-star hotel).

Existing government and legal forces

Governments cause much change in the business environment by taking measures to boost or slow down an economy. Governments use interest rates (monetary policy) and taxation rates (fiscal policy) to achieve these changes. Apart from central governments, there are many other levels of government that affect economic conditions—including local councils, health departments, public works departments, building and environmental planning boards, heritage bodies, and so on. The list of bureaucracies keeps growing, and the activities of these various bodies are a formidable obstacle to attempts by management to plan in anticipation of stable conditions for growth.

The hospitality marketplace can also be affected by government through its ability to dispense subsidies, both direct and indirect. Governments can choose to support and enhance industry development within targeted areas (although there are worldwide trends to reduce the role of government intervention in the marketplace). Most governments have also introduced laws to protect competition (which is viewed as beneficial in forcing businesses to make the best use of resources) and consumers (who might otherwise be subject to unfair business practices).

Apart from lobbying various levels of government, individual establishments have little control over their economic and political environments, and most establishments have to 'ride' the changing circumstances.

Ecological influences

The tourism and hospitality industry has not been exempt from the imposition of environmental controls. Environmentalism has become an international issue with international ramifications, and marketers must be aware of its implications. There are now international standards for good environmental practice (for example, the standard known as 'ISO 14001').

The marketing implication of ecological issues is clear. If a hospitality operation damages the surrounding area, it damages its own attraction to the guests who want to come and stay. If the environment is not protected, and is made unattractive by waste or overuse, visitors will go elsewhere.

Property owners who endorse environmental values enhance the value of their investment. Properties that have good environmental programs not only increase efficiencies of operation, but also gain important public-relations benefits, thus developing a marketing edge, through the promotion of minimisation and recycling programs. A hospitality operation that qualifies for 'green' labelling can advertise the fact. Consumers are becoming increasingly aware and supportive of such 'green' products, and the consumption decisions of such customers are affected by the environmental postures adopted by businesses.

Hotels in resort areas, or those close to natural features attractive to tourists, can use campaigns emphasising environmental consciousness as part of their marketing presentations. For example, the Sheraton Miramar at El Gouna on the Red Sea in Egypt, has taken responsibility for a mangrove-covered sandbank island which is a native habitat for bird life.[4] As another example, a resort development (including a golf course) near Khao Yai National Park in Thailand operated successfully for some years, but the deer in the Park were dying. Research discovered that the deer were eating golf balls, which proved fatal. The golf course part of the development was halted.[5]

Technological developments

Developments in IT have had profound effects on hospitality and tourism, just as they have in all areas of commerce, and these changes influence all aspects of the industry (as has been discussed above). It might be that IT developments comprise the most important issue facing hotel managers today, and the current era is rightly called the 'e-Commerce Age'. IT is all about information, and information provides knowledge for decision-making. As one writer has stated: 'Knowledge, knowledge, knowledge is what it's all about as the hotel industry frantically tries to reinvent itself for the 21st century'.[6] The same writer also claims that hospitality management has not been as quick or as ready as airlines and credit card companies to utilise new IT technology.

Increasing regulation

Ours is already a highly regulated society, and the spread of new government rules and regulations in all areas continues unabated as people try to create the 'perfect society' through legislation.

Health concerns—especially with respect to the consumption of alcohol, smoking, and food—directly affect the hospitality industry as governments endeavour to provide protection through new legislation. The industry responds to the changes by trying to turn them into customer benefits, or by providing facilities that meet customer requirements.

Physical location of the establishment

People's perceptions of a place are dictated by its location. Even being on the wrong side of a road can change people's perceptions. Is the place likely to appeal to businesspeople, to tourists, to locals, to country people, to interstate and overseas visitors, to sports enthusiasts, or to families? Whomever the hotel targets, the location must match the market's expectation in physical location, size, presentation, and facilities.

The competition

No business has a market to itself, or not for too long. The competitive environment materially affects marketing decisions on a continuing basis. The intensity of the competition, and how it intrudes into an hotel's market, determines the reaction required to counter it.

In the hospitality industry, what competitors should we consider, and how do we assess that competition? Management must consider:

◆ Have we decided on the market geography? That is, how far afield should we go in listing competitors?

◆ Have we decided upon the product? For example, should we consider the backpackers' hostel as a competitor to our new motel?

◆ Have we settled upon the form or task of the operation? For example, are we offering mainly accommodation, or are we primarily offering entertainment services?

◆ Do we have all the information we require? How do we get detailed information on our competitors? One author has suggested that 95% of the information on competitors required by a hospitality organisation to make marketing decisions is available and accessible to the public.[7]

The organisation's resources

Capital and cash flow are vital for survival. The ability to meet the long-term goals of marketing are often underestimated. For example, there is nothing worse than trying to earn a reputation for a service, a product, or a facility while operating with unreliable staff, money, and sources of supply. The presentation of the hotel's facilities have to be uniformly impressive, clean, fresh, and well maintained. Without cash flow, this can be difficult to maintain.

Each market has expectations that must be met. The ability of the staff to provide the service required by the market being targeted is critical. Measurable, consistent service standards are essential in hospitality, and careful staff selection and training are therefore essential. Management and staff must know and personally experience the market in which they intend to operate.

Impact of e-commerce

The operating environment of hotels has been revolutionised in recent times. This revolution has occurred because of the spread of the Internet which has had an influence upon almost all aspects of hotel marketing. Although the basic principles of marketing and the basic hospitality product have remained the same, the environment within which they operate has changed irrevocably, and businesses must 'keep up or perish'.

Figures from the Australian Bureau of Statistics for the period February 1999 to February 2000 indicate that 43% of all adults in Australia have access to the Internet. Of those who had access and purchased goods and services over the Net, the top spending category was tourism and hospitality products, comprising 12% of all online purchases. The Australian government has established a National Online Tourism Strategy to take account of the growing importance of the Internet to the industry.[8]

Internet marketplace

The marketplace for hospitality operations has been transformed by changes to booking procedures brought about by the spread of the Internet. The Net has brought about two huge changes to the way in which marketing is carried out.

First, the Internet means that consumers can now get information and make confirmed bookings at low cost and short notice, 24 hours a day, 365 days a year. In marketing terms, the Internet has made market conditions closer to those of a perfect marketplace—that is, one that has a large number of buyers, a large number of sellers, and perfect information exchange among them all, together with the ability to make instant contracts.

Secondly, by putting such information in the hands of consumers, the buyer has been given much more control over any given business decision. No longer can any hotel present a customer with a 'take it or leave it' option. If any hotel implies that a consumer can go elsewhere, that consumer can check out other possibilities on the Web, and can, indeed, decide to go elsewhere! The Internet has put customers in control. As one author has observed:[9]

> The first challenge of the 21st century will be to master the changes that come from customers being in control. Each company needs to develop an unprecedented degree of flexibility in order to offer customers what they want—when and how they want it.

Some of the players who are changing the marketplace are:

◆ Worldspan—a global distribution system that incorporates WAVE, a travel Intranet that brings hotel, airline, and rental-car bookings together;[10]
◆ Trust International—a subsidiary of a large media and communication company (Bertelsmann AG) that markets a given business segment and provides online reservations (at agreed rates) at 1300 hotel members in 685 destinations; in addition, Trust International has a database of 35 000 hotels with whom the business traveller can negotiate directly;
◆ Nethotels.com—a European-based company that can handle bookings for its (growing) database of 4000 hotels; and
◆ Worldres.com—a company that connects a number of travel and destination websites, agents, and tourism organisations.

The changing marketplace enables small and medium-sized hotels to compete in the e-commerce world. They can make contact directly with consumers more easily, instead of being restricted to negotiating separate contracts with different agents in different regions.

In the hotel Internet marketplace, some Web players offer more than hotel reservations. One site, <www.hotels-and-more.com>, operates as a hospitality employment agency matching job vacancies in hotels with applicants.[11]

Virtual hotel tour

One option offered by the Internet should excite marketers. This is the possibility of creating a 'virtual tour' of the hotel that can be transmitted to those browsing the hotel website. The virtual hotel tour can showcase the facilities that the property can offer, emphasise the quality of service, and highlight points of difference between the hotel and its competition. The problem with such virtual tours is that they are sometimes impeded by bandwidth constraints. The use of multimedia presentations can mean slow downloads of the page and this can be a disincentive for some people who are checking out the property.

Customer relationship management

Customer relationship management is a technology that allows an organisation to expand its links with current and previous customers to build up their loyalty and generate increased business. The use of websites, email, and online communication as part of a strategic marketing package has opened new possibilities for interaction with customers.

Essentially, the information that accumulates on customers and their purchase patterns enables the organisation to build up a marketing database. (For more on customer databases, see 'Building a database,' page 344, in Chapter 28.)

The concept of customer relationship management is not new. Other terms for the concept are: 'loyalty marketing', 'interactive marketing', 'one-on-one marketing', and 'wraparound marketing'. What is new in the e-commerce age is that the technology has greatly improved the means and information by which a business can enhance its relationships with preferred customers. The business is able to:

◆ identify different classes of customer—by origin, purpose of travel, and so on;

◆ offer the customer more information on the property;

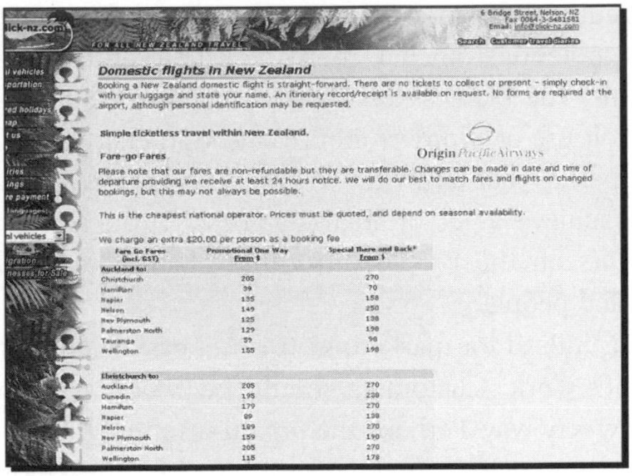

Figure 2.2 Internet marketing can not only represent the business, but also include details of current fares and offers.

Thanks to Origin Pacific airline of New Zealand for permission to reproduce part of their website

◆ develop various loyalty schemes;

◆ offer special products and promotions; and

◆ develop market-related hospitality products (a practice known as 'cross-selling').

Customer relationship management is particularly useful in niche marketing—focusing on narrow market segments. Through customised marketing offers or programs, the business can strengthen its personal relationships with its clients. It can treat classes of customers as 'special'. Customer relationship management is important in highly competitive markets—such as the hotel sector in urban areas—in which it is crucial for a property to be able to differentiate its product to attract business.

Chat rooms

One aspect of customer relationships that has always existed is that of word-of-mouth communication. In other words, people have always talked about inns, hotels, and restaurants to their friends and acquaintances, giving their opinion on the desirability (or otherwise!) of a property and its services.

When communication was person to person, through speech or through mail, word-of-mouth description was useful and important, but it was seldom a means of mass communication. The Internet has changed this. Through the use of chat rooms—interactive communication sites—one person can pass on views and opinions to hundreds of others. Chat rooms have become an important part of an organisation's marketing potential. However, they are, to a large extent, beyond the organisation's control. Participants in a chat-room environment are sensitive to efforts to manipulate the conversation, and can be resentful of inappropriate behaviour.

However, despite this difficulty, a business operation in the twenty-first century cannot disregard the potential of chat rooms for marketing. The producers of a low-budget film ('The Blair Witch Project') made their film a marketing success through adroit use of 'word of mouth' through chat rooms. In the hospitality industry, properties that target the low-budget youth market (such as backpacker hostels) achieve a lot of their business through their customers passing on comments on the property through chat rooms and through contact with like-minded people.

How can chat rooms be best utilised for marketing? It is not easy. A clumsy and obtrusive approach will not work. Customers should be encouraged to pass on their comments in a low-key way. Perhaps the organisation might give customers a card with their receipts, with a note suggesting: 'Did you enjoy your stay here? Why not tell others in your chat room'. Another means to make use of this marketing facility is to provide free and unlimited Internet access as part of the accommodation package. The cost will probably be recouped through the indirect advertising of the property that is likely to be achieved.

As in all aspects of marketing in a new medium, the use of innovative and imaginative strategies should reap rewards.

Risks of e-commerce

The spread of new technologies has brought risks for hospitality marketing. Some of these are discussed below.

Uneven spread of the Internet

A marketing strategy that is entirely dependent upon use of the Internet can result in some demographic segments being neglected. For example, older people as a demographic group are not connected to the Internet as much as younger people, and if an hotel has identified seniors as a targeted market segment, it will have to take this relative lack of Internet access into account.

A market segment based on geographics will also have to take into account the uneven penetration of the Internet. For example, according to South Africa's largest IT group, Dimension Data, sub-Saharan Africa has a low rate of Internet connection, due largely to problems with communications infrastructure and the costs of telecommunications.[12] The United Nations estimates that Latvia (population 2.5 million) has as many Internet hosts as Africa (population 780 million).

However, if demographic and geographic factors are taken into account, the Internet remains an effective way of communicating market information.

Crashing of systems

Many businesses recognise that e-commerce can revolutionise all aspects of their operations—including customer-to-stock supplier integration, a complete transaction system, and online business reporting. However, it is risky to attempt to update all of an operation in one move. There will inevitably be 'bugs' in the systems, and if too much is attempted at once, all of the operation might crash. If that happens in a hospitality operation, the business lost can never be recovered. A factory can delay supplies of a product, but hotels and restaurants cannot do this.

To avoid the risk of a total loss, update incrementally—a piece at a time— wherever possible. Bring in the problem-solvers to take on the small problems, rather than using a 'crash-through or crash' philosophy.

Security

Market information—such as client lists and market plans—can be at risk from hackers. In addition, an organisation's website can be vandalised. These events are more than an inconvenience. From a marketing point of view, such occurrences can put off potential customers for several reasons.

◆ The public 'face' of the hotel is spoilt and its image damaged.
◆ The fact that the hotel systems have been open to penetration by hackers suggests to potential customers that their own private personal information (as passed onto the hotel in confidence) could also be open to theft or misuse.
◆ Internet users tend to avoid websites that are known to have been defaced—for fear of importing a virus or a trojan into their own systems. The *Far Eastern Economic Review* has reported a 'wave' of hacking in Hong Kong, Singapore, and Korea, and has noted that the risk to website operators is the future avoidance of these websites by worried users.[13]

Marketing management must ensure that it keeps up to date with developments in combating hacking and computer fraud. A new problem that has arisen is that of hackers targeting mobile phones. The Telco NTT DoCoMo in Japan discovered that some of its mobile Internet subscribers were hit by an email virus that caused their phones to start ringing a large number of unknown parties. The only effective temporary solution was to take the battery out of the phone!

Lack of skilled staff

Because the IT sector has expanded in a short time, shortages of skilled staff have occurred. The supply of qualified people from universities and colleges has not kept up with demand. The implication for hospitality operations is that they should not 'bite off more than they can chew', and should avoid attempting to change systems without sufficient trained and experienced staff.

Consumer resistance

Not all of an hotel's regular clients will readily transfer across to a new technology. Many consumers are uneasy with some aspects of e-commerce. For example, some people are reluctant to transmit credit card details over the Web, for fear of misuse. An hotel must therefore take every effort to reassure its customers about its Web-based systems, and keep them fully informed. With respect to the credit card security issue, an hotel must ensure that it has appropriate encryption procedures, and should advise its customers of the fact. There are also other means of making payments over the Web without transmitting credit card details—for example, through a process called Ecash.[14]

Whatever problems are raised by operating on the Internet, the chances are that a solution has been found somewhere by someone.

Summary of the e-commerce marketing environment

All of the factors in the market environment have to be continuously monitored. Nothing in marketing remains static. Management's job is to monitor these factors and be prepared to make modifications or changes to the marketing plan.

An establishment might have to reposition itself several times during its existence to meet the changing expectations of the market, to meet the needs of new markets caused by environmental change, or to make use of revolutionary new technology.

To be successful in business, the following resources are needed:

- a consumer need;
- a large-enough market;
- an accessible market;
- a product that can turn a need into a want;
- a product that is competitive;
- production means and facilities;

◆ continuity of supplies, materials, and human resources;
◆ money; and
◆ a good crystal ball!

Questions for discussion or revision

1 If you won a trip to a tropical tourist resort on an island, what facilities would you expect to find there? What would you think if these facilities were not available?

2 You are the owner of a three-star hotel. It is recommended that you should change the style of the dining-room to cater for the tastes of an emerging market of foreign tourists. How would you react and what would you do about it?

3 Your three-star hotel has had a virtual monopoly of the business travellers' market for years. Suddenly, two highly regarded hotel chains build four-star hotels in your vicinity. What would you do? What e-commerce strategy would you implement?

4 A tourist resort in a dry area that has a superb golf course is stricken by drought. The cost of watering rises significantly and the course is losing a large amount of money. Would you advise the resort management to accept the losses until the next year, in the hope that conditions will improve? Or would you close the course down? What other alternatives would you consider, and why?

5 You have inherited a large house by the beach, near a big city. It is ideal for many hospitality uses. How would you go about making a decision on the best use of the place? How would you market it on the Internet?

Chapter 3

The Marketing Mix

Aims of this chapter

The aims of this chapter are:
- to expand the understanding of strategic planning;
- to explain the relationship of goals and strategy; and
- to describe how strategies can be grouped under the six main marketing categories of 6Ps called the 'marketing mix'.

Goal of goal-making

Mission statements

A business without goals is like a rudderless ship—likely to go anywhere or nowhere. Goals harness power and set the direction for an organisation. They give it purpose and motivation. McCarthy et al. (1994) noted that a business must define specific and explicit objectives, and should have three general goals:[1]

- to be socially and economically useful;
- to develop an organisation to carry on its activities; and
- to earn a profit in the long run.

However, a goal is virtually useless unless it has a measurable, quantifiable objective. To have a goal that says simply, 'To achieve profit', is almost useless. How much profit? A dollar? No? How about ten million dollars? Not possible?

What, then, is a reasonable expectation for profit that can be quantified and written down as a goal? When that question is answered, a goal is created—a goal that will generate the activity to attain it. A goal must be feasible and sensible. If it is too high, it can plunge those who have to achieve it into dismay or apathy. If it is too low, it encourages underachievement.

Athletes constantly strive to achieve better than their 'personal best', or to beat another competitor's time, or to set a new record. This is the stuff that makes champions. The adage, 'I'll give it my best shot!' is a statement uttered by someone who is being very coy or by someone who is already virtually defeated (having given up on the prospect of winning). This sort of statement is made by people who think the goal is beyond their capacities to achieve.

The other essential component of a goal is to have a time schedule. When is this profit to be achieved? Sometime in the vague future, or by the end of the calendar or financial year?

Without a quantifiable objective within a definite time frame, a goal is merely a wish or a hope, and a business cannot survive long on wishes and hopes. As an example of failure to achieve objectives, Impulse Airlines (set up in 2001 to compete against Australia's two established domestic carriers) was a good idea, but was not able to turn a profit from its operations in the face of price competition from the established airlines.

So, to have a meaning, a goal must be challenging, but achievable, and must have a definite time frame. For example, a meaningful goal might be expressed in the following terms: 'To achieve a profit of $250 000 by 30 June next year'.

The next question is: 'Is it feasible?'. A *feasibility study* is the only way of answering this question. A feasibility study is an accountable forecast of the likely outcome of marketing activity. Such a study cannot be done without considerable investigation into the market—known as 'market analysis'. If this analysis reveals opportunities that allow the goal to be achieved, the next step is to propose some strategies and plan the marketing in sufficient detail to satisfy those who have to decide whether or not to proceed.

Setting marketing objectives is the decision-making time in marketing—the moment when the marketer's credibility is on the line. Woolly forecasts (and unjustified expenses required to achieve them) will be quickly torn apart by the hard-nosed financial people who are accountable for the business's prosperity or who are accountable for providing the funds to be raised in pursuit of a goal. Before they grant a loan or an overdraft, bank managers are in the habit of asking questions along these lines: 'What makes you think that you can achieve this profit? What makes you think that you can make this number of sales?' Marketing objectives are a commitment, and they have to be accurate and defensible.

Strategies are the means by which marketing objectives are achieved. They are meant to answer the all-important question: 'How are you going to achieve this objective?'.

There has been debate on the accuracy of forecasts in the context of setting market strategies and objectives. Professor Tarras of Michigan State University was funded by the Hilton Corporation to report specifically on this question. His study, 'Accuracy of Project Evaluation Projections', found that only 29% of occupancy forecasts (of those he studied) were within 5 percentage points of the actual, and that 60% of projected net income figures were inaccurate.[2] The tendency was to *overestimate* occupancy and net income. Stephen Rushmore (1996) has argued that strategic studies provide third-party confirmation of factors related to a proposal, and also provide the credibility that is necessary to obtain funding. However, the problem is that 'hotel markets are highly dynamic', and circumstances can change very quickly.[3]

See Figure 3.1 (below) for an illustration of how mission statements are related to the objectives of an organisation.

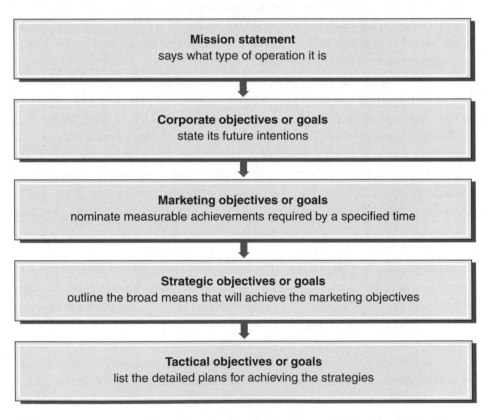

Figure 3.1 The sequence of steps involved in developing a marketing plan, defined by objectives
Authors' presentation

Tactics are the working mechanisms of strategies. *Strategies* are theories. Tactics make the strategies happen, and it is tactics that cost the money in a marketing plan. When goals and objectives are set, they become the measurement of performance, and that is why they must have quantifiable criteria. As a result of the feasibility study, the goals might have to be modified, or possibly even abandoned until a better set of strategies is proposed.

Having considered the general framework of mission statements and goals, let us consider some of the goals (or objectives) involved.

Organisation (or corporate) goals

Organisation goals are the overriding goals of a business that shape its future intentions. These goals change from time to time depending on circumstances. Here are some examples.

To achieve profit

'To achieve a profit' is the first and most obvious goal of a business. However, in difficult times, a goal might have to be written that restricts *loss* to a certain amount.

To increase market share

'To increase market share' is a corporate goal for an organisation in a highly competitive market. When quantified, it will state the amount of business that has to be taken from the opposition. It has even more meaning if the opposition is named.

To increase sales

'To increase sales' has an implied profit objective in the longer term, but it is primarily aimed at building the number of customers to form a customer base.

To achieve corporate growth

'To achieve corporate growth' is an objective that might come about when a company reaches the limit of its existing market, and the owners consider moving into other markets—taking over other organisations, or diversifying into other products.

To increase capacity

'To increase capacity' is an objective that is required when the establishment has reached the limit of growth with its existing facilities, and then sees merit in adding more rooms, or increasing the size of various products (such as restaurants).

Apart from the examples given above, other corporate goals might be:

◆ to reduce stock inventories;
◆ to capitalise assets;
◆ to offset competitive activity;
◆ to achieve takeovers;
◆ to provide finance or cash flow;
◆ to increase share prices or values;
◆ to enter new markets;
◆ to introduce new products; and
◆ to achieve product or corporate rationalisation.

Marketing goals

Corporate goals (discussed above) are broad in scope. In contrast, marketing objectives are more specific and spell out how the corporate goals will be achieved by the marketing mix. Thus, a corporate goal concerning profit might have one or several marketing objectives that relate to achieving profit by

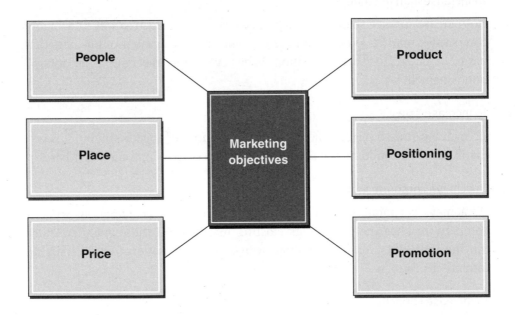

Figure 3.2 Strategies achieve marketing objectives
Authors' presentation

changing a particular product, by promoting it, by pricing it differently, by offering it to new markets, or by positioning it in new ways.

A marketing objective relating to a corporate goal for profit might read as follows.

To achieve the corporate profit goal

Let us take the case of a fictitious hospitality operation called the 'Yass River Sports Club', which operates a restaurant (the 'Yass River Restaurant') and club bar operation (the 'Yass River Club Bar'), as well as motel-style accommodation ('Yass River Accommodation') for its members and visitors. This organisation might express its corporate profit goal in the following terms.

To achieve the corporate profit goal of 25% by 30 June next year we will:

◆ increase food and liquor sales for the 'Yass River Restaurant' by 30% before 30 June next year;

◆ increase sales return from the 'Yass River Club Bar' by 21% immediately; and

◆ increase the return from 'Yass River Accommodation' room hire by 25% immediately.

Strategic goals or objectives

Strategic objectives are included in the plan that a business draws up for at least two reasons. These are:

◆ to define the target market (that is, who will consume the product); and

◆ to decide how the elements of the marketing mix will be determined (that is, the type of product and how it will be packaged) to satisfy the needs of the target market through promotion of the product.

Taken together, these should answer the questions of (i) what we want to promote and (ii) to whom.[4] It is also important to consider the context in which the business operates—its working environment.[5]

When drawing up its plans in conformity with business objectives, a hospitality organisation has four alternative courses of action in determining its future strategic objectives:

◆ product development;

◆ market development;

◆ market expansion; and/or

◆ diversification.

Each of these is considered below.

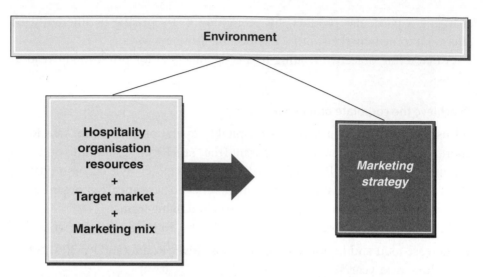

Figure 3.3 Environment and marketing strategy
Authors' presentation

Product development

This strategy involves developing and offering new services to meet the various needs of current customers. This might involve the development of enhanced facilities—such as free use of spa or gymnasium facilities.

Market development

In this case, the hospitality organisation seeks a new market for the organisation's existing services. For example, this might involve the seeking-out of new users for conference facilities—such as encouraging wedding parties to be held in the facilities over the weekend when there is limited business demand.

Market expansion

This strategy involves trying to sell more of the hospitality organisation's current service to current customers or, in the case of hospitality services, encouraging its guests to stay a longer period or to return frequently. This type of marketing can be done effectively through the use of sales promotions—for example, an offer to stay four days with the fourth day being free.

Diversification

This fourth strategy involves the hospitality organisation developing a completely new service for consumers in a new target market. For example, this might involve the renovation of a wing of a tourist hotel and rebuilding existing single units into business suites with a full range of support services.

The strategic objectives state how the increases will be achieved. They are detailed and might read as follows:

1. Food and liquor sales

To achieve an increase of food and liquor sales by 30% for the 'Yass River Restaurant' before 30 June 30, we will:

◆ make more tables available (a 'place' strategy);
◆ offer special deals (a 'price' strategy); and
◆ double the advertising expenditure (a 'promotion' strategy).

2. Club Bar income

To achieve a sales return increase of 21% from the 'Yass River Club Bar' immediately we will institute a 'price' strategy as follows:

◆ increase the prices selectively; and
◆ offer specials to offset negative customer reactions.

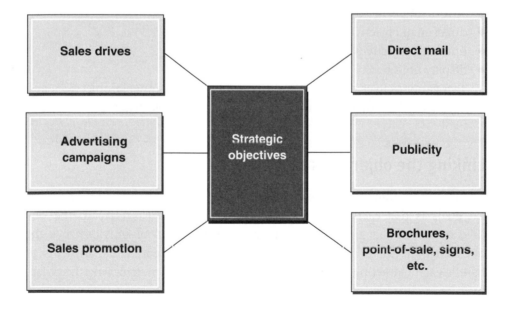

Figure 3.4 Tactics achieve strategic objectives
Authors' presentation

3. Room rate

To achieve the increase of 25% in 'Yass River Accommodation' room hire rate by 25% immediately, we will:

◆ adopt a price ranging policy by regrading the rooms so that there is a greater price differential between them (a 'product' and 'price' strategy); and

◆ have a range of premium-class rooms to attract more people from the senior executive levels (a 'people' strategy).

Tactical objectives

Tactics are the short-term, detailed courses of action that follow through from the strategic objectives. *Strategies* are broad, long-term means of achieving objectives whereas *tactics* usually involve specific activities and communication. Tactics therefore are concerned with the short-term, immediate needs of implementing product changes, selling, advertising, sales promotions, publicity, direct mail, public relations, signs, brochures, and so on.

Therefore, for the strategic objectives to be achieved, all the communicating departments of the establishment have their own objectives to carry out the intentions of the strategies. These objectives include:

◆ sales objectives;
◆ advertising communication objectives;
◆ direct-mail objectives;
◆ publicity objectives; and
◆ display objectives.

Tactical objectives are written in the same way as strategic objectives and must also have a time frame and measurable, manageable criteria.

Linking the objectives together

The important thing to remember when setting marketing, strategic, and tactical goals is that each succeeding set of objectives must relate to the one preceding it so that they link together to form a chain of activity. Once the objectives are set, in a large organisation that has separate departments to handle each marketing function, every person involved in achieving the objectives has a clear idea of what is required of him or her.

When all the objectives are assembled into a document they become the *strategic plan*.

For example, to achieve the corporate goals for the 'Yass River Sports Club' outlined previously, the marketing, strategic, and tactical objectives might read:

'Yass River Restaurant'

Marketing objective for the 'Yass River Restaurant'

The marketing objective is:

◆ to increase food and liquor sales for the 'Yass River Restaurant' by 30% before 30 June next year.

Strategic objectives for the 'Yass River Restaurant'

The strategic objectives are:

◆ to make more tables available (a 'place' strategy);
◆ to offer special deals (a 'price' strategy); and
◆ to double the advertising expenditure (a 'promotion' strategy).

Tactical objectives for the 'Yass River Restaurant'

The tactical objectives are:

◆ to increase the table capacity of the 'Yass River Restaurant' by 20 tables by eliminating ten of the private booths;
◆ to promote the restaurant by offering a special 'table-for-four rate'; and
◆ to offer a low-priced, hot buffet alternative for early diners.

'Yass River Club Bar'

Marketing objective for the 'Yass River Club Bar'

The marketing objective is:

◆ to increase sales return from the club bar by 21% immediately.

Strategic objectives for the 'Yass River Club Bar'

The strategic objectives are:

◆ to increase the prices selectively while offering specials to offset negative customer reactions.

Tactical objectives for the 'Yass River Club Bar'

The tactical objectives are:

◆ to increase the prices of spirits and cocktails by 21%; and
◆ to offer various cocktail and spirit 'specials' to offset the price increases.

'Yass River Accommodation'

Marketing objective for 'Yass River Accommodation'

The marketing objective is:

◆ to increase the return from room hire by 25% immediately.

Strategic objectives for 'Yass River Accommodation'

The strategic objectives are:

◆ to adopt a price ranging policy by regrading the rooms so that there is a greater price differential between them (a 'product' and 'price' strategy); and
◆ to have a range of premium-class rooms to attract more people from the senior executive levels (a 'product' and 'people' strategy).

Tactical objectives for 'Yass River Accommodation'

The tactical objectives are:

◆ to upgrade 100 rooms on the fourth and fifth floors to the premium rate;
◆ to package the present premium rooms and offer value-added products; and
◆ to promote the second-floor and third-floor rooms as discount specials and sell-up as many clients as possible.

Management by objectives

Management of the strategic plan involves several phases, and the decision-making process for setting marketing objectives follows the steps shown in Figure 3.5 (page 41).

Marketing-mix strategies

There are basically six main strategic elements (or groups of strategies) used in the marketing mix. Some marketing authorities stipulate only four 'Ps'—*product*, *price*, *place*, and *promotion*. However, because all marketing activity involves people and the selection of a target market, there must be strategies aimed at another 'P'—*people*. In addition, because people tend to buy images and not things, and because the minds of people are the principal concerns of marketing, there have to be *positioning* strategies as well. Therefore, there are *six* types of strategies involved in marketing planning. The six strategic elements that comprise the marketing mix are described as the 'marketing Ps'.

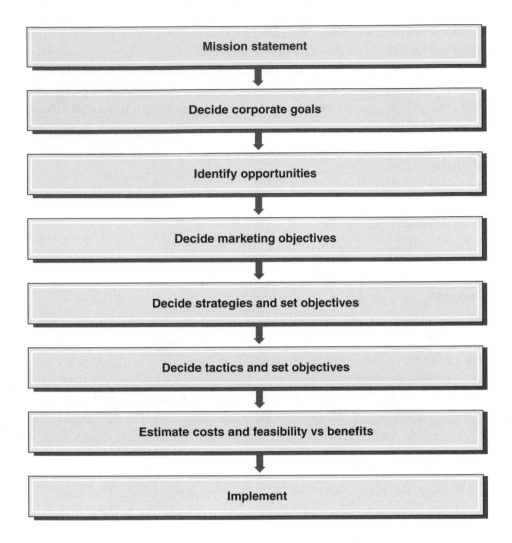

Figure 3.5 The decision-making process for setting marketing objectives
Authors' presentation

It is called the 'marketing mix' because it is a mixture of strategies that is used by management to produce a marketing plan. In the planning process, management has to make decisions about each element in the mix and determine how people will respond to the strategies separately and in combination. Tom Peters, author of *In Search of Excellence*, also compiled *The Shape of the Winner*. Peters theorised that the successful corporations in today's global economy had certain traits—the first of which was to seek niche markets to develop with a view to gaining an advantage over competitors.

In the hospitality industry, developing a product for a niche market requires excellent knowledge of the marketplace, and a flair for selecting a product that appeals to people in a particular place that no one has thought of before.

When devising the most appropriate strategies for a marketing plan, the sequence in which each element of the six Ps is considered is usually as follows:

- people;
- product;
- place;
- price;
- positioning; and
- promotion.

Each of these is considered below.

People

When you begin any marketing assignment, always consider first the *people* who will be your major customers. It is easier to develop strategies for the remaining Ps of the marketing mix when you have first focused on a clearly identified target market. Who are the consumers and where do they come from? An hotel or a motel might draw its guests from a national or even an international region. A neighbourhood restaurant might have a clientele that lives or works locally. A theme resort might draw its customers from a particular age group.

Having identified the broad target group, the organisation needs to ask itself about the likely *motives* of the target consumer group. This leads to a *people strategy*. People strategies can be broadly classified as being:

- undifferentiated (a mass-marketing approach);
- differentiated (choosing selective markets); or
- concentrated (choosing very specialised markets).

Undifferentiated marketing (or mass marketing) is now a strategy seldom chosen by large companies around the world. It means one product for everyone, but it is easy to understand why it has fallen out of favour. For example, these days it is hard to imagine a motor-vehicle manufacturer seriously believing that it can produce one model in one colour—like the Ford 'Model T' which was so popular in the 1920s. Even so, there are many operators in the hospitality industry who retain the fond illusion that their market is 'everyone'.

Differentiated marketing occurs when a company produces a product with model and style differences to satisfy selected markets. A five-star or six-star hotel, for example, aims at providing an experience mainly for a wealthier class of customer.

Concentrated marketing is targeting a specific group of people with a product. The best example in the hospitality industry is a vegetarian restaurant.

A thorough knowledge of the people who comprise the segments to be targeted is probably the most essential aspect of successful marketing. It is easier to develop the other five Ps (that is, appropriate product, price, place, promotion, and positioning strategies) when the marketer has already focused on specific groups of people, the needs they have, and the way in which they want those needs to be satisfied.

Product

Products are the things and the services that happen to, and for, the customers. It is what they get for their money. In the hospitality industry, the product is a service, and this means that it has certain characteristics that a physical product does not have. A hospitality product is:

◆ intangible (it cannot be touched);
◆ inseparable (it cannot be removed from the hospitality property and remain the same product);
◆ variable (it is never completely the same in all respects); and
◆ perishable (once the day has passed, the opportunity to offer hospitality for that date also passes).[6]

Therefore, how can the hospitality product be designed to ensure that it is exactly what the customers want? Strategies determine the benefits that the customers will gain from their purchase.

Product strategies can be classified under two broad headings:

◆ product growth strategies; and
◆ competitive product strategies.

Product growth strategies

Product growth strategies are generally aimed at producing a better or different product to expand the establishment's opportunities for increased market potential by attracting new or different customers. The corporate objective of a growth strategy is to improve the organisation's sales figures or to achieve greater profit contributions.

Competitive product strategies

Competitive product strategies are generally aimed at retaining customers by off-setting competitive activity with an improved or different product. For example, if a restaurant caters to the fast-food market, should it include hamburgers in its product offerings—purchased separately or as part of a take-away meal?

How should the hamburgers be made? Can the restaurant offer a hamburger that is distinctly different from that of competitors?

Place

Where and how the establishment sells the products is the purpose of *place* strategies. The site chosen for the establishment is a place strategy because it is from the *place* that it will mainly sell its products. However, it might have to sell its products from other places (such as travel agents) so that the products are more accessible for purchase by travellers coming from other districts or countries.

Manufacturers usually sell their products via intermediaries—such as wholesalers, retailers, and sales agents. In this case, place strategies are the means of using 'channels of distribution'. In the case of hotels, the channels of distribution are travel agents, tour wholesalers, and bus, airline, and train companies—each of whom sells rooms on behalf of hotels. Another important channel of distribution is the use of other hotels in the same chain. Hilton, for example, uses its wide spread of hotels around the world to sell sister establishments in other cities.

Price

The *prices* that an establishment decides to charge for its products, and the reasons for selecting these prices, are determined by the expectations of the *people* it chooses to target. The prices must match the sacrifices that the consumers are prepared to make to receive the benefits of the product on offer from the hospitality organisation. Usually, but not always, this involves the exchange of products for money. Sometimes benefits can be bartered. In the hospitality industry, accommodation for airline staff is often bartered for air travel for hotel employees. Prices are also influenced by the corporate objectives, the activities of the competition, the cost of the product, and external factors (such as the economic climate prevailing).

Positioning

The combination of the other P strategies in the marketing mix *positions* an establishment in the minds of people. The market's perceptions and expectations are the most important influences in determining the market's choice of products. Therefore, great care is required in *positioning* the establishment and its products competitively. Image and reputation are the result of positioning strategies. The 'information feeds' provided by good *promotion* thus make a major contribution to an establishment's *positioning*.

Information feeds are the means of getting messages to people. These include talking, writing, using the Internet (websites or chat rooms), broadcasting, putting up signs, mounting displays, and the many other forms of advertising.

There might be very little difference between two properties in reality. However, if in the customers' minds there is a *perceived* difference, and they therefore believe that one property is better than the other, this perception will be stronger than the reality. The property that is perceived to be superior will be the favoured place to go—whatever the reality might be.

Promotion

The means by which a marketer communicates the existence of an establishment and its products makes up its *promotion* strategies. A variety of communication channels, or 'message-delivery systems', are available to fulfil promotion strategies. The main ones are:

- personal contact (sales representation);
- advertising;
- sales promotion;
- publicity;
- point-of-sale displays and signs;
- the website of the establishment;
- direct mail and email; and
- the 'look' of the establishment and its staff.

Promotional strategies usually involve a combination of all the message-delivery systems. This is also referred to as the 'tactical mix'. Promotion can be linked with related entities—such as hotels in other regions. In the hospitality industry, personal selling (that is, through personal contact or telephone calls) is an important factor, because the product being offered is, after all, a personal service or experience. The linking of personal selling with advertising, other promotions, and merchandising makes up the 'promotional mix'.[7]

Interaction of the Ps

One element of the marketing mix cannot be treated in isolation from the others. All the elements of the marketing mix are inextricably tied together in the pursuit of a corporate goal, and every element in the marketing mix has an impact on another. For example, a *product* change might affect the *price* of the product. It might also change the *positioning* of the product in people's minds, or even bring different *people* into the market. The changed product will certainly require *promotion*, and might even need a separate distribution or *place* of sale.

Similarly, a new target market will necessitate a new strategy for each of the elements involved in the marketing mix and, consequently, will require different tactics.

Therefore, when writing a marketing objective, it is essential to consider all the marketing elements involved and the strategies required to achieve the objective. A marketer should go back and change the objective if the marketing mix strategies appear to be incapable of achieving it.

CASE STUDY

Ravi's marketing approach explained

Ravi says his food is the reason for the success of his restaurant. However, he has actually put together all the strategic elements of the marketing mix to form a competent and highly successful operation.

Ravi's *people* strategy is to target managers, supervisors, and secretaries—not a difficult decision to make considering that his establishment is located in the heart of a large city's business district. He also attracts young professionals and junior executives.

His *product* strategy is good-quality seafood—superbly prepared and presented. He has a team of carefully selected, fast, and efficient waiters. Another important strategy he uses is to make absolutely certain that his customers are served and fed within thirty minutes. All his customers know that they can be 'in and out' within their lunch breaks. All the waiters wear white shirts, black ties, and trousers. All of them can recite the menu from memory, and they use the 'specials' to assist customers in choosing their food.

Ravi's *place* strategy, apart from his location, involves the layout of the restaurant. This enables rapid access to the tables, the kitchen, and the bar facilities.

Ravi's *price* strategy is to maintain the prices just below or approximately the same as nearby competitors. Every dish is available as an entrée or main dish.

Ravi's *positioning* strategy is to be perceived as a place for high-quality food at reasonable prices, supplied with fast, efficient, and friendly service. Few customers are ever disappointed.

Ravi's *promotional* strategy consists entirely of an illuminated sign under the striped awning verandah, and a very large 'blow-up' of the menu in the window. He never advertises in the major media. Word-of-mouth advertising is enough. A nice tactical touch is to give everyone a miniature menu with next week's fish specials when they leave the restaurant.

Thus, although Ravi says that his food is the reason for the success of his restaurant, it is apparent that he has *all* the elements of a successful marketing mix—incorporating *people*, *product*, *place*, *price*, *positioning*, and *promotion*.

Questions for discussion or revision

1 To compete with a price-cutting hotel nearby, a large hotel decides to cut its own prices even lower. What impact will this have on other elements of the hotel's marketing mix?

2 A medium-priced restaurant in the main part of the city decides to upgrade its image, and endeavours to capture the 'top end' of the market. Why might it make such a decision, and what would be its marketing objectives?

3 An expensive but popular tourist resort in the mountains appeals mainly to wealthy chief executives. The marketing objectives for this resort read as follows: 'To enlarge our market base by 20% within the next twelve months, and to target the honeymoon market'. Develop some strategies to help the hotel achieve these objectives.

4 The market for a backpackers' hostel (formerly a bed & breakfast property) close to the city has been identified as young people on a holiday. The first problem is that liquor cannot be sold or served, and drinkers represent a high percentage of the potential market. In addition, the previous clients of the hostel have been older, conservative people who seek a quiet, restful place to holiday while being close to shops, theatres, and restaurants. Prepare a strategic plan to overcome the difficulties faced by the owners.

5 Using the example of Ravi's restaurant in the text (page 46), how would you advise Ravi in the event of his rent being raised to the point where he could no longer maintain his price strategy?

Chapter 4

Market Analysis

Aims of this chapter

The aims of this chapter are:
- to explain the purpose of market analysis;
- to describe how markets can be divided into measurable segments; and
- to describe the type of information required, its relevance, and its use in analysis.

Theory

Before you can make a decision you must have information. Market analysis is the information base upon which marketing planning decisions are made. The purpose of market analysis is to understand the dynamics of a market by segmenting it into convenient components so that it is possible to identify the opportunities that exist and, from this, make improvements to a property and its products.[1]

Market analysis is a detailed examination of the business environment in which a property operates. It has to be comprehensive to avoid overlooking important developments to the detriment of the property's sales and competitive position in the market.

In the continuing search for improved sales performance, an aggressive marketer uses market analysis to give direction to the marketing of its products, thereby attracting new customers. As part of the process, market analysis is constantly used to review and assess the market. The internal and external factors affecting the patrons of an establishment are constantly changing as a result of competitive activities.

Market analysis should therefore be an ongoing process of assessment and re-evaluation of a property's performance. This requires an information system so that there is a constant supply of vital information. (For more on this, see Chapter 14, 'Marketing Audits and the Marketing Information System', page 180.)

In market analysis, the people forming the market are segmented into various categories. The market's total size (in dollar terms and sales numbers) is measured, and market share figures are compared. The external and internal influences on the market are identified in search of any factors likely to affect the marketing mix strategies in the future. When armed with this vital knowledge, management can proceed with its marketing planning and make vital decisions that will ensure its future growth by building a bigger customer base.

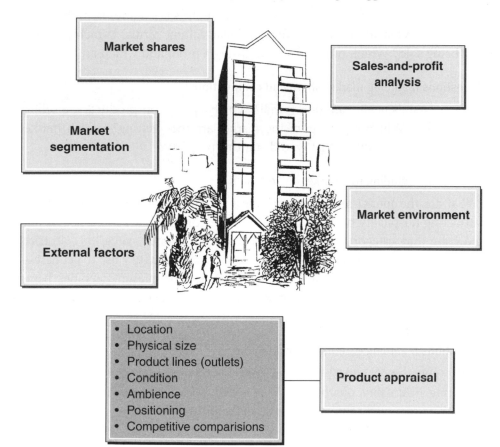

Figure 4.1 Market analysis
Authors' presentation

Main types of information required

Questions

The answers to the following questions need to be quantified—that is, compared with previous years or periods, compared with industry averages and, if possible, compared with the competition. Most of this information will come from a sales analysis, from reservations records, and from customer surveys.

Questions regarding market segments

Who is buying? What 'types' of people are they? From where do the majority of guests and food & beverage patrons come? What products are they buying? How often and when are they buying?

Questions regarding sales-and-profit analysis

What is the size of the customer base? What are the sales figures by numbers of unit sales? What are the sales figures in dollar-volume terms? Which products are being sold? Which products are returning a profit and which are not?

Questions regarding market share and competition

Which establishments are doing well? Which opposition products are selling well? Why? Which segments of the market are they getting? Which market segments do they attract that would suit this property?

Questions regarding the market environment

What are the tourist attractions, business activities, or other factors that are attracting hospitality business to the city or region? Who are these people and how are they categorised? In terms of districts, regions, states, or countries, from where are they coming? Which transport means do they use to get here— for example, which highways do they use? Are the present facilities being offered by the various properties in the city or region meeting the overall needs of customers?

Questions regarding external market factors

What government rules and regulations—both existing and pending—are affecting hospitality purchases? What social values or behaviour trends are occurring that might influence events in the future?

Questions regarding product appraisal

How does the property compare with the competition? How large is it? How many rooms? What is the composition of the rooms? How many seats are there in each food & beverage outlet? What other facilities are on offer—such as meeting-rooms, ballrooms, bars, shops, car-parking facilities, business equipment, and so on? What entertainment and recreation facilities are provided by the property? How do they compare with other properties? Where is the property located and how convenient is it? What is the physical condition of the property, its equipment, and its facilities? What is the ambience of the property, and how is it positioned in people's minds?

Market analysis is exciting because it invariably reveals opportunities and gives direction for marketing decisions. It also unveils unpalatable truths that must be faced, and indicates corrective action that must be taken. Frequently, analysis will point to the need for more information.

Gathering data involves a lot of work. But in marketing you can never have enough appropriate information.

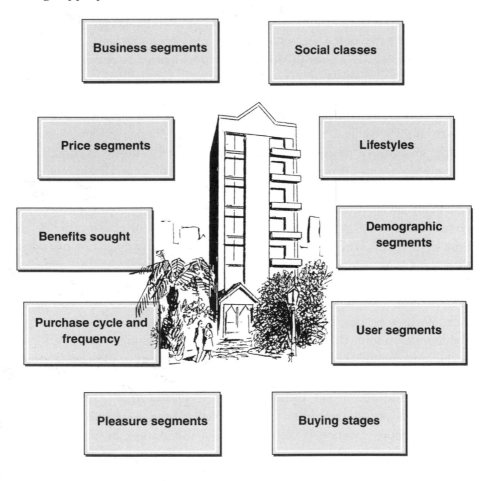

Figure 4.2 Market segmentation
Authors' presentation

Segmentation

People are the core of the hospitality business. Therefore, an essential part of market analysis is a thorough examination of the existing and potential customer base.

Different people prefer different products—even for the same purposes. Customers can therefore be divided into groups with various tastes and preferences on the basis of these varying consumption decisions. The marketplace can thus be divided into smaller groups—for example, those who seek a modest style (such as a backpacker hostel) and others who prefer luxury accommodation (such as a five-star hotel).

There are many ways of segmenting a market to form a complete picture. All markets consist of buyers who differ from each other according to their needs and wants, how much they are prepared to pay, and where they come from. For planning purposes they can be divided into demographic, geographic, psychographic, and behavioural segments.

Once the various segments within the product market have been identified, the hospitality organisation can make a decision on the selection of one or more of these segments as its target market(s).[2]

Unsophisticated managers of establishments simply segment their customers into 'travellers' and 'locals', or even into 'foreigners' and 'regulars'. Common industry practice is to segment customers simply as 'holidayers', 'corporate business clients', 'groups', 'packages' (people accepting special packaged deals), and 'frequent independent travellers (FITs)'. The last category essentially means that these people do not fall into any of the former categories. For many hospitality establishments, this sort of classification is the limit of their concern. Their attitude appears to be: 'Why does it matter where they come from as long as they keep coming?'.

This attitude is irresponsible and unprofessional. It *does* matter where customers come from, where they are travelling to, and why they are visiting the area. We assume that no one does anything without a reason. Marketing is about understanding these reasons and using the information to make better use of the opportunities presented. The essential opportunity is to provide greater customer satisfaction and, ultimately, to increase sales.

The Worldwide Hotel Industry Study[3] indicates that 52.6% of hotel room–nights are sourced from foreign travellers, and 47.4% from domestic sources. Leisure travellers make up 34.1% of the market, business travellers 28.5%, tour groups 17.7%, and conference participants 10.1%. These are worldwide averages, and individual countries show large variations.

Within Australia, most domestic travel is by leisure travellers. The motives for their travel are as varied as the people themselves. Business travellers are both private-sector and public-sector travellers, and this sector tends to be the most attractive to hospitality operators because of the frequency of their travel, their repeat business, and their relative lack of price-consciousness (because their travel expenses are being met by their businesses or their employers).

Some common market segments

Business segments

A business traveller can be defined as a person who is travelling away from his or her home base on matters associated with commercial purposes. Such people have particular needs—such as telecommunications (for example video-conferencing) and support services (such as small meeting-rooms for client appointments, or secretarial services). The guest-room should be able to function as a 'business-room' with in-room fax, on-call printer, access to the Internet, and two or more telephone lines. Video-conferencing and telebeaming facilities are becoming increasingly attractive to business travellers.[4] These facilities can include news services, and various e-commerce applications. To support these services, high-speed, broadband Internet access is essential.

The Bass Hotel chain (which includes Inter-Continental Hotels and Resorts, Crowne Plaza, Holiday Inn, and Staybridge Suites) has negotiated a deal for in-room Internet technology to cover 120 000 rooms outside the United States. The cost to a typical Australian user is approximately US$20 per day.[5]

A clarification of business travel reveals the individual reasons for choice of hospitality. Each category wants different standards and levels of food and accommodation—depending on their occupations, incomes, lifestyles, and positions. On this basis, most market segments can be further subdivided. Within the business segment, the main subsegments are:

- sales representatives calling on company customers;
- executives, professional persons, and public servants attending meetings or conferences;
- people attending conventions or training seminars; and
- itinerant professionals (such as marketers, lobbyists, entertainers, and individual sportspersons) on assignment for a limited period.

Pleasure segments

The cluster of factors forming the pleasure segments of the market include age, income, lifestyle, class, nationality, living mode, and means of transport. Some typical segments are:

- people visiting friends or relatives (VFR);
- honeymoon couples and lovers;

- individual pleasure-seekers who want to meet someone, play sport, gamble, or visit nightspots;
- people on holiday with a planned itinerary;
- people with children (of varying ages);
- package holidaymakers; and
- tour, coach, sporting, and social groups.

Geographic segments

This segment is influenced by the size of the drawing area of a hospitality operation. Many years ago, the local market area for an hotel was restricted to one or two hours' walk. A town could have two or three hotels or inns, and these constituted the local market area because prospective guests did not wish to walk all the way to the next town. Today, a discerning traveller can take advantage of readily accessible transport to travel on to another destination if services are not satisfactory in one venue. An hotel or a restaurant several kilometres away, or perhaps even a hundred kilometres away, can be a competitor.

Demographic market segments

Every age group has its own needs. Young people have quite separate requirements of hospitality from those of older people. Both groups need to eat and sleep but they prefer to do these things in contrasting environments. Family size changes people's needs. A couple with three children wants a different style and size of accommodation from that required by a single young person.

Demographic factors include age, income, sex, number of dependants, stage of family life-cycle (that is, young, teenage, or adult children), occupation, education, and so on. Not all of these factors are relevant in determining the target market. For example, the sex of business travellers does not influence their need for accommodation.

Income influences choice. Although people might want a particular type of accommodation, their desire is significantly modified by what they can afford.

Occupation affects choice. For example, a corporate businessperson or professional with an expense account usually aims for a higher standard of facilities than a small business operator.

Lifestyle segments

Psychographic or motivational segmentation is a more exact form of segmentation because differences in lifestyle often determine the choice of a particular hospitality experience. Lifestyle segments offer a marketer the opportunity to target their planning more accurately to people's needs, and to prepare a product mix geared to their wants.

Some lifestyle groups have been defined as:[6]

◆ school kids with income and purchasing power (known as 'SKIPPIES');
◆ mother older, baby younger ('MOBYS');
◆ double-income, no kids ('DINKS');
◆ dual-earners with kids ('DEWKS');
◆ poor urban professionals ('PUPPIES'); and
◆ well-off older folks ('WOOFS').

Under this heading of lifestyle segments, we include people's preferences, their attitudes, the rate of usage, their recognition of brands, their purchasing habits and frequency, and so on. In hospitality terms, we can look for the preferences of guests who have already stayed with us, and compile a register of likes and dislikes. We might list their preferred transport needs, preferred standard of accommodation, duration of stay, and times of year when they travel. When dividing the market according to lifestyle, we might identify groups with special interests who come for specific events—for example a floral festival or a cultural festival.

The length of stay is a significant factor in this segment, and this obviously affects an hotel's profitability per guest. Length of stay varies appreciably by different segments, and also varies according to international destinations. For example, the average length of stay in India is twenty-four days, whereas in China it is seven days, and in Hong Kong it is four days.[7] In Australia, different segments of the market have different average length of stay. Japanese package-tour visitors stay seven days, whereas backpackers stay, on average, forty-five days.[8]

Buying stage segments

Holidays and extended business trips are usually 'considered purchases'. This alerts us to the fact that there are various stages of readiness-to-purchase before people ultimately become customers. These range from being 'aware' of the property, to being 'interested', to being 'ready to buy'. Each stage is a market segment and each requires careful attention in hospitality marketing—to ensure that the transitions are smoothly handled by an establishment without the loss of too many potential customers.

'Benefits sought' segments

The market can also be segmented according to the benefits being sought by the customer. There are many factors operating here. People seek different benefits in terms of:

◆ certain styles of accommodation (quiet, busy, popular, big, small, luxurious, cheap, and so on);
◆ types of meals (gourmet, regional themes, smorgasbord, vegetarian, and so on);

- in-house entertainment (games, videos, gambling, and so on);
- locations (seaside, views, shops, casinos, night life, business, and so on); and
- facilities (golf, pool, sauna, tennis, and so on).

In making a decision on which market segment to target, a hospitality operator has to consider the attributes of the property. For example, is the property geared to meet the benefits sought by business, convention, or holiday travellers?

In the conference and convention sector, a hospitality organisation can seek further information on this market segment as it relates to the organisation's actual and potential customers. For conference travellers, relevant information to seek out includes the number of conferences held in the market area, the number of participants, the length of stay, and the level of spending of participants. For recreational or holiday travellers, a marketer might seek statistics on the average length of stay, level of spending, the length of the tourist season, and any potential changes to the season.

Purchase cycle and frequency segments

Most products have markets that are cyclical, and this is especially the case with hospitality. Some people have annual holidays (the 'seasonal holiday-maker' segment) and some have more than one holiday a year (the 'habitual holidaymaker' segment). Some lucky people manage to holiday all year round! Business travel drops off significantly during January and February.

What constitutes a 'holiday' varies considerably from person to person—ranging from a regional campervan trip to a world sightseeing tour staying at the largest and most expensive establishments.

Types of travellers are grouped into segments depending upon their worth to a marketer.

Business travellers are categorised according to their frequency of travel as 'heavy', 'medium', or 'light' users. Airlines promote products to the 'frequent-flyer' segment and offer incentives to attract members and their custom. Similarly, large hotels target the segment of 'heavy' users and offer discounts, room-upgrading, or special privileges to attract their patronage.

Understandably, restaurants and clubs always pay special attention to the 'regulars', and endeavour to address them by name: 'Good evening, Mr Spender. So nice to see you again!'. Casuals or 'drop-ins'—people they do not know by name—are called 'sir' or 'madam'.

User segments

There are many people who have a 'club' mentality—those who regularly attend a bar, restaurant, club, or hotel that they particularly like. These people can also be dubbed a 'loyal' segment. Others change their loyalty from time to time. These are called 'shifting loyals'. Those who have no sense of belonging to one establishment and constantly explore places for new experiences are known as 'switchers'.

Another large segment for the hospitality industry is the 'celebratory' or 'special occasion' segment—those people who use hospitality facilities for weddings, anniversaries, birthdays, reunions, and other special occasions.

Price segments

Everyone considers price. Most people seek value. Many people have no alternative but to pay less, and some pay less because they are careful with their money. In contrast, there are those who think that an expensive product must be a good product.

Business travellers tend to select an accommodation product on factors other than price, but holiday travellers, especially families, tend to be more selective with regard to the price of accommodation.

Hospitality establishments vary in the way they cater for these various price segments of the market. Lodging properties design their services to suit the prices of the various price-sensitive segments of the market, and this is usually reflected in the 'star-rating' of properties. A five-star property publicises its level of services and amenities and, in so doing, indicates that its product is aimed at a certain segment of the market. A budget motel also advertises a level of services differentiated on price.

Competing products and their strategic segments

An easy form of segmentation is to 'tag' the people attracted by certain establishments, and to refer to that market by that company's name. Thus there is the 'Sheraton market', the 'Hyatt market', and so on.

Not all products compete in exactly the same way. For example, there might be two motels, with almost identical facilities, located on opposite sides of a highway. Despite the similarity of facilities, each will attract a different segment of the available passing traffic. Of course, one will get the outgoing traffic and the other will get the ingoing traffic. Moreover, one might tend to get the 'commercial segment', whereas the other might get the 'family tourists'.

In all these segments, hospitality consumers have become more complex with respect to their needs. These trends have influenced the hospitality products on offer. Few hospitality operations stand alone any more. To meet changing needs, hospitality operations have embraced either 'vertical' or 'horizontal' integration of their services. The hospitality product now encompasses travel and entertainment as well as accommodation and meals. The product is marketed to consumers as part of a package that might include a 'fly–drive' holiday to a resort area, or a business convention booking with two-day side trips. The increase in brand recognition and consumer loyalty schemes means that these packages are often marketed through a preferred carrier, or through a preferred service supplier.

A simple way to segment customers

In an area with several similar establishments—for example, a big city with a number of four-star and five-star hotels—a simple way of segmenting the market is to divide the available customers into 'fors', 'againsts', 'indifferents', and 'unawares'.

'Fors'

Those who are 'for' an establishment are customers now, or are likely to be soon. Many will pass on the 'good word' and attract others.

'Againsts'

Those who are 'against' an establishment have been there and did not like it. These people are 'bad news' for the establishment because they are likely to tell others that they did not like their experience.

'Indifferents'

Those who are 'indifferent' to an establishment know about it, but see no reason for trying it. They are not convinced, and they go elsewhere.

'Unawares'

Those who are 'unaware' simply have not received the message. They do not have enough information.

The percentages in each of the above categories are important in this exercise. An establishment with a high 'against' percentage is in deep trouble. A place with a high 'indifferent' percentage is not competitive enough; it is not offering enough benefits. A high 'unaware' percentage means that an establishment is not communicating well enough; it has to work harder to get its message across.

In summary, hospitality enterprises attempt to segment markets because success depends on understanding what is going on in the minds of people. The market has been formed by what people know, think, feel, and believe. If hospitality establishments want to improve the chances of their products in this marketplace, they must understand the needs, wants, and motivations of each market segment.

Market measurement

The size of geographic market segments

All market segments have to be measured for their viability. As noted above, the size of a segment must be substantial to justify the time and effort to target it as a group. Regional market segments are significant only if they have sufficient numbers to warrant special marketing consideration. For example, Japanese, American, and German tourists make up large segments of the total tourism market, whereas people from the Falkland Islands do not. In a large city, some suburbs deliver a greater number of customers than do others. To conserve the marketing effort, it is wise to concentrate on the larger segments—unless there is a specific reason for targeting specialised segments (for example, if a property is seeking to establish itself in a niche market).

Sales analysis and IT systems

The collection (and analysis) of sales data is the main way of determining the trends of a business. Sales figures are helpful in identifying weaknesses and strengths of products, sales in particular geographic areas, the performances of sales representatives, the activities of agents, and the effectiveness of sales methods and advertising. To do this thoroughly, internal sales records and an analysis of bookings from each profit-earning centre are required, together with profit-and-loss results. In this respect, IT systems are very important in recording information on the guest cycle in lodging properties.

Computerised systems (such as Fidelio and Maxial) and a large number of specialised packages can be used to provide data on market segments. The use of these systems allows guest information and preferences to be tracked, and allows all relevant data to be included for billing purposes. In some properties, 'smart cards' have eliminated paper-billing of guests and customers. Ideally, a property should operate an integrated database system that includes records of reservations, property management, guest details, financial information, and various other statistics that can be adapted for marketing purposes.

Market-share comparison

Market-share numbers are necessary because these demonstrate how the business is going in comparison with others in the same area of activity. In the hospitality industry, this information is often shared to the advantage of all concerned. If not, market-share estimates have to be obtained by market research, by observation of supply deliveries, or by doing regular customer counts.

See Figure 4.3 (below). Daily sales analysis sheets like this provide a basis for accumulating data about guests—the types of people, where they come from, the reasons for their stays, what they used, and how much they spent. Over time, these data are also used to determine trends, and to ascertain product strengths and weaknesses.

Date: Tuesday 09 August 2003

Total Guests: 150

Room Occupancy: 85%

Client category		Method of payment	
Business	52	Visa	23
Convention	60	Diners	27
Leisure	38	Account	90
Total	150	Cash	10
		Total	150

Guest origin

Domestic	68
Asia	22
Europe	21
US/Canada	39
Total	150

Dining facilities used by house guests

Breakfast

Restaurant	75
Room service	60
Bistro	8
Total	138

Sources of business

Affiliated	92
Agent	28
Other	30
Total	150

Dinner

Restaurant	11
Banquet room	60
Bistro	12
Total	83

Room rate mix

Rack rate	16
Discount (1)	60
Discount (2)	14
Discount (3)	25
Discount (4)	33
Other	2
Total	150

Comments

Picked up good business from a local trade fair.

Figure 4.3 A daily sales analysis sheet
Authors' presentation

Performance comparisons

The customer comes first

The major concern of hospitality marketing is the customer. Market analysis identifies how well the various services of the property are being delivered.

In the hospitality industry, service is everything. How is the customer being treated by the establishment from initial contact through to the paying of the bill? Are the products performing to the standards required? More importantly, are the products meeting the expectations of the customers?

Service is a measurable function. Not only does the establishment's performance have to be measured but also it has to be compared with the performance of the competition. For example, Budget Rent-A-Car once promised: 'If the phone is not answered after the first two rings, your first day's hire is free!'. Pizza Hut promised that if a customer's order did not arrive in ten minutes, it was free! How would the average restaurant perform with that as an offer?

In nearly every case, the sum total of the customers' experiences over time determines an establishment's sales result and its market share.

In a large hotel or tourist complex with many products or profit centres involved in producing a total result, each product in the mix has to be analysed to ascertain strengths and weaknesses, and to find which areas perform better than others. To maintain an establishment's market position, the aim should be service of a uniform standard.

The external influences affecting the market

Government regulations, taxation, union activities, and supply issues all affect the industry. An establishment's market analysis must assess the measures to be taken in response to these issues.

Reactions to change are important. If a certain type of food becomes difficult to obtain locally, does the establishment endeavour to obtain supplies from further afield? If the excise on alcoholic beverages suddenly increases, does the establishment pass the additional cost on to the customer immediately, or does it wait and allow other establishments to give the customers the bad news in the form of increased prices?

Competitors' activities

A picture of comparative performances can be obtained by compiling records of the opposition's advertising (perhaps by a collection of newspaper cuttings and similar), by observing their sales promotions, by noting their products in action, and by observing the reactions of customers. A market analysis is not complete without this information.

Information sources

A business never works in isolation, and a hospitality establishment is always very visible in the marketplace. It is necessary to discover how suppliers, bankers, insurers, politicians, government departments, and influential people in the industry perceive the market, and to obtain their opinions on how the property is performing.

Trade publications, industry reports, government statistics (available through the Australian Bureau of Statistics), newspapers, and published marketing research are valuable sources of information. They often give advance notice of industry trends.

The performance of intermediaries—such as distribution and agency sales outlets—must also be part of the market analysis. Reports from (and about) every significant intermediary can be a goldmine of useful information.

Further analysis is needed to examine impending building developments, government interference, legal changes, economic trends, industrial action, and social trends. Even potential changes in weather patterns and climate should be considered.

Assessing the data

Market analysis means knowledge, and knowledge means power. Market analysis is a fact-gathering process. The sum total of the information gained provides a basis for management to plan future marketing changes and improvements.

Each market segment should be measured against the performance of each of the property's products. This analysis will reveal what the property is good at, and what the customers think that it lacks.

No segmentation system is perfect. There will always be some people who do not quite fit into the chosen categories. However, for measurement purposes, and for ultimate diagnosis of the condition of the market, a segmentation system can be considered sufficient if it is logical and if it covers most contingencies.

Questions for discussion or revision

1 If there is a gradual downturn in sales by an hotel, which areas would you examine and how would you discover the reason for the downturn?

2 Two five-star hotels in a city are competing for the lucrative business market. Prices have been maintained at a high level. Suddenly, a new contender builds a superior complex. Before it is completed, one of the pre-existing hotels does a full-scale survey and market analysis locally, interstate, and internationally. What is this hotel looking for?

3 Your hotel's market analysis reveals that a substantial number of people are unaware of many of your facilities. What does this tell you? What remedial action would you take?

4 A large guesthouse on the outskirts of the city, with accommodation for 120 people in private rooms, but with shared bathrooms, is considering applying for an hotel licence. Before applying, it does a market analysis. How would it go about this? Which aspects of the market should it investigate?

5 Many people complain about a particular hotel being too 'upmarket' for them. This is rather vague. How would you go about ascertaining the real problem?

Chapter 5

Segmentation by Purchase Motivations

================== Aims of this chapter ==================

The aims of this chapter are:
- ■ to explain the concepts of market segmentation;
- ■ to describe how to identify the segments; and
- ■ to identify the behavioural characteristics of purchasers and their decisions to buy.

Lifestyle factors

There is a huge number of people all around the world with the desire and the resources to spend on travel, accommodation, entertainment, and recreation. These people represent a diversity of nations, occupations, incomes, and personalities, and they have a wide range of reasons for wanting various hospitality experiences. Obviously, the market is too vast and diverse for one establishment to satisfy.

For practical purposes therefore, the total market is subdivided into many smaller markets and, by using market analysis, a hospitality establishment can determine which segments best suit its location, property size, property type, expertise, and resources. The selection of the most appropriate segments is called 'target marketing', and its purpose is to provide a focus for the whole marketing effort.

The preferred lifestyles of different people determine their behaviour and guide the patterns of their purchases. Not everyone wants to live in the same way, and these lifestyle preferences can be clustered to form market segments. Once management knows the thinking of these various market segments, it is in a position to decide which segments to target, and which strategies to develop. The targeting of these segments will be more incisive if management is armed with knowledge of the reasons for their various behavioural attributes and attitudes.

Trying to understand behavioural patterns of a whole hospitality market has never been easy, and has become increasingly more difficult in recent years. For the hospitality industry, only one thing is certain—people will continue to want places to eat, drink, and sleep. But how, where, and when they will want to do these things is a matter of continuing complexity.

Changes in attitudes to the environment and ecology are altering the demand for many types of products. Advances in technology are allowing the introduction of new products that are rapidly being accepted by consumers. The changes that information technology (IT) is bringing to hospitality marketing in the twenty-first century are, of course, a major theme of this book.

There is a growing sameness about cities, with the ubiquitous 'Coke' and 'McDonald's' signs emerging in the most surprising places. The development of satellite communications, the explosion of information on the Internet, and the intrusiveness of television have removed many of the mysteries that once surrounded the political, cultural, and geographical features of remote areas.

One of the trends made possible by the IT revolution is for the home to become the main source of entertainment and information. Shopping and access to a range of services is possible from home. Although older generations are not racing towards early adoption of this way of life, the younger generations are embracing it eagerly. Already there are ominous signs of younger people being far less interested in the wider world around them and, possibly, signs of a reduced desire to travel. The effects that these changes will have on travel and tourism have yet to be seen.

The way in which the industry operates has also changed. The majority of bookings for travel, for hotel and motel rooms, and for resorts are being made through agents. These agents, who act as 'brokers' between consumers and hospitality providers, often operate out of suburban shopfronts or commercial offices. Tourism agents might sell travel in general, or they might be specialised wholesalers (who reserve bulk reservations with airlines and hotels), or they might be corporate travel agents. Most countries and states also operate their own tourism offices to encourage visitors to travel to their regions. Private operators who specialise in a similar fashion are referred to as 'destination management companies'.

Tourism agents use computerised booking systems—some on a global scale called 'global distribution systems'. Because of the size of the systems required, and the number of agencies to make them effective, most computerised booking systems have been established by large corporations—especially airlines (which had a higher number of reservations than any hotel chain due to the number of flights involved). Examples of some computerised reservation systems are: Sabre (which is oversighted by American Airlines and has 100 000 outlets), Apollo, Galileo, and Worldspan.

These developments bring advantages and disadvantages for the various players in the hospitality industry, especially in relation to marketing. Although large hotels might seem to have a market edge, the developments in IT can 'level the playing field'. Smaller operators, who can compete by repositioning their hospitality properties to appeal to 'niche' markets by offering more specialised products, can utilise Internet opportunities. Smaller operators can develop websites that attract consumers in a cost-effective way and thus compete with the larger systems.

There are also changing trends in food and dining preferences. This is causing the demise of many fine silver-service dining-rooms as many people all over the Western world turn to a less formal dining experience in the form of cafés, brasseries, and bistro-style eateries. An article in the *Australian* observed:[1]

> People are choosing to eat out more casually, in places which are noisier and more fun, not in places which are constrained and where there is a mystifying barrage of cutlery . . . Rather than beautifully crafted dishes that demonstrate the skill of the chef, there is a tendency towards not cooked [food] but arranged food.

Chef Philip Searle of 'Oasis Seros' in Sydney was quoted in the same article as saying:

> As we move down the generations, this lack of formality is going to become more and more popular—service that is purely functional as opposed to service that is obsequious.

Searle concluded that it was his belief that people were going to become more 'eaters' than 'diners'.

Another lifestyle fashion is the trend towards privacy. In earlier times, there was a certain imperative to 'see and be seen', but now this is less important—although it still exists in parts of Asia and the Middle East.[2]

The real danger in referring to 'trends' is that they do not apply to everyone. The changes affecting the hospitality business indicate a further fracturing of the overall market into more segments of people—each with quite different purchase motivations.

The last chapter of this book ('Forecasting Market Demand', page 364) returns to the subject of trends, but with an emphasis on forecasts of trends to come, rather than trends that have come to pass.

Buying influences on behaviour

Before making a purchase, buyers go through a series of decision processes. In most cases, other people are involved in these stages in the decision-making process. The stages of purchase are the same as the stages used in selling—from awareness, to interest, to willingness to purchase. Before the purchase is made, however, there is a nervous period when most would-be buyers require convincing that they are doing the right thing. For this, they look for reassurance from others. Once their doubts are overcome they usually proceed to buy.

There is evidence from several research agencies in the United States that most advertising is read by people who have already made a purchase, and who seek reassurance that they have made the correct decision. The reason for this, the researchers claim, is that after the purchase comes another nasty moment when the purchaser worries whether he or she has made the right decision. Much luxury car advertising is of this nature. These post-purchase 'jitters' make after-sales service vital. The key to getting customers to come back, or to converting a once-only customer into a regular client, is to concentrate on making sure of satisfaction after the event. This is why every establishment should know the name and address of every customer and should maintain regular contact from immediately after the sale, and thereafter.

Lenses of distortion

Although they might be unaware of it, most people buy to please or impress others. Who they are pleasing or impressing varies. Spouses, parents, bosses, close friends, and relatives are the most common influencers. Thus, the product is perceived by the purchaser through *other* people's eyes, and this distorts what the purchaser is seeing—which is why the attributes of many products are overlooked by the buyer. This also explains why some people keep on making the wrong purchases. They are actually being motivated by their desire to impress or please someone else—perhaps even an imaginary group of peers that exists only in the buyer's mind.

'Where did you stay?' is a question frequently asked of the returning traveller. This is often followed by another question: 'How was it, any good?'. Everyone prefers to give answers that will impress the questioner.

Who influences the decision on where to go for the holidays? When a couple is going out to dinner, who makes the decision of where to go? If a family is driving along a freeway as night falls, who decides which motel they stop at?

The roles involved in buying motivation are:

◆ the *initiator*—the one who first suggests or thinks of buying something;
◆ the *influencer*—the one whose advice or opinion counts most in the decision to buy;
◆ the *decider*—the one who makes up the minds of others;
◆ the *purchaser*—the one who actually makes the purchase;
◆ the *user* or *users*—the ones who often have much to say about the purchase afterwards!

In hospitality, the person in a group who pays the bill might not be the one you are trying to please, nor the one who decides if the group comes back next time! Consider Figure 5.1 (below). Who initiated, who influenced, and who decided the choice of restaurant? Who paid the bill? Next time, the users might be the deciders.

Figure 5.1 Initiators, influencers, deciders, purchasers, and users
Authors' presentation

In the corporate scene, the identification of the key people and the roles they play in making a decision is more complicated—because there are usually many people involved in influencing and deliberating over the decision. An executive assistant might phone through the booking, but who was involved in making the choice of establishment?

There is always hesitancy when a prospective customer comes across a product for the first time. This might be a new product or new service introduced to the market, or an established product which the prospective customer has not experienced previously. In these circumstances, some people make decisions earlier than others. These people are called 'early adopters'. They are the first to buy a new gadget or a new car, or the first to try a new experience.

At the opposite end are the 'laggards' who make sure that everyone else is satisfied before they 'make the plunge'.

In between are the 'early majority' and the 'late majority'.

The job of a marketer is to identify these processes and to assist the purchaser to make an easy decision—remembering that word-of-mouth advertising (the 'good word' that is passed on by satisfied customers) is critical to an establishment's acceptance and eventual success. Therefore, every customer has to be seen in the light of his or her ability to affect thousands of future sales.

Purchase behaviour

Most people like to think that they are in charge of their own destinies. In fact, in making purchases, most people are motivated by two major factors:

◆ their aspirations to be certain types of persons who live particular ways of life; and

◆ the cultural and social influences of the society in which they live.

People are affected by a host of influences. These include their self-perceptions, their personalities, their desired lifestyles, the attitudes of their peers, their age-related needs, their gender, where they live, whether they are married, single, widowed, or in various relationships, their race or nationality, their financial resources, the pressures of parental and other relationships, and their varying levels of intelligence and physical capacity. These factors are a result of their genetic makeup and the environment in which they have grown.

People's identities and self-perceptions are revealed in their personalities. The word 'personality' comes from the Latin *persona*, meaning 'mask' (as in the mask worn by an actor). The Irish playwright Oscar Wilde said, 'It's not people themselves who are interesting—it is the masks they wear in society'.

A Greek philosopher, Galen (AD 129–199), also a physician, anatomist, and physiologist, recognised that people tended to be either extroverted or introverted, competitive or careful. He believed that the combination of these factors produces four basic personality types. For hospitality providers, these personality types can be recognised as customer types (see Figure 5.2).

Figure 5.2 Performers, followers, rulers, and thinkers

Performers

These are people who like to be noticed. Often loud and ostentatious, they are gregarious talkers and extroverts, and usually stimulating people to be with. They prefer bright colours, striking fashions, outstanding cars, and have lots of friends. They go out a lot and want to be 'where the action is' so that they can be noticed. They are very people-orientated.

Rulers

These people are less friendly, and are cooler and more calculating. They like to be in charge of people and situations. They are usually active, hard-working, and task-orientated. They seek (and usually obtain) positions of power. Their dress is formal, and their tastes in possessions are usually restrained and elegant, but often lacking in warmth.

Followers

These are friendly people, but are often shy. They like to avoid trouble. However, when they have to face up to problems they often do so with considerable determination. They prefer home and a familiar comfortable environment.

Thinkers

These are independent, preoccupied people who work at their own pace. They are systematic, task-orientated people who shun the limelight. They work to regulations because they like to know where they stand.

By observing the effects of personality and lifestyle preferences on purchase behaviour, it is possible to identify the above groups, and to predict the wants of each group for a hospitality experience. Consequently, when marketing to specific classifications of people, the attributes and benefits of a product can be made obvious to each lifestyle classification that is targeted. The advertising can thus enable prospective customers to recognise that an establishment is 'their sort of place' from the appearance of the establishment and the services and facilities on offer.

It should be noted that corporate motivations are different from private motivations. The business executive who uses a suite and entertains lavishly on an expense account, considerably modifies the budget when holidaying at the same place with his or her family.

Because marketing is all about satisfying the needs and wants of people, hospitality managers must concentrate their efforts on understanding the segments they intend to target. The next chapter discusses how to select the right customer mix for an establishment.

Questions for discussion or revision

1 Apart from thirst, what are the purchase motivations of a group of shift workers who regularly drink at the same hotel after work?

2 What are the most likely product attributes of a cocktail bar in a five-star hotel? Describe what should happen to and for the customers.

3 A family of four—consisting of two parents with two children (aged one and eight)—arrive from another town to stay the night in a motel. They have not booked, they have been driving for most of the day, and they do not know the town. Name the benefits you think are being sought by this family.

Chapter 6

The Customer Mix

Aims of this chapter

The aims of this chapter are:
- to explain how to base a customer mix on the segments;
- to list various segments in the category of 'reasons for travel and dining'; and
- to describe the customer matrix and how to use it.

Segmentation selection methods

Which available segments of the market, as revealed by market analysis, should management choose to develop, change, or eliminate? In other words, of all the many types of people and businesses in the hospitality market as a whole, which ones will suit the property best?

The customer mix is dictated by the type of property, and its size, location, and facilities. Management should attempt to match the resources of the establishment with the most suitable customer mix, rather than attempt to pursue a market segment that has no links with the existing customer mix and the property's prevailing resource base.

A property that assumes that the total market has a uniform set of needs and wants is adopting a strategy of *aggregation*. The belief of this property is that all people are basically the same, and that one product mix will suit everyone.

A more appropriate strategy is based on *segmentation*. Such a strategy proceeds on the basis that all people are not the same, and that the hospitality market, even in a small region, is comprised of many types of people who have different requirements to be satisfied by hospitality services.

Chapter 4 ('Market Analysis') described how to segment markets by demographic, geographic, behavioural, and psychographic criteria—thus revealing a wide variety of possibilities. Arriving at the best customer mix requires all these possibilities to be sorted and then narrowed to a choice of segments. All people (whatever their particular travel segment) have certain things in common—they all want a place to eat and a place to sleep. However, in fulfilling these basic desires, the members of different segments have significantly different requirements and expectations. A hospitality establishment should assess the segments it now has, and check these against potential segments that might be more attractive financially, while still suiting the resources and capabilities of the property.

For hotels, motels, and tourist resorts, the best way to select a customer mix is to begin with each segment's 'reasons for travel'—such as business, convention, holiday, sporting, cultural, compassionate, and visiting friends and relatives. The variables in each segment are then analysed by the targeting process to define and separate the benefits sought by smaller (but usually significant) submarkets. Variables affecting the final choice are the demographics and psychographics of the segments. These can be sorted through until the choice is narrowed to the final customer mix.

It is not possible to serve all segments effectively. They are either too diverse geographically (and therefore too difficult to access) or have particular requirements (which are too varied for one establishment to satisfy adequately with the same overall mix of products, facilities, and services). In other words, the location, resources, experience, and competence of an establishment cannot extend to meeting the needs of every potential customer.

Some types of customers do not mix well. High-profile, international business executives are seldom happy to be 'rubbing shoulders' with large families who have young children roaming the building and facilities. A place predominantly occupied by older people is not necessarily an attractive environment for younger people who have vigorous activities in mind. Contrasts in age, lifestyle, occupation, and social views can cause antagonism.

The only situation in which it is possible for a property to be 'all things to all people' is one in which there is no competition. This might occur in a remote country town, for example. However, even in this situation, people will choose not to go at all if the environment and customer mix is unsuitable for their requirements.

Customer mix percentages

A customer mix for an establishment is reflected in the percentages of each market segment it succeeds in obtaining. An establishment that attempts to satisfy a broad number of segments is said to be indulging in 'undifferentiated marketing'. If it concentrates on several, distinctly different segments it is involved in 'differentiated marketing'. If it aims at one major segment it is practising 'concentrated marketing'.

The total hospitality market (in terms of numbers of people and 'reasons for travel') is made up as follows:

◆ holiday;
◆ visiting friends and relatives (VFR);
◆ compassionate (death, illness, accident, and so on);
◆ convention or meeting; and
◆ business.

Overall, although there are more people involved in non-business travel, the business segments make up the largest segment of the travel and hospitality market, because of their higher frequency of usage. This is why most centrally located establishments adopt a policy of differentiated marketing in which they pursue the business segments ahead of other segments. For city establishments, the main market segments (in terms of frequency of usage and reasons for travel) are usually:

◆ business;
◆ convention/meeting;
◆ holiday;
◆ VFR; and
◆ compassionate.

In contrast, tourist resorts concentrate on the recreation markets. Despite this focus, business conventions and seminars still represent a sizeable proportion of their customer mix, and some resorts specialise in conventions.

In other words, the business segment is the smallest in terms of number of people, but is the largest user of hospitality because most businesspeople make several trips in a year. The recreation segments are larger in numbers of people but members of this segment make less frequent trips.

The percentages of each travel type within an establishment's customer mix vary from region to region—depending on an establishment's ability to market itself to each segment. For example, in a small city, hotel 'A' might have the following customer mix (averaged over a year):

◆ corporate business 20%
◆ business meetings, conferences 25%

- conventions, seminars 10%
- interstate vacationists 5%
- overseas vacationists 2%
- package tours 10%
- stopovers 5%
- local weekenders 5%
- miscellaneous and frequent independent travellers (FITs) 18%.

In contrast, the customer mix for hotel 'B', which is on the fringes of the same city (perhaps on a waterfront), might favour the leisure/pleasure segments, as follows:

- package tours 20%
- miscellaneous and FITs 17%
- interstate vacationists 15%
- corporate business 10%
- conventions, seminars 10%
- overseas vacationists 10%
- stopovers 8%
- local weekenders 7%
- business meetings, conferences 3%.

Customer mix assessment criteria

When choosing the customer mix, each segment has to be assessed on the basis of:

- size;
- location and accessibility;
- homogeneity;
- profitability;
- durability;
- expectations of the segment; and
- ability to service it.

Each of these is considered below.

Size

The corporate market is a popular target market because it is composed of a large number of frequent users. For this reason it is also the most competitive. The holiday market is also large. There are many segments and subsegments worth attention—provided that there are sufficient numbers to mount a worthwhile marketing strategy to obtain them.

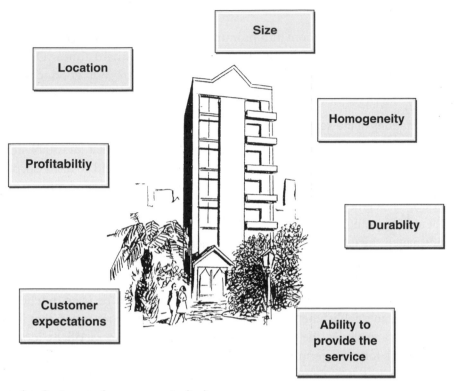

Figure 6.1 Customer mix assessment criteria
Authors' presentation

Location and accessibility

Most customers come from definable countries and areas. However, it is not always possible to reach them with cost-efficient communication methods.

Homogeneity

'Homogeneity' refers to a market made up of similar personality types, lifestyles, ages, occupations and incomes. This is mostly sorted out by the customers themselves who tend to choose a property that has a customer mix with similar lifestyle values to their own.

Profitability

The corporate market is most often targeted for profitability because of its size and frequency of usage. It is also the easiest to access with promotion. However, it is seldom the most profitable on the basis of dollar per unit sale because corporate customers seek discounts and concessions. The volume of this segment makes it attractive and viable.

Durability

Some segments mushroom into prominence when favourable economic conditions prevail, and then disappear at the first sign of hard times. Others are 'trendy' segments, and subject to change. These are not good customers around whom to build a permanent business.

Expectations of the segment

Some segments have preconceived ideas of the facilities that an establishment should have. For example, people from certain cultures and wealthy corporate groups might have definite requirements for food & beverage and other services. Specialist segments are good business earners if they are of sufficient size, but there is no point in competing for their custom if an establishment's facilities do not match the expectations of these segments.

Ability to service it

The resources and competence of an establishment can be overstretched. For example, an establishment might successfully bid for a convention that fills the place, but excludes the regular clientele. Such a move sacrifices long-term customers for short-term profit.

The objective of management should be to get the customer mix right and match it with the right product mix so that the hospitality standards and prices communicate the right message to the chosen market segments. The location of the property (that is, its proximity to entertainment, business places, special events, holiday infrastructure, and so on), its size, its facilities, and its image determine the choice of customer mix. Future chapters discuss how it then goes about developing strategies that attract the chosen customer mix.

Reasons for travel

Business travellers

Business travellers make up one of the largest and most important segments. In Australia, there are approximately four million interstate trips made by business travellers each year.[1] Once dominated by males, the business segment now contains many women.

The accommodation needs of business travellers range from a modest room to a suite of rooms with luxurious, self-contained facilities. Many hotels provide special meeting rooms, video-conferencing, computers, secretarial assistance, and fax facilities. They are offering a virtual 'office-away-from-the-office' to attract the corporate and public service markets.

The travellers' country of origin is an important consideration when targeting the business market. In Australia, the Japanese, American, and European markets are being sought by many hotels. Some are offering specific products to suit the expectations of the Japanese in particular.

CASE STUDY

Business services—the Concorde Hotel, Singapore

The Concorde Hotel in Singapore has 515 rooms and a marketing focus on business travellers, reflecting its situation on Orchard Road in the commercial district of the city.

To cater for its selected market, the hotel has a range of suites of business quality, and also includes some designed specifically to appeal to business guests from Japan and South-East Asian countries. The range of services offered include a fully equipped business centre, and suites are also provided with NHK and CNN news channels, and telephones with IDD service.

In addition to the usual facsimile, telex, and cable facilities that business travellers expect, the business centre includes secretarial and dictation services, photocopying, Internet connections, binding and printing services, library facilities, and presentation rooms with overhead and slide projectors.

The hotel also runs a shuttle service to the larger business and convention centres.

Conventions and seminars

The convention and seminar business is a huge market requiring medium-to-large conference areas and dining facilities. It is a highly competitive market and most establishments have to bid for it. For large conventions, especially national and international conventions, the bidding is done through a convention and tourist bureau, through a promotion or marketing company, or through a travel consortium. The bid assembled by these organisations is usually comprehensive—offering transport, recreation, and shopping in addition to the provision of a suitable venue. A hospitality establishment attempts to convince the organisation that it should be included in this comprehensive package being presented to the convention organisers.

If an establishment does not have the conference areas to cope on its own, it can become involved in this market if it is close to a convention facility, and thus obtain some of the associated accommodation and meals business which is so attractive.

Leisure and pleasure travellers

The reasons for travelling to a holiday destination are varied, and the subsegments that make up leisure and pleasure travellers are largely created by lifestyle and demographic considerations. These include single people, couples, couples with children, the young, the elderly, the wealthy, middle-income earners, and low-income earners. In Australia, each year there are more than five million interstate trips made by people taking holidays.[2]

Holidays and 'weekend escape' are among the most common reasons for travel in this segment. Other reasons for leisure and pleasure travel include sightseeing, health, sport, and honeymooning.

Income and the period of available leave-time are considerations for these travellers. Many people are on a travel schedule that allows for only short stopovers at various places.

The selection of a leisure and pleasure customer mix largely depends on the location of a property, its surrounding attractions (the natural and physical tourism infrastructure), and the facilities being offered.

Package holidays

Tour wholesalers are organisations that put together a number of holiday components and then sell the total package at a special discounted price. Most tour wholesalers are travel agents. In 1997, there were 3266 retail travel agents and international tour operators or wholesalers in Australia.[3] Wholesaling is also undertaken by airlines, bus and train companies, casinos, hotels, and motels. The products they create are saleable by anyone with access to a customer base. The packages encompass various combinations of travel (sea, air, train, bus, or hire car), accommodation, sightseeing, entertainment, sports, games, and special events.

Coach tours

Coach tours or bus holidays provide a continuing source of business for motels, hotels, roadside taverns, cafés, and tourist attractions of various descriptions. The customers are usually the young or the elderly.

Motoring holidays

People on motoring holidays represent the largest of all travel markets because this type of holiday is cheap and convenient. All that is required is a car, a map, some money (relatively modest compared with other holidays), and the will to go. Seventy-eight per cent of all domestic trips involving a stay away from home and a journey of least forty kilometres are made by car.[4] Although this segment is not a big 'money-spinner' for large hotels, its sheer volume feeds numerous smaller establishments. The quality of the business for a hospitality facility depends on the socioeconomic status of the traveller and the benefits sought along the journey.

Caravanning and camping

Caravanning and camping are undertaken by people who enjoy the freedom and convenience of having a 'home on wheels'. These holidays usually involve more planning, and many people make a pilgrimage to the same spot year after year.

Myriad caravan parks and adjoining tourist facilities service this segment. This is a market undergoing change, with increasing numbers of onsite vans and permanent cabins.

Restaurants and cafés benefit from this segment, but it is less significant for hotels and guest houses.

Backpackers

Backpackers represent a burgeoning segment of the tourism market. Backpackers come from all countries, and an estimated 500 hostels have emerged around Australia to service this growing segment. Many former hotels, motels, guest houses, and caravan parks have been converted to cater for these people.

Backpackers generate a high proportion of foreign-exchange earnings for Australia. In 1999, their average expenditure was $64 per person per day. They number 404 300 each year and most are aged between 20 and 40 and come from Europe, Asia, and America. They stay an average of 66 days. They seek low-cost accommodation and avoid many of the conventional tourist attractions, preferring adventure and nature, and often staying in smaller centres.[5]

Explorers and trekkers

Organised tours of the outback are the main attractions for explorers and trekkers. Although similar in some ways to backpackers in their desire for adventure, the members of this segment prefer a structured experience that guarantees what they will see and do.

Group travel

The group travel segment is made up of musicians, entertainers, theatre groups, hobbyists, and a variety of special-interest groups (including sporting clubs, social clubs, community service organisations, and pensioner groups). They require discounted group rates for everything, but they often fill rooms at opportune times of the year.

The 'reward market'

Many organisations reward their employees with travel holidays for good performances—especially sales performances. This 'reward market' is a good market to pursue. Prizes and give-aways for competitions for promotional purposes also form part of this segment.

Permanent users

Airlines, building companies, project developers, and many large corporations need a permanent or semi-permanent base for their employees, and such organisations usually request that accommodation always be available on demand or as a continuing reservation. The level of service that is required varies, but this is excellent business for most accommodation establishments.

Special events

For festivals, large sporting events, football trips, big concerts, state celebrations, and the like, establishments can produce special promotions as a continuing marketing strategy to attract customers. The usual strategy is to provide tickets, special group rates, and packages (including air, bus, and train travel). Proximity to the venue is a significant advantage.

'Compassionate segment'

The 'compassionate segment' is a diffused market without any particular segments of any size. The segment is made up of individual travellers with diverse reasons for travel—such as visiting friends and relatives, or attending functions including reunions, funerals, and so on. The benefits being sought by such travellers are so broad-ranging that it is difficult to identify a single group that is of a size worth targeting.

Seasonality

The customer mix of most establishments varies from weekdays to weekends, and changes according to the months of the year and the seasons. Business and convention segments usually require accommodation on working days—perhaps booking-in on Sunday nights and leaving on Friday mornings. The weekends usually attract holidaymakers or short-term trippers. In Australia, the months of December–January and June–July are traditionally slow months for business travel.

If an establishment targets a clientele of business and management people, and if its strategies have been effective in reaching this group, its holiday and weekend markets should be made up of the same types of people—because this is the sort of place they like. Many establishments offer inducements for business travellers to 'stay-over' or to come back another time. Attractive inducements are special rates, upgrading, and entertainment (such as shows, concerts, plays, sporting events, gambling, and special sightseeing tours). These establishments induce people to accept by offering family-plan rates, concert tickets, rental cars, tour packages, and discounted facilities.

CASE STUDY

A seasonal market—the Novotel Phuket Resort, Thailand

The tourist accommodation market on the island of Phuket in southern Thailand has approximately 400 hotels and accommodation facilities. Due to weather and temperatures, the market is very seasonal.

The Novotel Phuket Resort is a property with 210 rooms in Patong, which has one of the more popular beaches on the island. For five months of the year, the Novotel Phuket achieves an occupancy of more than 90% over the peak season, attracting mainly international tourists. From April, however, the demand falls off as the hottest time of the year approaches. From May to September, to maintain its market share, the hotel has to offer discount rates of up to 50%.

Local market

For many establishments, the local market is the main or only user of food & beverage outlets and recreation facilities. If the property is geared towards interstate business travellers, the local market can be targeted for weekend use of the facilities. Depending on the country, approximately half of the adult population never travels away from its home region or state, and a similar percentage seldom ventures from home to use the facilities of an hotel, a restaurant, or a café. Such people are not potential customers. Nevertheless, a substantial number of potential patrons exists in local areas, and an establishment can target locally the same segments as it targets in the travel market.

Some establishments spurn the locals. In doing so, these businesses forget the role of these people as potential influencers. Travellers planning to visit an unfamiliar city want information and reassurance on where to stay or which hospitality places to attend. If they know someone in the destination locality they might phone, email, fax, or write to seek advice.

Some establishments spurn the locals to protect their guests from unwarranted intrusions or to maintain exclusivity. Most international hotels for example, do not have public bars. Some make the restaurants prohibitively expensive as a means of restricting access to all but the wealthiest of the locals.

These are ill-advised policies. Because of the influencing role of locals, it pays to familiarise and encourage the indigenous market by offering full access to the facilities.

Modes of transport

Another way of choosing a customer mix is to assess the means of transport used by various segments. This makes sense for motels, for example, which are mostly dependent on car, bus, and commercial travellers. Hotels and motels adjacent to airports naturally target air travellers. Resorts are dependent on location, and the mode of transport of potential customers determines access to the property.

Points to remember

From the above discussion, the following important points emerge.

- ◆ Choosing the customer mix begins with an assessment of the reasons for travel of various segments. The final selection of segments is adjusted by considering the demographic and psychographic market variables of each segment.

◆ The customer mix is dictated by the establishment's resources, experience, and location.

◆ Each segment should be assessed on the basis of its size, location, accessibility, homogeneity, profitability, durability, and expectations. The ability of the establishment to meet those expectations must be considered.

◆ The usage rate by each segment of the market varies according to the wider environmental variables of the market—the most dynamic of which are economic and political.

◆ The cities, states, and countries from which the customers come must be analysed. This knowledge assists in the appointment of sales staff and agents, the planning of promotion and publicity, and the provision of facilities that suit the customers' requirements.

◆ The attitudes of the local market must be considered—especially its ability to influence the customer mix.

Customer matrix

Nearly all governments maintain records of tourists and travellers and, through customs and visa records, their reasons for travel to a country or region. Other data can be obtained from analysis of competitor's activities. These statistical data can be used to compare an establishment's customer mix, from its own records, with the total market potential. This comparison shows which types of customers are being lost to the competition and which market segments offer the best (and least) potential. This can result in modification to products and facilities, or the provision of new facilities.

Figure 6.2 (page 86) shows the sort of table that can be completed. Different organisations might record different categories of data, according to their individual needs. A quick appraisal of the data in Figure 6.2 indicates that our establishment is attracting more of the local clientele than the competitors, is more dependent on telephone bookings, and is more likely to be paid in cash or cheque. This might be appropriate to our strategy. Alternatively, we might choose to look at these data and reappraise our strategy. Other data could be accumulated, plotted, and used in such a reassessment. This sort of matrix is therefore useful in such assessments.

But in this e-commerce age establishments are less likely to use such a table, and are increasingly likely to use computer programs that enable them to call up data arranged in categories as required. An organisation might wish to call

Accommodation sales

July 2003, weekdays

Category	Competitor A	Competitor C	Competitor B	Our company
Sex **(% total this city)**				
Males	30	20	20	30
Females	25	25	30	20
Origin **(% total this city)**				
Local	10	20	20	50
UK	30	20	30	20
Japan	30	30	30	10
Other Asia	30	30	30	10
USA	20	30	30	20
Other	30	30	30	10
Reservation **(% this hotel's booking)**				
Telephone	20	20	20	50
Internet	40	40	30	20
Agent	30	30	20	10
Other	10	10	30	20
Method of payment **(% this hotel's booking)**				
Visa	40	35	20	10
Mastercard	20	35	40	10
Cash/cheque	20	20	30	50
Account	20	10	10	30

Figure 6.2 Hotel or motel accommodation sales (percentage of total)
Authors' presentation

up data on their sales according to the age group of guests, or according to the sex of their guests, or according to their origin (local, interstate, international). This information can be compared with sales data from other organisations, and with national data.

With increasing sophistication of such computer programs (already available and becoming more versatile almost daily), establishments can reorganise data and present these in various ways—comparing categories of people, places of origin, times of stay, and so on. Moreover, modern computer programs allow these data to be presented in various ways—as tables, column graphs, pie graphs, and so on—sometimes using colours and shading for extra clarity of presentation.

Restaurant segmentation selection

The method for selecting a customer mix for a restaurant or a dining-room in an hotel or a motel is very similar to that used for selecting an accommodation customer mix. It begins with ascertaining the reasons for people eating out and the benefits being sought. The selection of segments is then narrowed by analysis of each segment's demographic and psychographic attributes. Essentially, the customer mix is affected by the establishment's location, its physical and human resources, and the experience of management.

Each reason for dining-out is counted as a market segment. In the course of a year, some people have several different reasons for eating out. Consequently, over a period, it is possible to find the same group of people eating fast food on one occasion or dining in a luxury restaurant on another. However, the majority dine out according to habit. They find a restaurant that suits them and, for a certain time, consistently use the facilities, moving on only when they become disappointed with the outlet, or want a change.

The reasons people eat out

There are many reasons for people dining-out in a particular place. In each of the following examples, a different benefit is being sought. In some cases, several benefits are combined:

Convenience

Convenience usually means 'somewhere quick'—a place close to an hotel, motel, home, or office. Convenience can also refer to the availability of car parking near by.

Figure 6.3 The reasons people eat out
Authors' presentation

Escape

When people want to get away from it all—whether it be the home, the office, a difficult situation, or a particular person—they seek escape to a haven or retreat. Some people escape to a place where there is a crowd. They seek music, entertainment, a new environment, and possibly something exciting. Some establishments offer a pianist, a string quartet, a jazz group, a play, or fun characters waiting on the tables. Escape is also offered by unusual places—including ships, trams, or trains that have been turned into restaurants. People might seek a place with a high view, a country barn, or even a cave. There are many imaginative options for this segment.

To be with others

People sometimes seek places where they might find someone they know. This is a typical 'club approach', and some restaurants and cafés (and even some canteens) fulfil this requirement because they have secured a band of regulars who share needs and habits. Noise and activity are the requirements of this segment.

A meeting place

People who are seeking a meeting place are also usually seeking seclusion and exclusion. For example, a business group holding a discussion over dinner prefers privacy, as do couples or small groups of people who desire somewhere quiet, where they can talk and be alone together.

A food experience

People who seek a 'food experience' choose their restaurant for a food style—such as a steak, a fish dish, vegetarian, or a national food theme (Thai, Indian, Italian, Chinese, Japanese, and so on). Some people in this segment are entranced by the concept of an expensive gourmet experience with French cuisine and silver service.

A special occasion

People in this category are celebrating a special event—such as a business deal, an anniversary, a birthday, a win at the races—or are simply intent on impressing guests.

Somewhere casual

Seeking 'somewhere casual' does not mean that this segment wants cheap food. It could be as simple as not wanting to get changed into more formal clothes. These people are seeking a casual, relaxed environment that offers value for money. This is a growing segment all over the world. The requirements of the members of this segment might range from 'fast food' to a moderately expensive establishment—as long as it meets the criterion of being 'hassle-free'.

There are subsegments of each of these 'reasons-for-dining-out' markets. These subsegments are assessed by demographic and psychographic variables. The key variable is the income of the segment. Another variable is the type of food service—such as a smorgasbord, buffet, brasserie, carvery, table service, or more elaborate French or silver service.

An hotel should consider the overall 'umbrella' image of its property when deciding on a customer mix for their restaurants or dining-rooms. For example, a luxury hotel does not necessarily have to provide an expensive restaurant with French service, especially with recent trends towards a more relaxed dining experience. Perhaps casual elegance might be more suitable.

Questions for discussion or revision

1 If you were sales manager of a five-star hotel with a large business and professional clientele, how would you handle an enquiry from a football club that wants a group discount for a five-day stay? Explain the reasons for your decision.

2 Assume that you are the manager of a five-star hotel that has five floors of accommodation with four suites and a hundred rooms on each floor. Would you segment your guests by floors? If so, describe the criteria you would apply to differentiate the customers from each other on the various floors.

3 If you were the manager of an hotel with three bars, how would you organise the attributes of the bars to suit the four main people-types identified by Galen (page 70)? Describe the décor and service experiences that you would offer. Which of the four types would you combine in your deliberations?

Chapter 7

Target Marketing

=========== Aims of this chapter ===========

The aims of this chapter are:
- to explain how to target segments using the market menu and target market grid;
- to explain how to choose target segments; and
- to describe how to build a customer base and a sustainable competitive advantage.

Opportunities from market analysis

A hospitality establishment, like any business venture, can *create* a market, *discover* one, or *join* one. A tourist resort commencing in a new area and offering unique facilities is *creating* a market. An hotel that thinks it is catering for one type of customer can *discover* that it is gaining most of its business from an unexpected source. An hotel that sets out to capture a well-established market in the same location as several others is *joining* a market if it does no more than offer the same services.

A hospitality establishment can also *specialise* in one market, or it can *target several segments*. An hotel that caters for only the health-conscious is *specialising* in one market. An hotel that looks for a mix of business clientele during the week and short-term holidaymakers at the weekend is *targeting more than one segment*.

Targeting is selective. It fixes on market segments and makes it possible for products and strategies to be developed that are specific to the needs and wants of the people comprising the segments and that are offered at prices they are prepared to pay. Such targeting is more cost-efficient for the marketer's promotions than is a broad or undifferentiated marketing approach. It is about customising products and services. The enterprise chooses one segment of the market and focuses on satisfying the needs of that segment.

There are advantages in this—namely that all the enterprise's resources can be focused on meeting the needs of only one group of customers. The disadvantages are that the enterprise is putting all its plans for increased sales on one group and, if that group of customers decides that it no longer wants the enterprise's product, the enterprise is left without a market. External factors can affect this. For example, if airfares rise excessively, backpackers might not be able to afford to travel and backpacker hostels will lose custom.

In targeting, management develops strategies for each market. The rule is: 'one market, one strategy'.

Target marketing is the opposite of mass marketing. Mass marketing does not recognise separate preferences. The term 'mass marketing' (also called 'undifferentiated marketing' or 'aggregation marketing') is used to describe a hypothetical situation in which all possible customers might want to buy the product. Although mass marketing has some applications, it is usually impractical for most enterprises. One single market for everyone is very rare. Even a universally used product (such as Coca-Cola) can not and does not target everyone. Coca-Cola changes its strategies for each market it targets, including its container type and size, promotion, price, and distribution. Coca-Cola thus targets both sexes, and people of different age groups, lifestyles, and diet preferences. It is interesting that advertisements aimed at one group are seldom noticed or recalled by another. As with Coca-Cola, a hospitality enterprise can have several target markets for the same product—with each segment responding to different persuasions.

The purpose of market analysis is more than establishing the segments that form a market. It also involves identifying the segments that are to be targeted and exploited. The objective for the business is to consolidate, to expand, or to increase profitability.

When choosing the target markets that best suit a property or a product, the enterprise can define the people it wants by their needs, wants, preferred benefits, and the price they are willing to pay. *Needs* arise from people requiring security, ego-gratification, bodily comfort, escape, and the basics of food, shelter, and clothing. *Wants* are individual expressions of needs—as translated into things and experiences that suit people's ideas of colour, size, fashion, shape, and performance. People can thus also be selected according to their demographics (age, income, occupation, and sex) or their psychographics (personality and lifestyle).

Targeting is crucial to good marketing because it recognises the differences among types of people, and generates new products or changes to existing products that satisfy individual preferences. Precision is important in determining target markets because the attitudes of masses of people are often difficult to understand. Small groups are more predictable, and are therefore easier to satisfy with separate marketing solutions.

So much in hospitality relies on understanding and appreciating people. Targeting is thus the platform of a marketing plan.

Selection process used in targeting

The way to use target marketing at the planning stage is to follow the steps explained in previous chapters.

1 Conduct a market analysis and identify the key segments that make up the total market.
2 Sort them according to their demographic, geographic, psychographic, and behavioural characteristics.
3 Establish the sales volume of each product used by the various market segments.
4 Find out the reasons for each segment's product preferences.
5 Determine the segments that the property is now servicing.
6 Identify segments that the property is not servicing and decide which ones would be attractive to target.
7 Establish which competing properties are successful with the segments that have been identified for targeting. Find out if the people comprising those segments are happy with the level of service they are receiving. If they are not, there is an opportunity for exploitation by the provision of a better service.
8 Conduct a feasibility study. Ensure that the segments targeted are worthwhile. Assess each segment on the basis of its size, location, accessibility, profitability, durability, and expectations. Assess the establishment's ability to service the segment.
9 Commission research to fill in information gaps that are required to answer any questions arising from the assessment procedures.
10 Armed with the appropriate information, confirm the segments that are to be targeted.

11 It is probable that to meet the targeted segment's needs, it will be necessary to develop or modify the facilities or product mix. The cost of making these changes has to be weighed against the profits likely to be obtained, thus calculating the time it will take to recoup the outlay.

12 If all criteria are satisfactory, the marketing planning process then continues with the development of marketing mix strategies for each targeted segment.

The information gained from the market analysis usually suggests some segments that represent opportunities for the property to expand its customer base—the 'hard core' of customers who make up the bulk of an establishment's clientele. Before embarking on a plan, first be sure that your property is located in the right place and has the resources and capabilities to win the segments over. If it has, perhaps with some reasonable modifications to products, consider some strategies that might move a significant number of people in those segments over to your property.

Developing a target market grid or matrix from a market menu

The customer mix matrix or target market grid uses a *market menu* as a means of narrowing the selection process to one (or several) market segments. In the case of hotel and motel establishments, the process begins by selecting the reasons for travel. For restaurants, it begins with the reasons for dining out.

The market menu is the list of variable factors that have to be considered when selecting a market segment.

The hospitality market menu

Market segments

business	caravanners	explorers and trekkers
package holidays,	FITs	sport
tours	vacation, leisure	the reward market
convention, seminar	pleasure	sight-seeing
bus tours	backpackers	compassionate
meeting, conference	honeymoon	group travel
motoring holiday		
special event		

Mode of travel

aircraft	coach	self-drive
train	hire car	car and trailer/caravan

Reasons for dining out

convenience	a meeting	somewhere casual
escape	food experience	permanent users
entertainment	special occasion	local
to be with others		

Age

0–12	25–34	55–64
13–18	35–44	65–74
19–24	45–54	75–85

Sex

male or female

Desired price range

least expensive	medium–high
low	top of the range
middle of the range	

Occupation

small business owner	senior management	student
self-employed trade	middle management	unemployed
self-employed	supervisor/foreperson	casual worker
professional	clerical	home manager
employed professional	skilled worker	retired
senior executive	unskilled worker	pensioner

Income

$0–6999	$32 000–41 999	$86 000–99 999
$7000–13 999	$42 000–51 999	$100 000–149 999
$14 000–21 999	$52 000–70 999	$150 000+
$22 000–31 999	$71 000–85 999	

Living mode

dependent child	couple with young children
young single	couple with adult children
mature single	mature-aged empty nesters
young couple without children	

Departure place

local	interstate
country	overseas (name country)

Religious affiliation (if relevant)

name religion and describe particular requirements

Nationality

name country or ethnic origin

How reservations are made

through an agent	Internet
telephone	personal (that is, 'through the door')

The target market grid

Once the lists of important factors of the target market have been drawn up in the market menu, the target market grids can be developed. The grids are a form of database of the target market segment. From each list in the market menu, one factor can be selected to go into a target market grid and correlated with other factors or elements. The marketer can use one market grid, or several; having several will be useful. These grids should be kept as simple as possible and contain only factors that will be useful in making market decisions. This means that the marketer does not have to use all the factors in one grid.

If the grid is simple (and therefore quick and easy to use), it should not be time-consuming to fill one out from existing data once a week, or even daily, for each individual or group. If the organisation does not have a fully integrated computer system that can perform database functions and produce such data, an Excel spreadsheet is an ideal tool to use for the grid, with individual sheets totalled through to a master sheet.

If the grids are being compiled for a new organisation, the researchers might have to experiment with a number of formats until an effective tool for assessing the characteristics of the target market is developed.

When the grids are completed, a picture should emerge of the people comprising the market segment to be targeted. The purpose of the process is to bring the segment into focus so that it contains factors that can be used when assessing or redesigning services to meet the desires of the target market segment—rather than being merely a broad sweep of a demographic category. Demographic factors are too general to be of use in making focused decisions.

The following examples use existing data for an operation to redefine its service and assess how it is meeting its target markets. For a new operation, the grid could be compiled from information gathered through market research.

Figure 7.1 (below) illustrates a target market grid used by a backpackers' hostel for each individual guest.

Note that not every category must be marked for every person or group. The key is to be flexible—the target market grid is not an end in itself. It has to be something that is simple and clear enough to use. To create forms and diagrams that look good in a file is meaningless bureaucracy. The hospitality business is not bureaucratic. It deals with real people and their wants.

The grids made up for individuals can then be totalled, and the accumulated data might produce a grid like the one illustrated in Figure 7.2 (page 98).

Individual's name: *Mary Jones*

Date of stay: *25 September 2003*

Departure place	Sex		Mode of travel			
	male	female	aircraft	ship	bus/train	own car
Local		X				X
Europe						
UK						
Japan						
Other Asia						
USA						

Figure 7.1 Target market grid used by a backpackers' hostel (for each individual guest)
Authors' presentation

Period from: *20 September 2003*

Period to: *27 September 2003*

Total guests: *53*

Departure place	Sex		Mode of travel			
	male	female	aircraft	ship	bus/train	own car
Local	15	17	6	0	18	8
Europe	3	4	5	2	0	0
UK	2	0	2	0	0	0
Japan	3	5	8	0	0	0
Other Asia	0	3	0	0	3	0
USA	1	0	0	1	0	0
Totals	24	29	21	3	21	8

Figure 7.2 Target market grid for a backpackers' hostel (for a time period)
Authors' presentation

What does this grid tell us? First, most of the guests are local, but there are important segments within the market that could repay some time and attention. For example, most locals arrive by bus or train—which suggests that the hostel should advertise at the local bus depots and train stations. A small group of guests who originated in Asian countries outside Japan have also come from by bus, but the number is very small and could be a 'one-off'. Nevertheless, the hostel should monitor this and see if that trend develops in future periods. The hostel should also note Japan is a significant source of guests, and perhaps could improve its service to that segment by offering translations (into Japanese) of local tourist information. The hostel should also note that the majority of guests is female.

A hospitality establishment should not be too general in defining the target markets. Gross generalisations are useless in defining the wants and needs of a target group. A group defined as 'men aged 18 and over' is not even a market, let alone a target market. The members of such a group will have such different wants that it is impossible to target such a group.

In the selection process, not every item on every list will be applicable. Religious affiliation for example, is not always a factor in the various products used in hospitality, but sometimes it is important. Some groups might have special dietary needs, or there might be special days of religious observance to be noted.

In keeping with the flexibility of the grid, the establishment can use whatever factors it likes, and express the data as percentages (rather than raw numbers). Excel spreadsheets are again useful—because they allow easy copying of formats and creation of new grids. They also easy conversion from numbers to percentages.

See Figure 7.3. From this grid, the hostel has learnt that the overseas guests, especially those from Europe and the UK, stay longest. For a smaller organisation, an Excel spreadsheet can be a useful tool to calculate average length of stay by entering a list of individuals' length of stay. This grid also reveals that the Internet is the most common form of booking.

Does the hostel want to compile other grids? Perhaps it could survey its guests for information on income, and relate the guests by income in a grid. The possibilities are many.

A good acronym to sum up the use of these grids is: 'KTGS'—keep the grid simple. A simple tool is easy to use and allows flexibility. Consider a simple analogy. To drive a nail into a wall, you need a hammer—a simple hammer. Do not look for a power-driven, electronically controlled concussion device! You need a simple hammer. The design of a hammer has been largely unaltered since humans first discovered that it was a simple and flexible tool that achieves its purpose. Similar comments apply to the use of grids—keep the tools simple and effective.

Period from: *20 September 2003*

Period to: *27 September 2003*

Departure Place	% of Guests	Average Length of Stay	How Booked		
			Telephone	Internet	Personal
Local	32	9 days	5	15	12
Europe	7	34 days	1	5	1
UK	2	32 days	2	0	0
Japan	8	18 days	0	8	0
Other Asia	3	14 days	1	2	0
USA	1	28 days	0	1	0
Totals	53		9	31	13

Figure 7.3 Alternative target market grid for a backpackers' hostel
Authors' presentation

Figure 7.4 Internet marketing can enable even small operators, such as home-stay or farm-stay operations, to achieve worldwide exposure.

Thanks to Falls Farm of Tasmania for permission to reproduce part of their website

Even by using the conclusions gained from a target market grid to target a narrowly defined segment of people, those outside the target group might still receive the message. There is a radiation effect from any public promotion such as advertising, and nearly everyone knows whether or not a product or service is meant for him or her.

Overall, in assessing the use of market grids, the essential point is that when a segment is properly targeted, the service can be better designed to meet the demands of that section of the market.

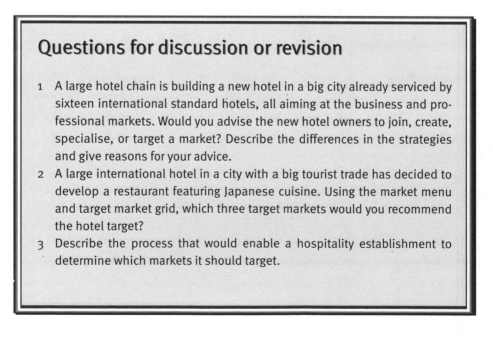

Questions for discussion or revision

1   A large hotel chain is building a new hotel in a big city already serviced by sixteen international standard hotels, all aiming at the business and professional markets. Would you advise the new hotel owners to join, create, specialise, or target a market? Describe the differences in the strategies and give reasons for your advice.

2   A large international hotel in a city with a big tourist trade has decided to develop a restaurant featuring Japanese cuisine. Using the market menu and target market grid, which three target markets would you recommend the hotel target?

3   Describe the process that would enable a hospitality establishment to determine which markets it should target.

Chapter 8

The Product Mix

Aims of this chapter

The aims of this chapter are:
- to explain how to assess a product mix;
- to explain how to match the product mix to the customer mix; and
- to describe the product life-cycle.

Achieving the right mix

A product mix is the range of facilities and the quality level of services that an establishment offers to its customers.

Every customer asks: 'What do I get when I stay at this place and how much will it cost?'. At a five-star or six-star world-class hotel, included in the daily room hire a customer will probably receive a full range of services—including the use of a tennis court, a gymnasium, a spa, and a sauna. The customer will also, in effect, be paying a portion of the costs entailed in providing the luxuries that surround guests in such an establishment—the marble interior, the plush lounges, the chandeliers, the palms, and so on.

At another hotel, the customer might get a cheaper rate, but with the tennis court, gymnasium, spa, and sauna being purchased separately. In this case, for the property to justify the existence of various products, each product on offer has to be regarded by management as a profit-earning centre.

Because of the expense involved in building and providing these products, a property has to be reasonably confident that the customers want the extras. The management of a five-star hotel might perceive the extras as being a necessary part of their product mix to attract custom—for example, a deluxe property might believe that having a wide range of products is an important aspect of its quality image. But this might not be the case for a tired businessperson who wants nothing more than a bit of attention, a nice meal, and a good night's sleep in a comfortable bed—without paying a huge price.

In matching the customer mix with a carefully planned product mix, the hospitality establishment makes a series of crucial decisions. It has to be sure which products to include in the normal room rate, which to offer as extras, and which not to have at all. The decisions depend on the customer mix that the property decides to target, and the expectations of that customer mix.

Essentially, having completed a market analysis, and then having selected the mix of customer segments for targeting, the facilities provided have to attract the customers who are wanted. This is customising the product to the needs and wants of known customers, as opposed to creating the products first and then looking for customers later.

Product lines

A *product mix* has width, depth, and consistency. A *product line* is a group of product items that are similar in their purpose and function. Every major hotel usually has three main product lines—its accommodation, its dining facilities, and its bars. The *product width* depends on how many additional product lines an hotel offers—such as shops, sports and recreational facilities, and hire cars. Some resorts have a wide product line and embrace an extensive range of services. Others keep it simple and inexpensive.

The number of items in each product line determines the establishment's *product depth of choice*. For example, an hotel with a choice of four dining-rooms has a depth of four items.

Consistency relates to the similarity of the product lines to each other in their appeal to the customer mix.

Each product line requires a marketing strategy, especially if the items are chargeable extras and have to pay for themselves. In contrast, some lines are subsidiary to the main promotions of the establishment—just by 'being there' they meet the needs of customers, and are not expected to make a profit contribution. The costs of these items are covered by the room-hire sales as part of doing business. The style and size of an establishment generally dictates its product lines, depth, and consistency.

Hospitality establishments provide a place where guests can enjoy almost the whole gamut of human experience. Guests can sleep, eat and drink, meet, have sex, talk business, exchange gossip, entertain friends, rest, relax, be private, be noticed, play sport, wash themselves, wash clothes, escape, celebrate, entertain, impress, gamble, shop, have fun, do nothing, do anything, be waited on, be massaged, have a sauna, dance, listen to music, wait, spend money, feel important, see important people, and so on. But no single guest wants to do all of these things. So does management spend time and effort in supplying the means to meet all of these activities? The answer has to be 'no'. As one hotel manager aptly put it: 'Sometimes you have to be prepared to walk away from business'.

Some customers are not worth pursuing because the investment involved in providing for them is unlikely to return a profit. For example, a large hotel will probably have a swimming pool—an item considered by many managers to be a mandatory item in their recreational product line. However, what if the pool is used by only a few customers each week? A pool is expensive to build and maintain, and occupies a large valuable space that might be put to better use. Many product lines are the result of marketing decisions based on industry habits, and can be pandering to a perceived customer demand that might not exist. An establishment without a pool might lose some customers, but might pick up many more by using the space for something else.

In contrast, a facility might not be much used, but might still play a part in the overall presentation of the property. For example, a gymnasium might be little used, but having these extra facilities might be important for the total image of the property.

Styles of operation

The primary accommodation places are hotels, guest houses, hostels, motels, and resorts. Each of these terms describes a type of place where guests can expect a certain product mix and style of service. However, there is some overlap, with some motels providing services competitive with highly ranked hotels, and some hotels offering resort-type facilities.

A star-rating is a broad classification used by the industry to describe a lodging place's product mix, price, and level of service. Management believes it has to live up to the rating—which might have been given to the establishment by management, or might have been assigned by an independent organisation that publishes an hotel/motel guide. Although customers use a star-rating as an initial guide, they base their final choice on personal experience or on the recommendations of others, and an hotel's reputation is ultimately earned by quality service. An establishment's occupancy rate and number of satisfied customers might have no relevance to its star-rating.

The star-rating reflects such aspects as location of the property, details of room amenities, and the room rate. In 1990, the system was reviewed by Standards Australia with input from Tourism Training Australia, and hospitality standards were brought into line with comparable international ratings schemes. The standard is entitled AS/NZS 3905.3:1994. The Australian Automobile Association has almost 16 000 properties on its rating system, under five categories—(i) hotels and motels; (ii) camping and caravan parks; (iii) onsite park accommodation; (iv) holiday units and cabins; and (v) bed & breakfast establishments and guest houses.[1]

The size of a large establishment has a bearing on its appeal to the customer only if the place has a width of product lines, and this is not always the case. Some of the largest merely have many rooms. Some of the smallest, such as boutique hotels, offer more personalised service and comfort.

The 'value engineering' concept of hotel construction is a phrase used to describe the concept of arranging a standard product mix that will offer value to any customer anywhere. This concept can produce a sameness in hotel design. The attempt to provide a multipurpose operation to suit everyone can, in the end, please no one in particular. This 'formula approach' to marketing is not using targeting to good effect, and is unlikely to produce satisfied loyal customers who will go away and 'sell' the place to their colleagues and friends.

The simple, cost-saving benefit of building a property around customers—rather than around expensive facilities—seems to escape many investors. The return from a multimillion dollar investment in a marble-lined foyer and related facilities can be as nothing compared to a modest investment in a smiling, helpful, and interested concierge supported by a willing staff. The customers will probably never come back to look at the marble foyer again, but they will come back to experience the dignity and comfort provided by caring service.

Keys to success

There is always a new property that seems to be brighter, bigger, and glitzier than the ones before it. Such a property will drag in the 'early adopters' who like change and want to be 'where the latest action is'. However, long-term survival depends on the lasting quality of the guest experience. For its ongoing financial health and wellbeing, every business has to conduct its operations in such a way that the main focus is on satisfying customers' needs and wants. If customers are not satisfied, they will not return to purchase goods or services from the business in the future, and the business will decline and eventually fail.

While the big places spend their money in a bid to gain the fickle 'switchers', a small lodging-house two blocks away can attract regular custom and make money consistently while watching with curiosity as the bigger places go into an ever-increasing debt spiral.

Location and distance

Location and distance is the primary determinant of an establishment's success. Not everyone can recover from being in a back street in the wrong end of town. Proximity to places where customers want to engage in other activities is always best—such as being near an airport, on a major highway (on the better side), next to facilities for shopping, sport, or gambling, next to the business centre, in the heart of a local community, or part of an attractive holiday destination.

Wherever the property is located, more business will come from the nearest customer sources than from the distant ones. And the customers will keep coming if they get what they want.

Product assessment

An establishment's facilities need to be constantly reviewed. There are two criteria—economic and strategic. The two work together.

Economic

Any establishment requires a huge investment in money and time. Investors are invariably looking for an early return even though they know that planning through to actualisation requires years. Management seeks to use the property and its products to achieve growth, sales, profit, and market share, and to make the best use of its capital and human resources. Each product therefore has to be assessed on its ability to make a contribution to management's objectives. This, in turn, is dependent on market size—the availability of customers.

Strategic

In the pursuit of economic objectives, management has to consider the competitive intensity—the expectations of customers. Management has to plan for maximum attraction of customers and maximum retention of customer loyalty. These considerations are reliant upon product and market homogeneity.

Decisions about products should be made on such *strategic* considerations of what the customers want and how the customer mix feels about each one, as well as considering the more pragmatic *economic* approach.

If the product mix is altered to achieve an economic objective, management faces the consequences of a change in the customer mix. For example, an hotel might abandon room service or allow it to run down badly because it is not making money. Such an hotel might be 'penny wise and pound foolish'—that is saving in the short term, but losing in the longer term. It is sometimes better to recover losses on a product that is essential to the needs of a market segment by maximising profit from other products.

The product mix formula

The simplest method for developing a product mix to match the customer mix is to ask the customers. Why sit around guessing what the customer wants?

If management has decided to target a segment, it should have a good idea why it has done so. The decision presumably has been based on that segment's reasons for travel and its expectations of product (or service) and price. A consumer survey of the targeted segment will fill in the missing gaps of knowledge.

Armed with knowledge about the groups that comprise the targeted customer mix, the product mix becomes a combination of items selected from the product lines noted below. (Remember that each item must satisfy the economic and strategic objectives of the property.)

Accommodation product line

- self-contained, fully serviced apartments or suites (large, medium, or small);
- separate condominiums, shacks, caravans, cabins, boarding houses, or huts;
- two-room or three-room self-service suites;
- room (large, medium, or small) with ensuite or shared bathrooms;
- bedroom layout: family, twin, double, or single beds.

Dining product line

- banquet rooms;
- restaurants of varying nature;
- cafés and bistros;
- coffee shops;
- room meals.

Beverage and bars product line

- room service, room mini-bar;
- cocktail bar, lounge bar, private bar;

◆ club bar, front-of-house (or street) bar;
◆ restaurant bars.

Entertainment product line

◆ night club, band, dancing;
◆ live theatre or variety show;
◆ gambling;
◆ movie hire;
◆ games.

Business services

◆ meeting rooms, conference facilities;
◆ e-business services;
◆ fax, secretarial, photocopying services;
◆ translators.

Shops

◆ wide variety of themes and items.

Personal services product line

◆ valet;
◆ hairdressing, nail-care, grooming;
◆ drycleaning, laundry, ironing, clothes hire;
◆ crèche, baby-minding, playgrounds, mothercraft nurses;
◆ in-house doctor, chemist, naturopath, chiropractor, nurse.

Recreation amenities product line

◆ swimming pool, swimming lessons;
◆ sauna, massage;
◆ gymnasium, aerobics.

Sports facilities product line

◆ tennis, golf, squash, handball, and so on;
◆ skiing;
◆ boating.

Leisure and pleasure product line

◆ hire cars, limousines, mini-buses, boats, and so on;
◆ sightseeing tours;
◆ tickets for theatre, concerts, and sports events.

Signature product line

◆ toiletries, towels, gifts, souvenirs, and so on.

When choosing the product mix, management must bear in mind that each product line comes with a cost for the customer one way or another—either in the total charge-out rate or by separate charges for each product used. How many customers will pay the price?

By using targeting to arrive at an ideal customer mix, the profile of the segment's basic wants becomes apparent. Management must add further in-depth research into each segment's wants. Taken together, the profile and further research allow the product mix to be decided with confidence.

The customer knows what is value to him or her. The bottom line is always cost, and customer value is arrived at by the simple equation:

$$value = costs \div benefits$$

Product life-cycles

Any establishment seems to have a limited life-cycle, and so do its products. Hospitality, even though it is a fundamental aspect of civilised life, is subject to fashions, moods, and trends.

The four stages in a product's life-cycle are *introduction*, *growth*, *maturity*, and *decline*.

Introduction

At the *introduction* stage, the new property, having gone through the early assessment stages of market analysis and feasibility, is launched and brought to the attention of the targeted customer mix by promotion.

Growth

If the property and its products are acceptable, it will achieve *growth* and some degree of prosperity.

Maturity

At the *maturity* stage, the property will have reached its maximum growth, and will stabilise. It should, by then, be returning some profit on the original investment. This might take several years.

Decline

The *decline* stage is reached when other places enter the market, when the facilities of the original property become tired and need refurbishing, when the market's needs and wants change, or when changes occur in the location surrounding the establishment.

The length of a product's life-cycle varies, and some concepts have more durability than others. For example, some well-known restaurants in capital cities have not changed their basic formats for many years, but there have been subtle adaptations to the needs of the customers over time.

How to handle change

In handling change, a property might target a new customer mix, or perhaps subtly phase-out one segment in favour of another. This will probably lead to some changes to the product mix—with the dropping of some items in a line or the addition of new ones. A restaurant that is no longer serving the needs of most segments can be refurbished, restyled, and renamed. There are always new fashions in hotel design and development. As previously noted, one of the trends of the mid 1990s was a 'boom in small, offbeat hotels where the interior design is cutting-edge or richly opulent'.[2] These were also termed 'boutique' hotels and catered for people who had the wealth and inclination to seek something different and exclusive.

A property and its product mix should be constantly under review. When the point is reached for a change to any of its product-line items, there are four basic decisions to be made—build, hold, harvest, or divest.

Build

If the market demand for a product is increasing (for example, bar, dining-room, or accommodation), and if the product can be expanded to cope with the additional business, it makes sense to *build* or extend the product. This depends on confidence (from various market, economic, and industry indicators) that the upward trend will continue.

In some cases, when the demand warrants it, management will extend its line—that is, add more items to the product line. For example, management might increase the number of bars, perhaps with differing prices and presentation. Another example might be an hotel extending its recreational facilities—perhaps adding to an existing golf course, or adding some tennis courts, badminton courts, squash courts, and so on—thereby providing a full mix of sports alternatives.

Hold

Holding (or maintaining) a facility makes sense if, for economic and strategic reasons, nothing is to be gained by making any change. Unfortunately, for sentimental reasons or fear of change, management sometimes holds onto a product for too long, despite dwindling customer numbers. Often there is a belief that additional promotion will solve the problem. In these cases, management is often 'throwing good money after bad'.

Harvest

Harvesting makes sense if more profit can be gathered by simply maintaining a facility. For example, this would apply in the case of a dining-room that fills regularly and in which patronage would not suffer if the prices were raised marginally over a period.

Divest

If a facility is losing money and has no strategic advantage, it might be time to *divest* it. For example, an hotel ballroom occupies valuable space in a hospitality building. If it is under-utilised for its original purpose—catering for balls, concerts, displays, or other functions—the space might be better used for another purpose.

Another approach is to franchise out a facility—for example, the laundry or valet service—to a supplier. A bottle shop might be relocated away from the main area so that it is available to customers, but not be seen as part of the main hospitality function. This is often done to avoid confusion about the establishment's position in the market. As previously noted, food & beverage outlets might be contracted out in 'innovative, symbiotic relationships in hotel dining that help build incremental revenue and foster brand identity'.[3]

A drastic change for a declining property to make is to refurbish, rename, and reposition the property, and target an entirely different customer mix. Some former convents and religious houses have been redeveloped in this way. The Hotel Costes in Paris is a former eighteenth-century convent, and the Casa de Carmona in Seville was a seventeenth-century mansion.[4] In Sydney, New South Wales, an Inter-Continental Hotel was developed within a large building that was formerly a department store operated by Grace Brothers. Sometimes it is better to sell the property and start afresh with a new one.

Most properties need redecorating, but this should not be delayed until the place starts to look tired and worn. Redecorating is required whenever it is necessary to maintain a contemporary sense of style that is compatible with the property's customer mix.

Drastic change to the property or its product mix can lose customers. Frequent customers develop a feeling of 'ownership' about a property and, like a relationship with an old friend, they do not like to see it change.

The problem for management is that nothing stands still in the hospitality business. Not to meet the challenge of external change is fatal. However, the important detail is to recognise what the changes mean, so that any change is made for a reason. That reason should always be to meet the expectations of existing customers, and to attract new customers. 'Change' can be a bad word to use with existing customers. However, if an establishment improves or does things better, customers will understand and appreciate the need for change.

Questions for discussion or revision

1   Your hotel has only one public bar and it always overcrowded at peak times of the day. Someone suggests a 'line-extending strategy'. What does this person mean by this term?
2   You have been asked to make an assessment of an hotel's recreational product mix—its pool, squash court, tennis court, and billiard room. Describe the criteria you would employ in this assessment.
3   Devise a product mix for a new hotel that is targeting a non-drinking, non-smoking, health-conscious segment of the market.

Chapter 9

The Service Concept in the e-Commerce Age

Aims of this chapter

The aims of this chapter are:
- to explain what service really is;
- to describe the service culture; and
- to describe how to match strategies, procedures, and the service product.

Theory

There is a lot of talk about service. Everyone says how important service is in the hospitality business. And yet, in an industry that claims to be totally committed to service, the disappointment of customers with the service they have received, and complaints reflecting their disappointment, are still prevalent.

What is the problem? Are customers expecting too much? Are they being educated to expect service beyond that which can reasonably be supplied?

Some of the problems are caused by the fallibility of human beings—our inability to work consistently to a standard. However, although this explains some of the difficulties, the problem is more likely to be due to management not knowing what service is. Management often thinks that service is something that the staff does, and that it simply means being pleasant and helpful to the customers.

Most books on management and marketing fail to give service more than a passing mention, and merely acknowledge its importance. Only a few books set out to define service as a product that requires objectives, strategies, and measurable management criteria.

Service: both a product and a strategic imperative

The objective of a hospitality business is to provide guests with a place where they feel welcome and appreciated, and where they can relax and have an enjoyable experience. Service is what an establishment does to and for its guests to achieve this objective.

Service is not about smiling, servility, and unctuousness. It is a strategy that considers the customer while serving the interests of the establishment. Service excellence gives an organisation a competitive edge. Outstanding service makes a lot of money for a hospitality establishment because the business of a hospitality establishment is people.

The intention of a service strategy is to manage the customer's experience. The services that an establishment provides are products and, like a product that is manufactured, a service has to perform to a measurable standard and fulfil its purpose all the time, every time. Who would buy a washing machine that works only on some days and, when it does work, washes better on some occasions than on others?

Service is not something done only by the staff. It requires commitment from the top. In an organisation committed to a service strategy there are only two types of staff members—those who serve the customer and those who help those who serve the customer. Service inverts the traditional hierarchical management pyramid in which the managing director is at the top and there are levels of seniority leading down to the customer at the base of the pyramid. Instead, with the pyramid inverted, the customer is at the top, and the full responsibility for the customers and those who serve them and help to serve them rests on the managing director. Service promotes a 'flatter' management structure, promotes teamwork, and makes the cleaner and the dishwasher as important as the managing director.

Imagine being in a high-class restaurant. As the food is about to be served, you notice that the fork has a small piece of old meat stuck to it and the wine glass still has lipstick on the rim. It is hard to feel positive about the food is these circumstances! And this has occurred because the dishwashers failed to do their job properly, and/or because the person setting the table failed to check the cutlery and the glass.

The products provided by a hospitality establishment are nearly all service-orientated. The product mix—consisting mostly of accommodation, restaurants, bars, and a range of ancillary products—has to perform to a satisfactory level. If this does not occur, the customers will not return. The product mix cannot be good on some days, and poor on others.

Lodgings, restaurants, and bars are obvious service products because they are direct profit-earners. Less obvious, but just as important to the customers, are the products that indirectly make money by substantially contributing to the customers' service experiences. These include:

◆ safety standards;
◆ stock and inventory control;
◆ cleanliness;
◆ financial planning;
◆ credit control;
◆ operational systems; and
◆ layout appeal and efficiency.

Each of these is considered below.

Safety standards

Safety does not make any money in itself. However, without adequate safety procedures, an establishment can lose a considerable amount of money. Safety for the staff and the customer is a product that performs without being seen to perform.

Stock and inventory control

Effective *stock and inventory control* is important to the service product. Service is significantly diminished if the establishment runs out of a customer's favourite wine, if the kitchen runs short of tomato sauce, or if replacement crockery is not there when it is wanted.

Cleanliness

Cleaning is not usually considered to be a profit-maker for a hospitality establishment, but the standards of cleanliness can help an establishment earn a good reputation, or can ruin its reputation. Most of us expect cleanliness where we stay and eat. When a place is obviously dirty, the establishment has failed to meet our expectations.

Financial planning

Financial planning is essential. If there is insufficient money for proper maintenance—the age-old excuse of management—there is a long list of things that should happen, but do not happen. Repairs to the premises, attention to plumbing problems, renovations to the kitchen and its equipment—all are left until later. Management should not believe that customers do not notice. They do. They notice the poor fixtures and fittings, and they experience the sudden breakdown of a small service that occurs because a piece of equipment was too old or was not fixed. Customers accept this sort of thing once or twice, but not if it happens again and again.

Credit control

Some establishments refuse to take certain credit cards, or ask for deposits, or insult customers in some other way—because someone in the organisation has been too lazy or inefficient to check a credit rating in advance. Such actions encourage customers to go away and never return. Proper *credit checks* are sound business practice. However, when such checks become unreasonable impositions on the patience and understanding of customers, the system is unacceptable.

Attempting to achieve perfect credit control will cost an establishment money. Relaxing credit controls slightly might cause the property to incur some bad debts, but it will also win many extra customers. Casinos in America have known this for years, and some credit managers have been dismissed for achieving a bad-debt percentage *smaller* than 3%!

Operational systems

Agreed *operational systems* are a good idea, as long as they improve the experience for the customer. But too many operational systems are designed for the convenience of the staff or management—rather than for the customer. For example:

◆ room-cleaning—which must be done at prescribed times and does not consider the customer who does not want to be disturbed;
◆ the tables—which have to be rearranged for another function while customers are still eating at another; and
◆ a docket system for meal-ordering—which is designed to prevent items being missed on the bill and to avoid petty fraud, but which causes a five-minute delay to the customers' meals.

Layout appeal and efficiency

Layout must be carefully considered. Many places seat the customers near the kitchen so that staff members do not have to walk too far, or they seat the customers in a way that makes the place look busier than it is. Sometimes the reception desk is just outside the general office not because it is closer for the customers, but because it is closer to the manager's office.

Many establishments make their front-desk staff responsible for answering incoming phone calls, as well as being responsible for serving customers face to face. Consequently, customers are often left to stand and wait while the phones are being answered—the phone calls always taking precedence. In reality, these establishments would be better advised to have the manager and the manager's secretary answer the phones. Which is more important—to avoid interrupting the manager or to service the needs of the customer at the desk?

Managing the service products and e-service

In the course of their stay, customers are part of a series of activities from when they come through the front door (or perhaps from when they first encounter the hotel through a computerised booking system) until they eventually depart. Each activity in this series is handled by a different department and the customer is passed from one to the other. Many different service products are involved, but in too many places no one is responsible for making sure that the transitions happen smoothly. The duty manager waits for a complaint, but meanwhile assumes that all is functioning as it should.

Some hotels have implemented a fully automated check-in process, stepping back from personal contact and relying on an electronic process to meet the customer's needs. The arriving guest need only swipe his or her credit card and be automatically allocated a room. The guest's card is debited with the accommodation charge. The same process generates a coded card that allows access to the room. This process, which is part of what is sometimes called 'e-service', suits some market segments, notably the overnight traveller, but it should not be relied upon to replace personal service entirely. Similarly, the booking system that preceded the guest's arrival might not have involved any personal contact, but might have been completed through the Internet—which suits some, but not all customers.

The whole service experience for the customer is the sum total of myriad smaller experiences. For all the service products to be supplied effectively and concurrently to the guest's complete satisfaction, several control factors are necessary at the service level, including the e-service level.

◆ There has to be a strategy that identifies when, where, and how the service product will perform.

◆ There have to be systems with measurable criteria for each of the working procedures involved in providing the service. If a service is to be managed it must be capable of being measured.

◆ The people providing the service have to be 'people-people'—those who are interested in others, care for their welfare, and make their comfort and satisfaction the top priority. Understanding the perceptions of the customers is crucial to service success. Procedures are only as effective as the people performing them.

◆ The people providing the service directly to the customer must have the support of everyone else. The organisation must exist to serve the needs of the people who are serving the customer. Management's primary function must be to monitor and maintain the service standards and to ensure that nothing impedes the delivery of service. Management's role is not merely the giving of instructions. Rather, it is to help those providing the service. If there are delays or upsets, what or who is causing them? Is it a procedural problem? Is there a weak link in the staff chain? Is extra training needed? Perhaps the person is wrong for that job? Would a new or different item of equipment solve the problem?

Services that satisfy wants

Some consider the service culture to be reactive to customers rather than proactive. This is wrong. Customers look for leadership from the establishment and want it to provide them with a quality experience. A service strategy aims to involve the customers and staff so that the service mix works to everyone's satisfaction. This is a process of drawing together the expectations, needs, and wants of both the customer and the provider—such that the customer gets value and the provider gets money.

This sounds simple, but why does it fail so often?

Part of the answer lies in the arrogance of some people who are not really interested in other people's thinking. It is an attitude of 'we know what is best for you'. Such an attitude can result in management putting products in place which the management thinks are for the benefit of the customers, but which the customer neither wants nor expects. Such managers are rarely successful in the hospitality business. For example, a restaurant once put on a special three-course meal for a very low price in anticipation of creating an influx of business—only to be disappointed when the influx of customers did not eventuate, and those who did come never came back. The restaurateur added more choices, but still failed to increase business. After two or three weeks of this he finally snapped at a table of uninterested customers: 'Well what the hell do you want then?'. They proceeded to tell him, and he finally realised that he had not been taking notice of what the customers wanted. He had not taken the trouble to review what the customers had been consistently choosing from his normal menu, and nor had he ever bothered to talk to his customers about their preferences.

The wants of the customer mix should always drive the service strategies. Providing service that the customer wants 'means spending considerable time listening and observing in the field'.[1] Equally as important is the *anticipation* of the customers' wants, and the occasional provision of something that they did not expect.

Secondary services—the competitive edge

Effective service products achieve increased business by *laddering*. This is gathering from the total market people who are transformed from potential customers into advocates for the establishment.

The objective of laddering is to identify and target the best prospects. With the help of promotion a percentage of them will become customers. From this point, the objective of service is to provide these people with a quality experience that turns them into regular patrons of the establishment who will become advocates and 'sell' the place to their friends and acquaintances.

Most dining establishments provide good food and reasonable service at prices that suit their customer mix. This is called 'primary service'. It is the small extras, the 'secondary services', that elevate an average customer experience into something beyond the expectations of customers. These extras might include a special brand of coffee, bread, or biscuits that have been made on the premises, or perhaps a complimentary appetiser.

The primary service product usually does its job of satisfying the customers without much comment. It is the extras give the establishment a competitive edge. These are the things that customers go away and talk about. In Berry's words, work for the 'service surprise', that little extra that exceeds expectations and makes the customer say 'wow'.[2]

Planning by working to an objective

Measurement by outcome

Service has to have measurable criteria. It has to have objectives and perform to a prescribed set of rules and standards. The purpose of measurement is to define precisely what will happen to (or for) a customer, when it will happen, and who will provide it. Measurement is achieved by deciding the required outcome of the service.

What do you want the service product to do for the customers? The answer to this question determines the objective. Forget the money objective. The money objective is an overall corporate objective. The service objective is a *product* objective, and its outcome—what actually happens and how this is accepted in the minds of the customers—is what counts.

To state such a product objective succinctly might require several attempts. For an objective to have meaning it must contain measurable criteria of achievement within a stipulated time frame. Set the tasks to be done in the time allowed. For example, a restaurant allocates staff numbers by customer numbers—depending on the style of service of the establishment. One waiter might be allocated to fifteen customers. Three chefs might be required to cook for 150 customers. The service standard that is set might require each customer to be served with drinks within two minutes of sitting down, to have the first course on the table within five minutes of ordering, to have the second course on the table no later than twelve minutes, and so on. If this is not being achieved, management must find out why, isolate the difficulty, and remedy it. 'Whatever it takes' is the rule that governs the provision of a service standard.

The measuring criterion in this instance is keeping account of individual performances and comparing them with the average. Staff members who lag behind the standard must be trained, encouraged, and helped until they come up to the standard required.

Describe the team work required

Hospitality is teamwork—people working together to achieve the objective of an excellent guest experience. A team leader is essential. This person must be a catalyst for the smooth functioning of the procedures required in delivering the product. Each person must know exactly what is expected of him or her, and each person's performance must be constantly acknowledged. Achievement is a reward on its own, but good performance deserves the extra rewards of money and privilege for a job that goes beyond the standard required.

Set quality standards

Not every action or function can be directly translated into dollar terms or measured by customer reaction. Much of what happens in a service product goes unseen by the customer. Because it is the culmination of little things that ultimately counts in the overall assessment by the customer, the contributing functions need a 'points-rating' system—from 'poor' to 'excellent'. It is surprising how standards are lifted and enthusiasm develops when staff members are performing to known criteria. Everyone likes to know where he or she stands in a situation.

Measure the level of satisfaction

The extent of the customers' satisfaction can be measured in terms of increased sales and repeat business. These are the basic measures of a product's success.

Customer satisfaction can also be measured by constant research of customer attitudes. Such research can find out if the number of complaints is being reduced, and whether the customers appreciate the various experiences being provided. Guests usually do not mind filling in brief questionnaires.

Set a goal for dollars earned

Although the objective is to meet the satisfaction of the customer, money has to be made. At the end of a service period, the dollars earned by a product have to be checked to ensure that services meet corporate objectives. A non-profit product (such as cleaning) can be measured by a points-rating system, and it can be judged by what it does *not* cost in terms of customers who would have otherwise been disappointed (and perhaps lost).

Analyse costs involved

Although customer satisfaction is paramount, accountants insist that a product service has to be cost-efficient, and customer satisfaction has to be balanced against the costs incurred and the profits made. Accountants are understandably concerned about profit. However, this concern can be allayed if turnover is good. A high turnover always contains the promise of profit.

Developing a service strategy

In developing a service strategy, certain steps are necessary to provide a sustainable competitive advantage over the competition. See Figure 9.1 (page 121).

Establish customer needs and wants

The first step is to *establish customer needs and wants*. This is done by market analysis and segmentation. It leads to a target market whose particular needs and wants the establishment intends to satisfy.

Ask the customers

Ask the customers. Nothing beats the simple research technique of talking to a representative sample of customers, existing and potential, and asking for their opinions and advice. Managers who do this will be overwhelmed with opinions and ideas!

Review existing products and procedures

The next step is to *review existing products and procedures*. In the light of new knowledge supplied by research and analysis, many existing ways of operating will be found wanting.

Set objectives for improvements

Set objectives for improvements or changes. Decide the outcome you want from a product or series of products.

Identify key strategies

The next step is to *identify key strategies*. You must decide how you are going to achieve the objectives and realise the outcomes required.

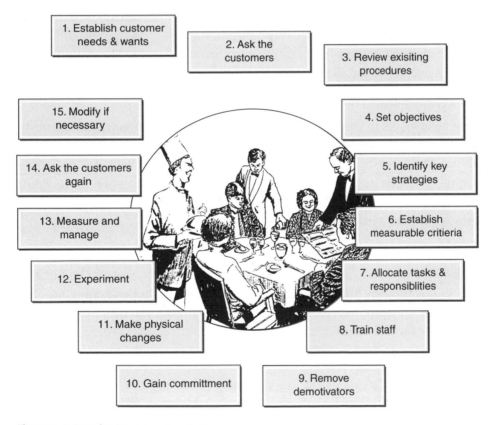

Figure 9.1 Developing a service strategy

Authors' presentation

Establish measurable criteria for the strategy

As previously noted (this chapter, page 118), it is important to *establish measurable criteria* for the strategy. If it cannot be measured it cannot be managed.

Allocate tasks and responsibilities

It is important to *allocate tasks and responsibilities*. Decide who is going to perform the functions involved in producing the outcome. Choose 'people-people'—those who can share the 'gift of friendship'. Look for team leaders—catalysts who lead and encourage a team effort.

Train staff

The next step is to *train staff*. Anything new requires careful explanation and careful supervision in its establishment. Then it must be monitored thereafter. Even high-quality service can deteriorate into mediocrity if left unmanaged.

Remove demotivating systems and staff

Remove demotivating systems and staff. Every organisation has a number of systems designed for the convenience of the operators. Seldom do these help the customer. In fact, most of them are 'customer-hostile'—in the sense that they create adverse reactions from customers in many instances. These must go! So must managers and staff members who insist on tasks before people.

Gain commitment to the objectives and strategies

The next step is to *gain commitment to the objectives and strategies*. Without the active support of all staff members, service becomes a bore and a nuisance for them. Only by involving the staff totally can this problem be overcome. Communication at all times is critical. Never hold information back. Praise those who are doing it right, and help those who do not come up to standard. Always aim for a team effort. Lead by example.

Make physical changes where necessary

Make physical changes where necessary. Any physical object, part of a building, or piece of equipment that prevents a service product from performing properly should be changed, moved, or replaced. Never allow a physical problem to be an excuse for lack of service.

Experiment with the changes

It is important to *experiment with the changes*. Do not go charging in with a whole host of new concepts. Test each one first. Involve staff and the customers to see if it will work as expected. When it works to expectations, and performs according to customers' satisfaction, it can become a permanent operation.

Measure and manage

Once a change is instituted and established as part of the operation, *measure it and manage it*. Management's role is to monitor carefully, and to step in to help staff members whenever necessary. Continue with the measuring criteria already laid down. Without appropriate monitoring and management, the initiative will become unstuck.

Ask the customers

Ask the customers. The ultimate test of a service product is its satisfactory performance for the customers. Maintain a regular research program with customers so that management is informed of progress at all times.

Modify where necessary, and measure again

If measurement suggests a need for further change, the service product must be *modified as necessary*, and then measured again. Not every product will serve the customers' wants indefinitely. Conditions change, expectations change, and moods and fashions change. A viable establishment that is committed to a service culture for its customers will change with the customers, and will not 'sit' on past achievements. If the organisation does not move with its customers, the customers will move—elsewhere!

Training strategy

One of the principal laments of managers about implementing a service strategy is that they lack the lack of cooperation of staff, and that staff members are not consistent in their implementation of the strategy. 'We tell them how to do it. We spend money on training. We try to motivate and enthuse. But, in the end, we find the staff members going back to their old habits, and we give up in despair. What's the use? It's a nice concept but it isn't realistic. People are people.'

Another common management lament is similar. 'Our staff know what is expected of them. They don't always do what they should, but they know what is expected.'

These and similar management complaints are often heard. Staff members often appear to be consistent only in their inconsistency! Management believes that staff members have been trained, but staff members do not deliver.

So what is the problem? The assumption that staff members know what is expected of them is often a false premise. The truth—from formal research, and even from informal random interviews with staff members—is that in many cases they do *not* know what is expected of them. They might know the rules, and they might know the procedures they have been taught. However, in many cases, members of staff think that performance strictly according to these rules and procedures is enough. But the delivery of an effective service product requires more than adherence to rules. It requires commitment to service.

Moreover, the imposition of a set of rules and procedures can be an invitation to rebel. Staff members, like all human beings, like to be treated as individuals and not as a group of robots. Occasionally they will deliberately flout the rules and procedures just to prove that they are individuals. After a while, flouting the rules can become a habit. And if rules and procedures are broken, and things go wrong, people who lack a sense of real teamwork can begin to blame one another—it is someone else's fault, not their own.

There can therefore be problems with staff members who think that working to regulations is enough, or problems with staff members who have lost respect for the rules and for one another. In both cases, the underlying problem lies with bad management.

Some service people perceive that they are working for remote and uncaring management, or for remote and uncaring shareholders—neither of whom have any interest in staff members at all. People working in this sort of environment do enough to avoid being dismissed and enough to ensure that they are paid—and this is all that matters to them. This is an understandable attitude in such an environment.

Good management gives staff members more than rules and regulations. Good management gives them responsibility for their customers. When staff members realise that the people whom they serve could be theirs for a long time, and that their real job is to keep these people as their own customers, they change their attitude to the procedures presented to them by management. They know that the procedures are there to help them build their own customer base. Staff members can also be given financial incentives—a bonus for every customer they retain, or a share of the money spent at the establishment by particular customers. They should also receive praise for their efforts in establishing and retaining loyal customers. In these circumstances, these staff members become people who are working for themselves as well as for management.

Notice what happens when customers request that they be served by a particular waiter whom they like. That waiter is flattered, and he or she responds with additional personalised touches of service. Often a handsome tip is the reward. However, it is better if management supplies the reward, so that there is a standard recognition for retaining a customer and providing outstanding service.

This approach does two things. First, it personalises the service—the staff get to know the customers by name. Secondly, the customers receive better service because every person who walks in, phones in, or writes in, is worth money. Staff members scramble to get to the customers first and claim them for their own! The ones who do not scramble are the ones that management does not want. Instead of management saying that staff members are all the same, it becomes apparent that they are not all the same.

Some managers might baulk at this concept because they fear that service people could become mercenaries who are paid to serve. But this misses the essential point—that the staff are an integral part of the product being sold. Staff members must be given individual respect by managers as being vital contributors to the shared prosperity of staff and the property. Unless this is done, customers will be at the mercy of many staff members who are unmotivated and uncaring.

Most motivational training is wasted. Staff members often see this type of training as an insult to their intelligence—and often it is! Most staff want to be pleasant to customers if they can, and they think that they already provide 'service'. Even those who want to do better, and who know how to do better, are often restrained or demotivated by the system in which they work. No one asks them for their opinion.

All too often there is little management supervision, but only authoritarian direction. Systems and procedures are often put into place without staff consultation and without recognition of the problems that such systems might pose for staff members. Profit and expediency often come first, and the staff comes second. Usually there is no means of measuring service, or what the staff do, except by casual observation.

As a consequence, most service training begins with the premise that it is the front-line people—those who procure sales and those who provide customer service—who need to have the right attitude. This is wrong. Management needs to have the right attitude—an attitude of respect, support, and service towards the front-line people.

Service is a marketing product that requires strategies beginning at the top. Training should be conducted around these strategies and should involve the people who will implement them. This requires staff acceptance and commitment to the concept. To achieve this commitment, an 'us and them' approach is not appropriate. The correct approach is a joint deal for mutual benefit—with the primary objective being guest satisfaction with the total experience of the property.

Questions for discussion or revision

1   List some of the most common examples of service failure in an hotel dining-room.
2   Is the customer always right? Give some examples of occasions when the customer's demands go beyond the provision of normal service. Discuss which of these are appropriate and which are inappropriate.
3   Explain how service strategies can overcome the shortcomings of room size, tired décor, and old-fashioned fittings.

Chapter 10

Service Strategies

Aims of this chapter

The aims of this chapter are:
- to explain the processes involved in developing service product strategies;
- to describe how to meet the competition; and
- to put the concept of sustainable competitive advantage in this context.

Service first, property second

The construction of a good business should begin with the service strategies, with a specific series of target markets in mind. It should not begin with the property and its facilities. Many investors believe that if a property looks good, has the right style, and is well located cleverly, lots of people will want to stay there, eat there, and use the facilities. They are not altogether wrong. There is some truth in this; but it is not the whole truth.

Where are they wrong? There are many places that have an impressive façade, lots of style, and excellent location—next to business centres, shopping and entertainment streets, or rivers, lakes, seas, mountains, and islands. The trouble is that many of them are not full, or even remotely close to being full. In the equation for success, there is something else that investors do not always recognise.

The fact is that the property itself is really only the shell in which the total service experience for the guest happens.

It is difficult for some people in the hospitality industry to appreciate that marketing is part of product development. Many in management believe that marketing people should be concerned only with selling. Such people think that their 'grand design'—the location and the style of the property—will dictate the customer mix, and that marketing people are merely communication tools between their property and their potential customers.

Their belief is that management is solely responsible for such matters as the environmental theatre of the place—its impressive design and associated features—and all its products and facilities. This attitude overlooks the fact that the choice of markets and the development of products for those markets is essentially a marketing process. This is why some properties are destined to fail before the first surveyor's peg is put into the ground.

In these circumstances, management's solution to a 'down period' is fairly predictable. Salespeople are told: 'Go out there and sell your heart out! Do deals; cut prices; do what you can to bring in the customers!'. The salespeople go into top gear. They ring up their main customers; they contact travel agents; they brief advertising agencies and PR firms. In short, they do all that can be done to promote the place. The drive and impetus of the sales team, backed up by some sharp deals, often does bring in a stream of customers. But what about service? Where are the special experiences that will retain customer patronage? All too often, the customers get more of the same service as they have been receiving nearly everywhere else. As these customers move off to competitors, the downturn resumes, and the expensive selling drives have to start all over again.

Salespeople need something more than just a story about size, style, and location. All the competitors have these. The competitors have most of the other things too—the club discounts, the special rates, the upgrades, the special hire rates, and so on.

So, what does retain the customers?

Points of difference in service

The things that make a property really successful are the points of difference— the unique selling propositions that make for a sustainable competitive advantage. Price-cutting is not sustainable; continuous quality service is.

Points of difference are in the products that are sold. In the case of a service product, points of difference can be established in the way that things are done, and in the people who do these things. These are service strategies. These points of difference are small in comparison with the huge investment in buildings, style, glitz, glamour, and location, but they usually work better and for longer.

CASE STUDY

Rick Angeletti—the 'perfect concierge'

The Southern Pacific Hotel Corporation (SPHC) ran a network of 67 hotels of varying descriptions. One of the hotels in the group, the Parkroyal in Adelaide, was an old small property of about a hundred rooms and did not fit the image of SPHC's 'new age' of hotels.

SPHC purchased another hotel in Adelaide with a similar name, the Hindley Parkroyal. It was newer, bigger, and closer to the business, shopping, and entertainment areas of the city. Because there was little that could be done to refurbish the older Parkroyal property to make it fit the SPHC style, the company decided to sell it, with a view to convincing as many customers as possible to use the newer Hindley Parkroyal in future. This was a tricky situation because the old Parkroyal had a strong loyal following of customers who had been using it for many years. A major change to any business can produce a loss of customers because a proportion of them will take the opportunity to seek fresh fields and new experiences.

Within twelve months, 90% of the old Parkroyal customers had made the transition to the Hindley Parkroyal—a phenomenal result. How was this achieved?

Much of the credit went to one person—the concierge, Rick Angeletti. When Rick went to the Hindley a large percentage of the customers moved with him. Rick Angeletti had a unique personality and bubbled with enthusiasm. But, more importantly, he liked his customers and knew every one of them by name. He treated them with respect and interest, and asked after their families and their hobbies at every opportunity. Rick was the perfect concierge.

The secret of a 'perfect concierge' such as Rick Angeletti is always the same—a deep interest in people and an impressive ability to remember names and personal details. Imagine walking into an hotel that you have not visited for more than a year and being greeted by name by the concierge. You will feel important, flattered, and welcome. Regrettably, in too many places, this sense of welcome stops after the concierge hands you over to other staff. Too often it is back to the ordinary from then on, as indifferent employees go through the motions of service.

Personalising the service

A service strategy is required for each product in an establishment's 'product line'. Although there should be an umbrella strategy for the whole establishment, each product needs its own strategic plan because each is aimed at a specific segment of the customer mix.

With accommodation, the service strategy begins with the initial contact between the customer with the establishment. Being welcomed by name is the first service that a customer notices—before he or she sees a room, has a drink in the bar, or experiences anything else being offered by the establishment. This is where a person such as Rick Angeletti (page 129) becomes so important. The point of difference in some places can simply be the concierge. A property can build a whole strategy around a smiling happy concierge—by extending that initial rapport throughout the organisation.

The concierge's example can be emulated by all staff members—who call the customer by name, and remember important personal details and customer preferences. Let us suppose that the customer's name is Mr Lee. The porter carries up 'Mr Lee's bags' and puts them in 'Mr Lee's room'. When the cleaner comes the next day, he or she is to clean 'Mr Lee's room'—not *the* room, but *Mr Lee's* room. The room, in a sense, temporarily belongs to Mr Lee, and that room can be invaded only with his permission. A different staff attitude emerges. The cleaner *asks* when it would be convenient for Mr Lee to have his room cleaned; this is no longer an automatic function. Similarly, with a dinner reservation, the table does not have a 'reserved' sign on it. Rather, it has a sign proclaiming 'Mr Lee's table'. The waiters call Mr Lee by name. In turn, every staff member wears a name tag so that Mr Lee can return the compliment and call each of them by name.

A side-benefit of this strategy (of wearing name tags) is that it is far easier to build, among staff members themselves, a sense of belonging and being appreciated. In a large organisation, with so many people carrying out so many different functions, many staff members do not even know each other by name. See the case study on 'The importance of name tags' (page 131).

Product knowledge of staff

Teaching the staff about the products the establishment has to offer is another simple strategy that does not cost much money. If management wants the staff to sell, staff members have to know what they are supposed to sell.

The additional business created by staff information and recommendations is huge. Familiarising the staff with the products not only helps the selling process but also builds a sense of pride in the whole organisation.

> **CASE STUDY**
>
> ## The importance of name tags
>
> James H. Lavenson once gave a speech to the Executive's Club of Chicago and recounted many amusing stories about his experiences when he first took charge of the Plaza Hotel in New York. The vignettes of his speech were published in *Dun's Bulletin*.[1]
>
> Lavenson made a very strong case for the simple strategy of calling a guest by name and of having the staff members wear name tags. When he moved into his new position things were far from right at the hotel. There were 1400 staff members and, as Lavenson observed: 'How would they ever know all the people working there, who were the guests, who was just a burglar smiling his way through the hotel while he ripped us off? I can assure you that in the beginning if he smiled and said 'hullo' he was a crook! He certainly wasn't one of us!'
>
> Lavenson went on to explain what happened after the Plaza affixed name tags to the chests of all staff members: 'Believe it or not, Plaza people began saying 'hullo' to each other by name when they passed in the hall or in the offices. At first, of course, our regular guests at the Plaza thought we had lost our cool and that we were having some gigantic convention there. But now the guests are also able to call the bell person, the maids, room clerks, and the manager by name. And we began to build an atmosphere of welcome with the most precious commodity in the world—our names and our guest's names.'
>
> 'When someone calls you by name, and you don't know his or hers, another funny thing happens. A feeling of discomfort comes over you if he calls you by your name twice, and you know you're not world famous, you have to find out his name. And this is the phenomenon we saw happening with the Plaza staff name tags. When a guest calls a waiter by name, because it is there to be read, the waiter wants to call the guest by name.'

'Selling' is sometimes perceived to be a 'bad' word. It can imply pressuring clients into buying something they might not want. Michael Hurst, who runs the very successful '15th Street Fisheries' restaurant in Florida, USA, does not believe that staff should 'sell', but that they do have to inform and advise, and to do this they must intimately know the products they are offering. Informing customers about what is available and asking them if they would like it, is not 'selling'. It is, essentially, simple courtesy. It is supplying knowledge that can be used by grateful customers to make a decision.[2]

CASE STUDY

Orientation for staff

James H. Lavenson reported in his speech (see case study, page 131) that when he took over the Plaza Hotel he made a few calls to the various departments, posing as a potential customer.

'What's the difference between your $85 suite and your $125 suite?' he asked.

'Forty dollars.'

'What's the entertainment in your Persian Room tonight?'

'Some singer.'

'A man or a woman?'

'I'm not sure.'

The whole experiment made Lavenson wonder if he'd be safe going there! Why is it that hotel staff members do not act towards customers in the same way that a family of hosts acts towards guests who have been invited to stay at their house?

Lavenson introduced a week of orientation for the staff. This orientation included a visit to the night club, a night in the various rooms, and a meal in each of the restaurants. Today, everyone knows who is singing in the nightclub, and everyone knows the difference (apart from price) between the $85 and $125 rooms!

Lavenson's experience at the Plaza (see case study on 'Orientation for staff', above) can be observed in many restaurants. The 'moment of truth' for an establishment is often reached when the customer asks the waiter about the wine. A frequent answer is something along these lines: 'Wouldn't know, sir. Don't drink wine myself.' What is the point of a drink waiter who cannot advise the customer on the choice of wine?

Another favourite customer question is: 'What is this dish? Can you tell me something about this?'. Unfortunately, the waiter often frowns, desperately tries to remember something about the dish, and finally admits with a sense of despair (or indifference) that he or she has never tried it. The waiter might then add with a smile: 'But it looks nice!'.

Waiters are not there merely to note down orders from customers. They are there to advise and assist the customers with their product selections. How can they do this if they do not know the menu or the wine list?

Like Lavenson and leading operators around the world, Michael Hurst makes sure that every waiter tries every dish before he or she serves a customer. The waiters cannot sell products about which they know nothing. Before the waiters go on the floor the kitchen must tell them about the whole meal, and how it has been designed and prepared. If there is something new, the waiters must try it so that they can tell the customers.

If everyone in an establishment is an expert on its products, sales soar. If staff members are enthusiastic, their advice is infectious, and customers get the message that products could be worth trying. Teaching staff about products, and encouraging them to share their enthusiasm with customers, is a simple strategy for management to use in building a business.

Little extras that make a big impression

Little extras can make an impression out of all proportion to their apparent importance. See the case study on 'The importance of lemon soap' (page 134).

Although the story told in the case study on 'lemon soap' might seem silly, lots of seemingly 'silly' little things (like a special lemon soap) make the all-important points of difference between places to stay. It is not the large issues that concern the average person so much as a sequence of seemingly inconsequential small issues. Freshly ground coffee might be such a point of difference, or perhaps coffee that is brought down by mules from little village high up in the Andes and shipped especially to the property. Or perhaps it might be flowers that are grown by a little old lady in the hills—especially for the hospitality establishment.

The name 'Country Comfort Inn' sounds like a non-alcoholic, private guest house run by a quiet hotelier in the sheep country of Australia. It is actually the name of a chain of successful city hotels, all owned and operated on the basis of a management philosophy that targets the corporate business market. Some marketing people confronted with the name 'Country Comfort Inn' would be tempted to reject it: 'What sort of name is that? Change it!'. But several surveys of customers have said the opposite: 'Keep it!'.

The Country Comfort Inn (CCI) management team has a special way of doing things, and all of them are aimed at providing what the name suggests—comfort. When CCI took over the former Parkroyal building in Adelaide it

CASE STUDY

The importance of lemon soap

Michael Hurst tells a story about a man who sat next to him on a flight to Denver.[3] Without knowing where Michael Hurst was staying, the man proceeded to 'sell' Hurst the idea of staying at a particular hotel. Hurst's companion explained that one of the main reasons for his enthusiasm for the place was the special things it did. The thing that stood out most of all for him was the hotel's lemon soap!

made some interesting changes. The marble and slate entrance foyer was covered in plush carpet because, as manager George Jones explained, ' . . . marble and slate are cold. They are also noisy. Women especially don't like their heels clacking over the hard surface. Carpet is warm, inviting.' In the foyer, a real fireplace was installed, with comfortable chairs grouped around for the winter. Tables with chess sets were made ready for those who like to relax and play. Games of cards, draughts, and checkers were made available. 'We treat our customers the same as guests in our own home,' said George Jones.[4]

In the rooms, anything that detracted from the ambience of serenity was removed and the décor was changed to a relaxed, warm colour scheme. In the restaurant, emphasis was placed on good nourishing food—rather than on exotic gourmet dishes. 'If someone wants a plain steak and chips they can have it,' George Jones explained. 'The mistake many make in this business is to think that a high-powered senior executive lives the high life and demands rich food. In most cases their tastes are ordinary. Many prefer meat and two vegies to a richly spiced foreign dish.'

Another aspect of the CCI way of doing things relates to the provision of service by staff. In the words of George Jones: 'Nothing is too much trouble. What the customers want, they get, and it is everybody's job to do that. No one says, "That's not my job, another person does that". So, from the manager down, if the floor has to be swept we sweep it. If help is needed in the restaurant anyone can be called to pitch and do it.'

When we were children we were told to come to the table the moment the food was ready. We sat down to eat. This does not happen in most restaurants. We sit down and wait. We wait to order our food. We wait to order a drink.

We wait for someone to bring it to us. This experience gives the word 'waiter' a totally different meaning from its original meaning! In too many places it is bad luck if we are hungry or thirsty. Meanwhile, the waiter performs the meaningless task of putting napkins on our laps. What for? It might be twenty minutes before it is needed. In many places, the waiter gives us our menus and says that he or she will be back in five minutes to take our orders. Meanwhile, we are left with an incomprehensible jumble of descriptive phrases that we have to convert mentally into an appetising meal. When the waiter returns, usually having taken much longer than the promised five minutes, he or she flips over the next page of the docket book and asks: 'What are you going to have?'.

Secret strategy that can make a place great

When customers go somewhere to stay or when they go out to a restaurant, they expect to be given some special treatment and be made to feel good. Often they seek a distraction—a temporary refuge from business, work, home, or a situation they would prefer to put to one side for a while.

If they are paying 'big dollars', they expect to be treated as though they really matter. But for most people, the places that really stand out are not always the most expensive, biggest, or most glamorous locations. Little things can matter. One restaurant had a special way of doing things with coffee and desserts. The waiter stirred the coffee to make it spin and, while it was spinning, slowly poured the cream to form a concentric pattern. They offered a range of different coloured, refined sugars, and followed this with the appearance of a trolley loaded with an appealing range of rich cakes and desserts. The enthusiasm of the waiters in carrying out this series of little procedures was infectious. They enjoyed what they were doing, and their enthusiasm made a special treat of everything the guests ate and drank. The whole experience was enhanced by a pianist who also quietly sang popular ballads. Her obvious joy in entertaining the customers reached out and grabbed everyone.

It is people who make the real difference between places. For a good concierge, looking after the customers is not a job. He or she enjoys every minute of talking with the customers.

The joys of staying somewhere are provided by people, not by things. The marble and slate of the imposing atrium rising to the heights are impressive, and they certainly provide a sense of occasion. But people cannot sleep on the marble and they cannot eat the slate. If they wanted only an imposing and impressive ambience they could visit a cathedral and stand in the nave with its soaring arches, stained-glass windows, and vaulted ceilings.

A value-added package that offers a free bottle of French champagne and discounted restaurant rates and free laundry, is all very well. But it loses its appeal when the champagne is brought by a depressed-looking waiter who announces: 'Here's your champagne. Sign here to say that you got it!'. The champagne, placed on a tray on a side table, goes flat—and the sense of occasion goes flat with it. Services performed in a perfunctory fashion with feigned smiles take the sparkle from the enjoyment of any experience—even in the most impressive places.

It is people who make an occasion special. The secret of a successful establishment is its people. The foyer, the procedures, the efficient service, the value, the location, and the extras (such as pool, spa, sauna, and massage) are all important. But to make the occasion really happen, people have to make it happen. Staff members with the 'gilt of friendship'—charm, wit, and engaging personalities—make an experience memorable. There are plenty of staff members who can whiz through the orders and get the work done faster than most. But if they leave behind them a trail of disaster of ruffled guests and irritated cooks, what is the point?

Someone who turns up for work with a problem—suffering from 'flu', or grieving the death of a friend or relative, or trying to cope with a 'bust-up' of some sort at home—should not be allowed near a customer! The cloud of worry hovering over that staff member could ruin the hospitality experience of a guest. It is better to pay such a staff member to stay at home—rather than lose a customer.

CASE STUDY

Selling Irish coffees

Michael Hurst at '15th Street Fisheries' hired an Irish lady for a specialised task—to sell Irish coffees. He hired her because of her beautiful accent and her fascinating personality, and her ability to spin charming tales about the effects the various Irish whiskies would have on the customers.

She talked about ancient spells and the 'drop of magic' from old Ireland that was in every nip. It was all nonsense of course, but the customers loved her, and they wanted a little bit of the magic to rub off on them. Michael Hurst said she had to sell a quota of Irish coffees to justify her place on the staff, but that she had no trouble at all in meeting the quota.[5]

Some people in the hospitality industry say that good service should go unnoticed. Although there is some truth in this, it can suggest that service is an expectation that is noticed only when it is not there. The trouble with many places is that service is more likely to be noticed if it *is* there! A lot of hard work is required before a place achieves the smooth-running excellence that meets the expectations of customers. Exceptional service—the 'extra something' that gives a place a competitive point of difference—is usually provided by the personalities of the people who provide it.

Making the whole service experience work

First contact

Service for the customer begins with the very first contact with the establishment. This initial contact might be with a travel agent. A property cannot directly control what a travel agent says or does, but it can indirectly influence the travel agent's advice by ensuring that the agent is armed with information to pass on to the customer. This information should be more than a mere description of the property, the number of rooms, and the going rates. It must include the points of difference and the benefits. It must encourage the travel agent to recommend the establishment to the enquiring customer. Proper briefing of the travel agent is not just a selling strategy; it is also a service to potential customers via an intermediary.

The initial contact could also be with the establishment's website, or through an Internet directory. It is crucial that these also provide the right impression that fits the targeted market segment. Various customer services and promotional offers can be targeted to segments using information drawn from usage of the website. (Chapter 11, page 142, considers website issues in more detail.)

As noted above, the handling of an enquiry by an establishment should also be perceived as a service to the customer. Most customers want helpful information so that they make a decision as to whether to stay at one place or another.

However, some establishments apparently do not see themselves as providing this sort of helpful service at the time of initial contact with customers. One of the authors of this book once conducted a 'ring-around' in Sydney and Melbourne. The results were interesting. At the time, the world was in a recession, and establishments presumably wanted as much business as they could encourage. Despite this, in most instances, a simple enquiry about the availability of a room at a particular rate resulted in a reply along these lines: 'No such room available'. Nothing more was offered. No additional helpful information was provided. And these replies came from some of the 'best' in the country! In one case the phone rang off without being answered. Those who did respond properly to the enquiry handled the situation by first quoting the rack rate and then going on to mention some of the packages they had. But not one respondent added any reason suggesting that the enquiring customer should consider its establishment ahead of the rest. No benefits or points of difference were mentioned. Apart from being bad examples of selling, the responses of the establishments also showed a lack of interest.

When this situation was related to some hotel managers the usual response was a denial that it happened! Others attempted to excuse themselves: 'Must have been busy'; 'Ah, yeah, it must have been an off day; we all have them'; 'Probably struck the wrong person'; 'I'm really surprised—our people are excellent as a rule'. No one seriously considered what could be done to improve the situation. Most did not even admit that something should be done!

First impressions

The moment of truth for customers occurs when they arrive at a property. How much preparation has there been for the guests' arrival? For example, were they told in advance what to do about parking?

Most establishments are very good at making first impressions when guests arrive. Building appearance, décor, cleanliness, and the reception by the door-person, the receptionists, and the concierge are normally fine. This initial contact is when an establishment's well-oiled machinery goes into operation, and there is usually evidence of good training at this point. The porterage and room-delivery systems also work satisfactorily in most cases.

Why is this? Perhaps it is because the front desk is like the cockpit of an airliner—where everything is controlled. Perhaps it is because these contacts take place right outside the manager's door!

When the new customer reaches the room, his or her impression of the establishment is affected by the initial impact of the room—its décor, lighting, smell, size, layout, cleanliness, tidiness, and facilities. The customer notes the bed, the music, the television, the mini-bar, the tea & coffee facilities, the bathroom, the toilet, the linen, and so on. All of these items contribute to the overall impression.

This moment of first impression is very sensitive. The customer either feels at home at this stage, or wants to leave. A judgment on the quality of the whole hotel is often made at this moment. A good service strategy is to explain to the guest how the room works—an 'induction course' on where things are and how they work. This can include advice on switches and appliances, information about the facilities of the hotel, and advice on additional services that are available. This is an opportunity for reassurance to be given on the customer's decision to choose this hotel. Moreover, it is a time to establish rapport with the customer and to prepare the way for 'selling' other services.

Ideally, the person doing the 'induction' should be the continuing contact for the guest during his or her stay—so that advice, information, and 'fix-it' situations can be readily handled by one person, or by another designated person when the original contact is off duty. Unfortunately, most establishments divide the hotel into a number of departments that work as separate profit-earning outlets, without anyone assisting the customer in the choice or use of the various facilities.

The list of service items that form part of the overall strategy can be extended according to the size and nature of the establishment. Every detail is significant. A service strategy is not someone else's job—it is a total commitment by everyone. The objective of a commitment to sustainable competitive service strategies is obvious—management and staff want the guests to return and to recommend the place to others.

The dining-room

The proximity of an hotel's eating establishment—whether it be a fine dining-room, a bistro, a carvery, a café, or perhaps all of these—should ensure that a high proportion of accommodation guests use these facilities. The problem is that such places are competing with others in the streets nearby. So, it is not just enough to be close by. Each hotel eatery has to offer a really exciting benefit to win a share of its own guests and add customers from elsewhere.

Dining should be an important part of the total guest experience of an establishment. A strategy for this product requires close attention to first impressions—comfort, familiarity, welcoming staff, pleasant décor, and style. It should build on the ambience and quality experience provided by the rest of the hotel. Hiring people with the right personality is important. So are little extras—such as having a child's chair, having cushions for the elderly, having music to create an ambience for the place (and not merely to fill a sound vacuum), and having the smell of freshly ground coffee and freshly baked bread and rolls. Most importantly of all, the quality of the food must make the place a really great experience.

Getting the fundamentals of food, wine, and service right is basic to the business of a restaurant. But this is not enough. There are many establishments that do the same. Doing the fundamental things in a better and different way is about style, and style combined with attention to every small need of the guest produces guest satisfaction.

Consider the following possibilities.

◆ The bar is not just a place where a guest can have a drink. A service strategy can be developed so that the bar is the beginning of a dining experience. For example, while the customers drink, the food order can be decided, taken, and prepared, so the meal is ready as soon as people go to the table. Meanwhile, a skilled and personable bartender can be offering cocktails that enhance the anticipation and enjoyment of the food to come.

◆ The wine list can be a feature—offering distinctive wines of the district, wines of selected vintages, or special house wines.

◆ Meals and presentation that exemplify local tastes can offer guests a gourmet experience not offered elsewhere.

◆ The menu can be considered part of the presentation. A restaurant should take the time to prepare an exciting and entrancing menu. There are many specialist menu designers, some of whom offer their services over the Internet.

◆ Special theme nights and promotions lend interest and excitement to eating occasions, and provide reasons for guest participation. Celebrity speakers and performances by entertainers are further suggestions for making the dining experience special.

The sum total of these experiences is the strategy for attracting and retaining customers. An establishment must have points of difference—what is unique about it, what is special, what is exciting, what is distinctive, what is worth talking about. And if a place has nothing to talk about, it has a problem! If this is the case, there will be no word-of-mouth advertising. A restaurant in an accommodation establishment will achieve some business through convenience of location, and it might be financially successful to a modest degree. However, in terms of building an establishment that is truly a vibrant living thing, things for people to talk about are essential.

Questions for discussion or revision

1   Describe the strategies you would employ for a cocktail bar that caters mainly for American tourists.
2   The hotel you manage has a small kitchen that can cope with a hundred à la carte guests at a time. Renovations will be required in twelve months' time. Without losing customers, explain the service strategies that could satisfy the needs of 300 guests requiring the dining-room on a busy night. For example, would you offer an alternative method of service such as a buffet, or arrange several sittings for dinner?
3   Some people are better at giving service than others. Describe the service strategies you regard as being essential when training people for front-desk reception work.

e-Commerce Strategies

========================= Aims of this chapter =========================

The aims of this chapter are:
- to explain the changes to hospitality marketing due to e-commerce;
- to detail the design and uses of a website in hospitality marketing; and
- to discuss issues of website operation.

Hospitality and e-commerce

Recent technological advances have changed the way hotels can operate, in addition to changing the way they are promoted and marketed over the expanding Internet. More than 50% of Australians are now regular users of the Internet, and the chances are that these make up more than 50% of the users of hospitality. The Business Council of Australia released a report in May 2001, compiled by its e-Business Roundtable, that estimated e-commerce could add $30–35 billion a year to Australia's gross domestic product within ten years.

Because many intending travellers use the Internet and online information when planning their travel, virtually every hospitality enterprise now needs its own website (ideally with a strong word function to allow speedy access) and its own e-commerce strategy if its operators wish to compete effectively in the wider marketplace. On their websites, some hotels not only offer information on prices and facilities, but also include pictures of their rooms and even panoramic scans of the views from their properties. Best Western Australia is just one example of an hotel chain that has developed an e-commerce strategy, and a reported 85% of its properties are prepared to adopt the strategy.[1]

The huge advantage of a website is that it allows the hospitality product to be accessed, examined, and contacted by an audience that is literally world-wide. In addition to researching accommodation and other hospitality options, the prospective tourist should also be able to check visa and currency information on your hotel's website, as well as physical aspects of the destination—such as the weather and local attractions.

After intending travellers have researched their destinations and itineraries, they can then check availability, make bookings by email and make deposits electronically (although care must always be taken when transmitting credit card details). This form of customer self-service is not only convenient to the customer, but is low-cost for the hospitality operation. If they so choose, intending travellers can also use online travel agents. Online agents in Australia usually have an Australian licence, and consumers therefore have a degree of protection because such licensed agents support the Travel Compensation Fund.[2]

Apart from the convenience of accessing this sort of information from their office or home connection, there are additional advantages for travellers in using the Web for arranging travel. Among these advantages are information on special deals—in some cases, Web-only deals offered to the online market.

It is apparent then, that a crucial part of the marketing campaign of an hotel or restaurant must involve a website—an electronic address that can be accessed by users of the Internet. A website can be accessed at any hour of the day or night, from anywhere in the world—which makes it an invaluable and indispensable marketing tool. The site can be offered in different languages, and aid the strategic marketing campaign of the property.

A website gives an hotel far greater exposure in the marketplace than does attendance at any number of trade shows. It can give more information than any other form of media, and allow users to pick and choose which information appeals to them. It can include—in separate pages on the site—brochures, guides, itineraries, and even video and sound messages about the property.

Apart from websites, changes in information technology (IT) have also had an impact upon the nature of the hospitality product itself. Rapid changes in technology mean that connections for television, computers, and business telecommunications might be desirable in guest-rooms. Smart-card access systems can enhance and monitor guest security and monitor the movement of staff. Computerised reservations and check-in/check-out functions can change the way in which front-office facilities are designed and operated. Database management and warehousing can be used to tailor approaches to prospective guests and can then be used to customise their stay. Subsequently, database management and warehousing can offer guests loyalty benefits.

But, for now, we return to the importance of the website as a marketing tool.

Designing and using a website

Input from the IT specialist

Any hospitality operation that is about to design and use a website must take one first crucial step—it must obtain professional advice on how to set up and operate the site. The establishment should use this professional advice, and read the following material, so it can become a partner in the design process and so ensure that the website is right for its needs. The hospitality establishment will have to supply the IT professional with the proposed information and content of the website. The successful use of the website as a marketing and promotional tool will largely depend on the information that is supplied to the IT specialist.

Appropriate software is needed, as well as a personal computer with Windows or Macintosh. An Internet connection is also a requirement. Software is available that can be customised for smaller properties (fewer than ten rooms) and for larger properties. The software providers are able to guide hospitality operators through the set-up procedures.

Essentials of design

From a marketing point of view, ensure that the website is designed with the following features.

Top-quality graphics

Top-quality graphics that are clear and informative are essential. Do not stint in this area.

Headings and subheadings

Headings and subheadings must be logical and take the user from one topic to the next consistently. These headings should be simple and convey the necessary information. 'Smart' or 'clever' phrases turn people off. Users do not appreciate grandiose statements such as: 'This hotel is the best in the country'. They will instantly click to somewhere else.

Appropriate paragraphs

Paragraphs should be short, and should be limited to one idea or concept. Users do not usually read long paragraphs with a solid block of text.

Bulleted lists or dot points

Use *bulleted lists or dot points* to convey the message. Be much less 'wordy' in compiling a website than you would be in compiling, say, a newspaper advertisement. Be as concise as possible.

Highlights

Highlight important parts of the website with various colours and typefaces. Have some movement in the website, such as rolling keywords that emphasise the theme of the site.

It is crucial that the website is credible from a marketing perspective. The website should not contain exaggerated claims. 'Shouting' at users will turn them off. The users of hospitality websites tend to be people who are seeking information on which to make a decision—often an expensive decision. For such a decision they need quality information that has an air of objectivity. It is waste of time to pitch 'spiels', as if the website were a platform for a 'snake-oil salesman'—a term used to describe a person who uses 'hard sell' to make the audience buy a product of dubious value. Any hospitality operation, and the potential customers, deserve far better than that.

The information cycle

In considering the information to include on the website, and the various pages of the site, it is important to take account of the psychology of website reading. There are five stages to this process—sometimes called the 'customer development cycle'.[3]

Introduction

The visitor is *introduced* to the website—probably after finding a website address on promotional material or through a search engine. The visitor should be given encouragement to send an email query, so that the hotel can record the contact details.

Comparison

The visitors *compare* your hotel with the competitors, using their impressions of the website information. It is essential that the website provides what they are looking for and offers credible and consistent information.

Transaction

At the *transaction* stage a booking is made, and money or credit card details are transmitted.

Fruition

At *fruition*, the person who was a website visitor becomes a guest of the hotel. Now this person must be encouraged by the quality of the service.

Relationship

An ongoing business *relationship*, with repeat business, is encouraged— perhaps through a variety of loyalty programs or incentives (such as upgrading).

Common mistakes in the design and use of a website

Mistakes in website use and design ruin the impact of a powerful marketing tool. Such mistakes include:

◆ using backgrounds and colours that make the site hard to read;
◆ using graphics that might be 'dazzling', but that do not fit the needs and the tastes of the targeted market segment;
◆ using graphics that are not related to the logo and colours of the hotel or restaurant, and that therefore do not add to brand or product awareness (or perhaps even cause confusion as to the identity of the product);
◆ not providing a way to make contact with the hotel or restaurant through the use of an email address; this is like placing a newspaper advertisement and failing to include a telephone number; and
◆ not including any human dimension to the website—such as pictures of actual people, or names and experiences and comments of real people.

Positioning the website

After the design, the next most crucial e-commerce issue in setting up an effective and workable website is the positioning of the site on a search engine. A common mistake in positioning a website is listing it in inappropriate directories. According to one estimate, only 1% of websites are optimised correctly for search engines.[4] It is essential to have as many links as possible and to have the website included in as many search engines and as many bookmark files as possible. A website that cannot be found is like an hotel tucked away in a back street with no signs out front to allow potential customers to find it.

One out of every two users who access websites have found the address through the use of a search engine. The site must be designed by an IT specialist (with input from the hospitality operator) to ensure that it is 'search-engine friendly'. This can be achieved through key phrases that differentiate the website from competitors. The IT specialist must be knowledgeable about the best search engine or search engines on which to place the site, but the specialist needs assistance from the hospitality operator regarding which aspects of their business are best highlighted to pull Web traffic to the site.

Another important consideration is where the website will be listed when presented by the search engine. Key phrases are also important here, linked with the name of the business itself. It is important that the website appear listed in the first twenty or so listings that are presented to the user. If it is listed much further down the list, the visitor will not go to it—indeed, the visitor might not even notice it.

Using the Web as an information centre

The Web can be a source of a range of information on an hotel or a restaurant. The hotel can incorporate a virtual hotel tour (see Chapter 2, page 24), or a restaurant can incorporate full details of its menus and ingredients for the interest of potential customers.

Travel and accommodation specials are often marketed exclusively on the Web. The lower cost of doing business in cyberspace means that services such as airlines and cruises can reduce their prices to those who are prepared to use the Web for information and bookings. Internet travel analyst Phocuswright estimates

---

CASE STUDY

The importance of good websites

Henry Harteveldt, analyst for Forrester Research, states that two online travel agencies, Expedia Inc. and Travelcity.com, are well positioned for growth—due largely to good website design.

'[These two online agencies] appeal to a wide variety of consumers. Their websites are well-designed, and they are constantly evolving and innovating.'[5]

that online bookings in the near future will total around US$20 billion—11% of the United States travel market, up from 1% of the market in 1996.

But the Web can offer much more than bookings and virtual tours. It can offer newsletters, for example. Newsletters and house magazines are really in a category of their own. Their intention is to build rapport with customers by keeping them informed of the property's people, its products, and new developments, and by providing news about its performance as a hospitality establishment (including promotions, happenings, and visits by famous personalities). Online newsletters are cheap and can be continually updated, without the expense of committing to print runs of several thousand at a time. Moreover, increasing numbers of people, especially in business, are in the habit of accessing them. Insurance company AMP produces 'eCommerce Report' and noted that the number of people accessing the newsletter and visiting its website increased by 600% following its introduction.[6]

Newsletters and house magazines have to contain news and items of interest to the receivers. If they do not, they will work no better than a brochure. If they are merely publicity organs, full of self-interested publicity and sales messages, they will end in a place where all such indulgent pieces go—in the garbage bin. In the case of the Internet and email, the equivalent of being consigned to the garbage bin is being deleted into the electronic wasteland. Everyone is interested in news, pictures, and people. Long boring pages of type will not attract readership. Some of the best examples of house magazines are published by airlines. Although this type of material is beyond the budgets of most properties, even a single webpage with well-designed menu, text, and pictures can be very effective.

The intention of newsletters and house publications is to assume friendship, to involve the customers, and to give them a sense of belonging to the establishment. They work very well, especially when used in conjunction with enclosures about special offers or appealing new developments.

The website can be used for the gathering of information, as well as imparting it. Users can be questioned on the services they prefer, and their reaction to offers can be posted on the site.

New technologies

There are continual changes in IT technology. This is hardly a secret! Indeed, even writing about the topic in a book such as this runs the risk of being outdated—even before the book is published. Some changes have already opened new options in customer service—such as the paperless check-in. There have also been advances in management control—such as automated stock-control and ordering systems.

To take just one example of how changing technology could affect some aspects of marketing, consider the area of voice-recognition technology. Voice-activation call centres might change the way in which direct telephony services operate. The Kelsey Group, a US management analyst, estimates that the global market for speech-recognition products will grow to US$14 billion (AUS$26.7 billion) by 2005, and that customer-relationship services will make up US$11 billion of this amount.

Web-enabled wireless devices will increase in number and capacity, allowing a marketing director to keep in continuous touch with agents and marketing officers. Research firm IDC estimates that the number of Web-enabled wireless units will be more than 60 million within the first five years of the twenty-first century, up from 7.4 million in 1999. High-speed access to the Internet is crucial to business and Internet users, and it is essential that a properly equipped business suite can offer the very latest technology with such access.

One change in technology and the way of doing work that might impact adversely upon the hospitality industry is the increasing use of telecommuting in business, and the use of associated technologies (such as video-conferencing to link executives and professionals worldwide). This might reduce the incidence of business travel. However, there are other factors operating—such as the overall effects of increased globalisation—that should offset any potential reduction due to these technological factors.

Because of the degree and scope of change, there is a heavy responsibility on marketing managers to keep abreast of changes in the IT marketplace, and continually to assess how they can improve their marketing strategies.

Questions for discussion or revision

1 A website should be designed to be used and browsed by as many people as possible. It must be 'all things to all people'. Do you agree with these statements?

2 Use a search engine to search for a local hotel on the Web. Note where the hotel appears in the listing. Visit the site and note down three items of information you think would be crucial in making a decision to stay at the hotel.

3 Search for a restaurant that markets itself as a speciality restaurant. Is the product on offer clear and attractive? Has the website any of the mistakes noted in this chapter?

Chapter 12

Marketing Management

The aims of this chapter are:

- to explain how to implement the necessary control procedures to keep a marketing plan running;
- to explain various corporate approaches to marketing management; and
- to outline job functions in a marketing department.

Service-control procedures and computerised control

A marketing plan can be effective only if:

- management has the ability to manage;
- the organisation has the right staff to service the customers; and
- the staff has the capability to implement the marketing program.

Because the hospitality business is so directly dependent upon service, organisational control and the maintenance of standards is critical. Any establishment is totally in the hands of its people and their skills. Hiring the right staff is therefore vital.

Staff should not be treated as a commodity. The hospitality business is about people. The customers and the people who serve the customers have to like each other. This means hiring staff members who can share the gift of friendship with their customers. The secret of a successful operation is having good people. You can always teach procedures to a friendly person, but you cannot teach friendliness to an unfriendly person. A person without the right personality for the work can go through the motions of smiling and saying, 'Enjoy your meal', or 'Have a nice day'. But that is exactly what they are doing—going through the motions. The customers know the difference.

Management by measurement

A good manager does not 'control' people in the sense of using fear or heavy authoritarian direction. Effective management is about giving direction by setting goals, by allocating tasks, and by facilitating—that is, making it possible for staff members to do their work effectively and efficiently. This involves management by measurement, and negotiation with individuals when there is conflict.

In a restaurant, each person's work is particularly dependent upon others doing their work. Teamwork makes an operation 'click'. If one person is causing a hitch in the procedures, not only will others in the chain be affected, but also, ultimately, the customers will be affected.

According to Blanchard and Lorber,[1] authors of the *One Minute Manager*, the following management systems are effective:

- ◆ acceptability—everyone has to be clear on what he or she is being asked to do;
- ◆ data system—performance information must be gathered to determine how well people are doing;
- ◆ feedback—feedback must be provided to people so that they can continue to do well or redirect their efforts;
- ◆ recognition—good performance makes a difference, and good performance must be recognised; and
- ◆ training—people must have the skills to perform well; high expectations without skills (or ability) lead to frustration and poor performance.

Management's job is to ensure that each of the five systems is in place and functioning appropriately. Management must constantly observe and monitor each person's work, and step in to help someone who is in trouble. To achieve this there must be a job description of each person's function—an 'average expectation' of how and when an activity should be accomplished—against which the performance of an individual can be measured. The degree of competence required to perform a task therefore has to be measurable. 'If it can't be measured it can't be managed.'

The 'employee performance appraisal' illustrated in Figure 12.4, page 166, is one of several forms that can be completed by a supervisor for the purpose of assessing an employee in a general way. The gradings used in this form are: 'U' (unsatisfactory); 'S' (satisfactory); and 'E' (exceptional). (This will be considered in more detail below.)

Those who are 'unsatisfactory' need counselling or training. However, on some occasions, a person performing to an unsatisfactory level is unable to perform because of factors beyond his or her control. For example, sometimes other people in the service team or a piece of unreliable equipment are obstructing the procedures. The procedure itself might be a problem, and might be incapable of fulfilment in the time allocated. Having taken these factors into account, if a person proves to be incapable of performing the task according to the performance criteria, other tasks will have to be allocated, or the person will have to be dismissed. The customer outcome must be achieved.

The aim of 'control' by management is the development of a working culture—a working culture that eases the interaction between people, smooths the handling of procedures, and maintains the momentum of service delivery. As a 'facilitator', management must provide information, advice, training skills, and staff development, and must make changes when necessary to bring the marketing process into line with the marketing plan.

In most service teams there are people who are natural catalysts around whom the service tasks flow more easily. They should be constantly acknowledged and rewarded. Unfortunately, there are also the odd 'rotten apples'—people who might be efficient enough at what they do but who are critical of management, find fault with others, and are generally disagreeable. Regrettably, these people must be removed. Their presence has an effect directly opposed to that of the catalysts, and causes friction and unfriendly feelings.

Objectives of marketing control

The objectives of marketing control can be listed as follows:
◆ to make it possible for each person involved in the marketing mix to perform efficiently and effectively to achieve the marketing goals;
◆ to measure the performance of each element in the marketing mix and take the appropriate action to correct divergences from the marketing plan;
◆ to have an efficient marketing information system with regular and accurate reporting according to a strict timetable; to ensure that the reporting system is regular and transmitted without delay (to avoid damage to the plan);

◆ to have a friendly environment for the customer and the employees—friendliness, pride, and willingness to do what is required being the attributes an employer must instil in the staff; the hiring of the right people in the first instance is essential to the process; and

◆ to offer praise and reward good performances.

Management by motivation

Having approved the marketing plan, management then has to provide the required resources to fuel ultimate realisation of the plan. A shrug of the shoulders and an acceptance of difficulties is seldom appreciated by disgruntled clients, and quickly leads to a rapid downturn in sales and profits.

The decision-making process of control involves the setting of realistic sales and profit objectives, and the ability to measure those objectives with:

◆ internal information;

◆ external information;

◆ performance comparisons;

◆ advice and opinions from those concerned with the marketing function and its implementation;

◆ the decision-makers' knowledge and judgment; and

◆ timing of the action.

Here, financial management and marketing management have to work together. In any well-run establishment, systems are in place for a reason other than keeping the customers. They are also essential to avoid unnecessary losses. Lax management can lead to staff members' dispensing free drinks or pilfering. In contrast, a staff that is motivated by friendly, caring management is less likely to be involved in petty pilfering.

Motivation and control go together. What motivates people? The motivations for staff members in a hospitality establishment are the same as the motivations for people involved in any enterprise:

◆ a desire for approval;

◆ a desire for belonging;

◆ a desire for achievement;

◆ a desire to fulfil a purpose;

◆ an interest in the task; and

◆ a pride in the task.

Figure 12.1 Management by motivation
Authors' presentation

Virtually everyone enjoys being appreciated—by being explicitly congratu-lated on doing a good job, or simply by receiving a friendly acknowledgment. And virtually everyone enjoys the feeling of being part of something worth-while. A sense of achievement, having a purpose, and doing interesting things makes life and work worthwhile.

So many organisations ignore these fundamental human needs. So many managers regard employees as functionaries—human robots who are 'paid to do what they are told'. Ignorance of basic human motivation leads to staff discon-tent, indifference, dissatisfaction, and poor service. This, in turn, can have disastrous financial consequences.

Intelligent organisational control therefore requires management to put into place the following:

◆ staff-orientated policies and administration;
◆ appropriate salaries and incentives;
◆ helpful supervision;
◆ friendly working conditions;
◆ understanding of the personal lives of individuals;
◆ proper recognition of status;
◆ supervisors with appropriate skills with people; and
◆ job security.

Although these factors are generally not considered to be the province of marketing—being usually assigned to general management, unions, and human-resource management—the absolute reliance of the hospitality industry on these sorts of human factors indicates that the marketing plan cannot function without them.

Fear and coercion are motivations of last resort. A working culture that provides people with esteem, pride, and satisfaction will always prevail. Appropriate wages, fringe benefits, and safe working conditions are essential. However, these factors do not, by themselves, bring lasting satisfaction. Motivation comes with recognition and rewards commensurate with contribution, with high organisational standards, with good internal communications, and with the opportunity for self-correction when errors occur.

Many car manufacturers around the world are throwing out the production-line approach to building cars and are using the team method. Self-managing work units are formed to make up a team that builds a car from beginning to end. The units compete against each other in terms of productivity and quality control—to build a better car and build it more quickly than the others. There are incentives for the teams to do better. The results have been outstanding. The team members are happier, there is less sickness, they earn more, and they have pride in what they do. All of this occurs because they are involved and are rewarded for their efforts.

Michael Hurst at his '15th Street Fisheries' restaurant builds the same pride among his staff. At the beginning of each busy Saturday night, the cooks want to know how many meals they have to do, and at the end of the night they want to know how many they did. The waiting staff are the same. Everyone is imbued with the desire to do better and reach a standard of excellence to keep improving on his or her personal best.

Productivity—a much-vaunted and overused term—is not achieved by systems alone. It is nurtured and encouraged by competition, job satisfaction, acknowledgment, praise, and rewards.

Organisation control

A successful organisation requires management of the marketing plan as well as good marketing strategies. A number of establishments begin with the right ideas and then lose their way because they become opportunists instead of sticking to the original game plan and controlling the strategies that made them successful.

See the case study: 'How to go downhill' (page 157). The point of the example is not only management's original error in changing its product mix, but also that it fails to understand what is happening when things go wrong. It fails to understand this because it does not have the necessary checking and control procedures in place.

A marketing plan has to be constantly monitored—otherwise it goes off track. This applies to a smaller establishment as much as to a larger one. Of course, the larger organisation has more people to attend to the various marketing functions. Someone running the small place has to 'wear several hats'—or in many cases, 'wear all the hats'. This makes it harder on the small business operation because many skills are required. But the marketing strategy should not be neglected because of this excuse. The larger organisation also has difficulties. Even though the load is shared, the efforts have to be coordinated, and this places a special responsibility on those whose task is to 'manage the people who manage'.

Elements of a successful performance strategy

Five elements are required for a successful performance strategy—strategic objectives, structure, systems, staff (including staff skills), and corporate culture. The essential features of each of these is as follows.

◆ *Strategic objectives* determine what the organisation wants to achieve.
◆ *Structure* determines the human and physical resources required to achieve the objectives.
◆ *Systems* determine the methods used to achieve the objectives, and the deployment of human and physical resources in support of these methods.
◆ *Staff (including staff skills)* refers to the number, experience, and skill levels of the human resources.
◆ *Corporate culture* refers to the type of operation conducted by the establishment, and how it wants to be perceived by its customers and the general public. This includes concepts of commitment to customer satisfaction, staff loyalty, occupational health and safety, maintenance, progress, and profit.

CASE STUDY

How to go downhill

Here is an example that is as old as the hospitality business. It is about a restaurant that originally targets a middle-income group of aspiring young executives and professional people aged between 25 and 35, a market that dines out frequently. The owners get their service strategies right and the target market appreciates the casual style and the modest prices they implement.

Before long the business succeeds and makes a profit. After a year or so of steady gains in customer numbers, the management becomes greedy. The prices are increased by a few dollars, the meal portions are limited, and staff numbers and hours are reduced. Before long, the customers realise that they are not getting the same value for their money and begin to drift away.

'It isn't the same any more,' the customers say. 'The place is going downhill.'

Management blames the customers for being fickle and resorts to advertising to 'get the customers back'. This does not work, and the restaurant goes on a slide and becomes just another restaurant struggling for survival.

A sympathetic managerial climate and open communication are essential. This is sometimes referred to as the 'corporate culture'. This culture determines, both consciously and unconsciously, how staff members regard themselves, their employer, their customers, and their workmates.

Marketing organisation structure

A performance strategy requires an organisation structure, and this can take several forms. In marketing, there are ten primary functions to be performed. These are:

- marketing planning (development and overview);
- new product development (future planning);
- direct sales representation (to corporate customers and travel agents, locally, interstate, and internationally);
- advertising (direct with media or using an advertising agency);
- sales promotions (usually assisted by outside consultants or agencies);
- direct mail and email (usually assisted by outside consultants or agencies);

◆ market research (usually assisted by outside consultants or agencies);
◆ public relations and publicity (usually assisted by outside consultants or agencies);
◆ product management (overview or separate product managers for each profit-earning outlet); and
◆ customer services.

Who performs these tasks depends on the size of the operation, and on the structure and systems decided by the owners. Sometimes the structure and the systems evolve as the needs arise or as growth occurs.

In the case of a marketing organisation structure for a large property there are five main alternatives for a marketing management system:

◆ a sales-only department;
◆ a sales department with ancillary advertising and promotions;
◆ a marketing department separate from sales;
◆ a marketing department with sales as subsidiary; or
◆ a modern marketing structure.

A sales-only department

Under this structure, the managing director handles most of the marketing functions and requires only a sales force to make direct contact with existing and potential customers.

A sales department with ancillary advertising and promotions

In this instance, the managing director appoints a sales manager to handle a sales staff and the advertising and sales promotions. The main planning functions are controlled by the managing director.

A marketing department separate from sales

This structure usually occurs when an operation grows in size and the managing director (or the board) realises that specialised assistance is required for most of the marketing functions. A marketing manager is appointed to work with the sales manager. The managing director retains control of planning. In this case, marketing and sales are seen as separate and equal functions.

A marketing department with sales as subsidiary

Marketing in this variation of structure is perceived to be a holistic function with sales being one of several functions. This is close to the modern concept of a marketing structure.

A modern marketing structure

Under this structure, a marketing director is appointed with full responsibility for all marketing activities. This person might have several specialists—one for each of the various functions—reporting to him or her.

Organising the marketing functions

There are four ways of organising the marketing functions—again depending on the size of the operation and from where it draws the majority of its business:

◆ functional departments;
◆ regional management;
◆ product line management; and
◆ market management.

Each of these is considered below.

Functional departments

Various marketing specialists report to a marketing manager. This means dividing the ten marketing functions (this chapter, page 157) into people or departments. In a large international hotel, the advertising manager plans for all markets and regions. This is centralised control.

Regional management

Under this structure, each region is self-sufficient and responsible for itself. For example, a large centre such as Sydney might have a complete marketing structure and control all functions for the state of New South Wales. Melbourne might have a similar marketing structure. Adelaide and Perth, being smaller markets, might share functions. This is decentralised control.

Product line management

Under this structure, a product manager is responsible for the marketing functions that affect each product. This approach appeals to most middle-line managers. It means, for example, that the food & beverage manager does his or her own marketing without direct interference. The person is given a target and a budget. Similarly, the convention and banquet managers, restaurant managers, and so on all work on the same basis. The overall marketing of the hotel as a corporate umbrella campaign might be vested in the managing director, the marketing director, or the sales manager.

Market management

Under this structure, separate marketing exists for various customer groups. This approach divides the hotel's customers into groups with a separate person responsible for the marketing functions affecting those groups. Thus, the corporate market is handled by a separate department, the holiday package market by another, the meetings, seminars, groups, and function markets by another, and so on.

Management control approaches

The owners and senior executives of operations often have differing views on marketing and how it should be controlled, including the part that it plays in the total running of the operation. Some owners believe that marketing is just another function and that it ranks equally in importance with financial control, operational control, and human-resource control. Others see marketing as being merely a 'selling' function and give precedence to operations and finance. The attitudes of senior management (and, therefore, the management system put into place in large hospitality establishments) affects the structure of the marketing division and the roles of the managers of each function.

The main control approaches are:

◆ market control;
◆ profitability control;
◆ strategic control; and
◆ product control

Market control

Under this approach, sales, markets, market share, and profitability are viewed together by senior management as being interrelated (as they are).

Profitability control

Under this approach, the emphasis of senior management is on sales and profits, the belief being that high sales mean high profits. This is a simplistic approach with inbuilt problems.

Strategic control

With this approach, markets, product mix, market shares, sales, and profitability are constantly monitored and analysed.

Product control

Under this approach, senior management places most emphasis on productivity, and on the cost-efficiency and profitability of each line of the product mix.

Depending on the structure and system employed to achieve the corporate goals, the order of the line management and the responsibilities of each job description will be different. The usual organisation structure found in leading hotels around the world is illustrated in Figure 12.2 (below). A typical marketing department structure is organised along the lines of Figure 12.3 (below).

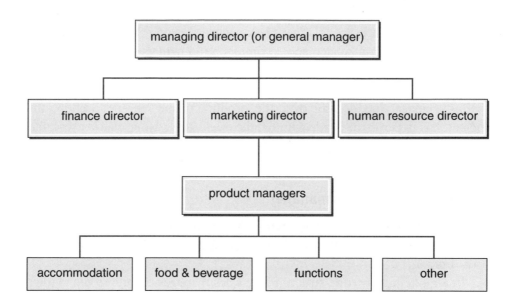

Figure 12.2 Classic organisation structure
Authors' presentation

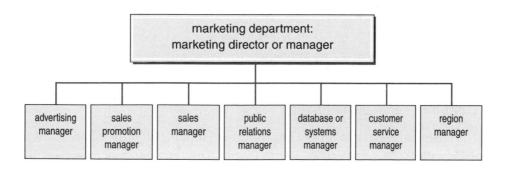

Figure 12.3 A typical marketing department structure
Authors' presentation

Job descriptions in brief

Marketing director/marketing manager/director of marketing and sales

This person is responsible for fulfilling all the marketing functions and meeting the sales objectives set by senior management. This person usually reports to the managing director, and coordinates his or her activities with the finance controller and administration manager.

In many hotels, the product managers (such as the food & beverage manager, seminar & function manager, and accommodation manager) have equal status with the marketing manager—who liaises with them.

In contrast to this arrangement, in a modern marketing structure the marketing manager has control over the product managers. In addition, this person has department heads who handle sales, advertising, market research, customer services, sales promotions, and public relations.

Sales director or sales manager

A sales director or sales manager reports to the managing director, and might also be responsible for the whole marketing function in a sales-orientated organisation.

In a modern marketing structure, the sales manager reports to the marketing director. This person is also responsible for all the direct-contact functions, and has a staff of sales representatives (also called 'account executives') and sales clerks. This department is required to develop corporate customers, groups, seminars, functions, meetings, and packages, and is required to contact travel agents and tour wholesalers.

Operations manager

This is an optional position. It refers to someone who is in charge of all the products or outlets in a large property.

Customer services manager

The customer services manager has the task of looking after the customer from the moment he or she makes a booking. This person is often called the 'accommodation manager' (mainly because, in hotels, accommodation is the premium product). This person can also be the administration manager.

Public relations manager

The responsibility for the image of the hotel is on the shoulders of the public relations manager. This person is responsible for contact with the organisers of conventions, with visiting celebrities, with politicians, and with government departments. This person is also responsible for organising large parties and big accounts. Indeed, all senior level contact is part of the function of the public relations manager. In addition, liaison with the media and the public is required to ensure favourable publicity whenever possible. This person is also responsible for the maintenance of the hotel's website—which must be continually updated. (In passing, it should be noted that it is 'off-putting' for users to find that a website has not been updated for a year or longer—probably because no one has had the responsibility or the skills to do it.)

Advertising manager

The advertising manager is responsible for the development and placement of all forms of advertising in the media. In addition, he or she must organise the creation of brochures and literature for the establishment. An advertising agency is generally employed for creating campaigns, for preparing the materials, and for placing them in the media.

Sales promotions manager

Because promotions are such a large stimulant for business, the sales promotions manager has to create the promotional concepts and follow them through. The position is often included in the duties of the public relations manager, and sometimes the advertising manager—functions that are closely aligned with promotions.

Website and email manager

The role of the website and email manager is a specialist area and one that is growing as establishments use websites, direct mail, and email techniques more frequently to maintain contact with existing customers and to achieve further market penetration. Maintaining a database of customers and potential customers is part of this function. Great skill is needed to gain the maximum results. Direct mail agencies are often employed. Often this job is included in the duties of the advertising or sales promotion manager.

Telemarketing manager

The role of telemarketing manager is another area of specialisation for some places. This manager backs up direct mail functions, sales promotions, and advertised package offers, or makes direct contact with customers to sell particular products. The telemarketing manager usually has a team of part-time phone people to control, advise, and encourage.

Product line (or outlet) managers

In a large establishments, the managers of the divisions of accommodation, food & beverage, banquets & functions, restaurants, entertainment, and recreation are also members of the marketing team—even though, in most cases, they report to the general manager or an operations manager.

Importance of interaction

Every function in a large property is directly involved or affected by marketing activity. A close working relationship is therefore required because the customer is part of a transfer of skills (doorman to concierge to porter, and so on). Unless the lines of communication are carefully planned, there can often be scope for problems resulting from ambiguity or demarcation disputes. This is another argument in favour of a modern marketing department structure—with a key person being responsible for directing and coordinating the various functions.

Using competency-based strategies

Service is a product. This product is the means by which a property provides the customers with an experience that is special and memorable. A service strategy has to state precisely what will happen to and for the establishment's customers, and this strategy has to be consistent and measurable.

The best way of achieving these objectives is to translate the strategies into competency-based criteria that detail every action involved in providing the service. The establishment of a competency-based service strategy requires a series of decisions that answer the following questions:

◆ What is the desired outcome for the customers?; and
◆ What are the details of the service that can be itemised as performance criteria?

Evidence of satisfactory performance of the service strategy is obtained from:

◆ observation by management;
◆ customer reactions from surveys or discussion;
◆ improved sales or customer numbers; and
◆ staff feedback from discussions with management.

The success of the strategy relies on the abilities of the staff members who perform the service, and on the feasibility of the demands of the performance criteria. Some amendments might have to be made to achieve consistency.

The concept of competency focuses on what is expected of the service and the people who provide it. To be competent, the staff members must:

◆ have the skills to perform the service functions;
◆ provide the service to the satisfaction of the customers in the time allowed;
◆ handle irregularities and respond to special guest requirements; and
◆ work as team members and interact with others such that the customer benefits from a smooth transfer of information in the service chain—from reception, to waiter, to kitchen, and so on.

Three grades of evaluation of the outcomes and the performance criteria are recommended:

U unsatisfactory, meaning the service is not being effectively provided as stipulated by the performance criteria;
S satisfactory, meaning the service is meeting the performance criteria; and
E exceeding, meaning the service is exceeding the expectations of the performance criteria.

Each person involved in providing a service has to have a written chart that outlines the desired customer outcome and the performance criteria. The 'restaurant reception service assessment' (Figure 12.4, page 166) is an example.

A service strategy such as that illustrated in Figure 12.4 is not inflexible. It is a guide to be followed, but customers should not be 'processed' in a mechanical fashion. Management must aim to create a service procedure that produces a happy, interesting, and even exciting outcome for the customers—an experience that is different from, and better than, that provided by other establishments.

Fast-food chains such as McDonald's, Pizza Hut, Hungry Jack's, and KFC work to highly successful formulae. In the case of these establishments, there is a certain degree of 'processing' of customers, However, it is not the 'processing' that is the clue to their success. Rather, it is the satisfactory and consistent outcome for the customers—fast, convenient, and cheap eating gratification. A fine dining establishment is different because it is offering an eating environment and a service experience. However, the outcome for the customers has to be planned just as carefully.

Customer outcome	Performance criteria	Grading		
		U	S	E
Greet on arrival	1. Greet customers within 30 seconds of arrival.			
	2. Open door for customers.			
	3. Greet cordially by name if known. If name not known, say: 'Hello, my name is . . . , may I have your name?'			
	4. Check name against reservations. If reservation, acknowledge: 'Of course! Mr & Mrs . . .'. If no reservation, enter name in reservation.			
Give a table	1. Make out a table place name.			
	2. Indicate a table, describe location, and enquire if OK.			
	3. Escort to table, making conversation.			
	4. Beckon to waiter who is responsible for table			
Introduce to waiter	1. Introduce customers (by name) to waiter (by name).			
	2. If no other customers waiting at reception, remain at table until customers comfortable.			
	3. Before departing, wish customers a 'happy occasion'.			
	4. Return to reception.			

Figure 12.4 Restaurant reception service assessment
Authors' presentation

Questions for discussion or revision

1 Three skills are essential to the success of a commercial organisation. What are they? How important is each one?
2 What are the respective advantages and disadvantages of each of the four ways of organising the marketing function?
3 There are three management control approaches. Each one places an emphasis on one aspect of management. Which approach would work best for an hotel that is targeting the business traveller?
4 List the objectives of marketing control.
5 What are the assessment procedures required for an effective management control system?

Chapter 13

The Planning Discipline

<table>
<tr><td>

Aims of this chapter

The aims of this chapter are:
- ■ to explain the components of a marketing plan;
- ■ to detail how to use a step-by-step process to bring these components together to market a product or property; and
- ■ to describe how to write a marketing plan.

</td></tr>
</table>

Why have a plan? What is it meant to achieve?

The planning discipline is the way in which management handles change. Change does not always represent growth; it is often an adjustment to altered circumstances.

Anyone involved in a business should always be thinking of strategies for maintaining or improving it. This is marketing planning, and it has to cover the short term, the medium term, and the long term. The overall marketing of a property—especially a large property that can take up to ten years before it returns a worthwhile profit—involves a long-term view, as well as considering immediate short-term progress. Good marketing planning should allow for contingencies to cover possible situations. Product lines are considered to be medium-term matters, whereas product items tend to be more short-term items, because they can be changed without affecting the customers' overall perceptions of the property.

It is worth remembering that in business, as in war, failures are often caused by growing too fast and entering additional territories with inadequate resources. This is, in a word, greed. The basis of the business should first be secured. Then, with careful planning, the operation should be expanded or extended.

The outcome of planning is a master plan that guides and directs the operation through change. The purpose of a marketing plan is to apply *discipline* to the strategic process. This avoids costly errors, and ensures that nothing is overlooked.

The benefits of a master plan are:

◆ it demands up-to-date facts upon which marketing strategies can be based; (the importance of using a website as a source of information should be emphasised here);
◆ it pulls together all the available information and the thinking behind the marketing efforts to create a documented plan of action;
◆ it provides an opportunity for all involved to question existing practices and seek improvement; and
◆ it integrates all elements of the marketing mix, such that all contribute to the overall corporate goals.

Critical path

The marketing plan and important issues

A marketing plan must be produced as a written document. It should:

◆ consider the company's mission and its corporate goals;
◆ recognise the financial, physical, and human resources available;
◆ examine and review all the available market information;
◆ analyse comparative strengths and weaknesses of each product in the mix;
◆ identify problems and opportunities;
◆ target the most appropriate customer mix;
◆ select the best match of products with the customer mix;
◆ decide on realisable marketing objectives;
◆ set marketing budgets;
◆ develop strategies for each of the elements in the marketing mix to achieve the marketing objectives;
◆ outline detailed operational tactics and costings for each element;
◆ establish management controls and review procedures of the marketing plan; and
◆ propose long-term future developments.

The discipline of 'ORGANISATION' described in Chapter 1 (page 11) is an easy way of remembering the main steps.

Flexible planning procedures

A marketing plan should be completed at least annually. However, when an opportunity is presented by an altered circumstance in the operation's micro-environment (internal factors, such as a failing product) or its macro-environment (external factors, such as new legislation, the demise of a competitor, or the emergence of a new market opportunity), the plan might have to be revised or a new plan devised to cope with the change. If so, the planning discipline should be followed for the reasons outlined earlier—to avoid costly mistakes and to ensure that nothing is overlooked. The planning discipline does not always follow the critical path in the same sequence. Nevertheless, it is essential that *all* steps be considered before a new plan is approved by management.

The planning process might start with a market opportunity and lead to an examination of target markets and the development of strategies. In this case, the planner must work 'backwards', and must test the feasibility of the market opportunity and all the other factors requiring analysis along the critical path—before finalisation and the preparation of a documented report.

CASE STUDY

The Pudong Shangri-lan hotel

An example of a new marketing venture established to meet strategic planning goals is the Pudong Shangri-Lan hotel, opened in August 1998 in a new region in Shanghai, China, called the Pudong district.

The Pudong Shangri-La was conceived as a five-star 612-room property and the decision to proceed with construction in 1994 was made in conformity with a long-term strategy of the company developing markets in fast-growing regions or Asia, rather than meeting short-term profitability targets. Shanghai can be termed a 'gateway' market, and the strategic aim is to obtain a foothold in the gateway with a view to being able to become a major participant in the market.

Customers and markets

Ronald Nykiel outlines some questions which concern specific steps to include in the marketing program.[1]

External operations

- Which market segments relate best to your product or service?
- In which areas of need are your products perceived by your current customer mix segments to be strong? In which areas are they weak?
- In the areas in which you have strong competition, what are their major strengths and weaknesses as perceived by your customer segments?
- With which products can you exploit a competitive weakness or capitalise on your own strengths?
- Which existing product lines offer an opportunity for expansion?
- Which new product lines or items show growth trends and could be introduced to your existing customer mix, or used to attract new customers?
- Are there any growing markets that can be exploited?
- Are there declining markets for some products requiring replacement or scaling down?
- What new developments are coming which represent a threat or an opportunity?

Internal operations

Questions to be asked regarding internal operations include the following.

- Are there selling difficulties with some products?
- Are there service and quality problems?
- Are the pricing levels and deals being offered attractive and competitive?
- Are some sections of the property in need of refurbishing?
- Is a change of image needed to reposition the property, or to reposition a product line or item?
- Are costs exceeding expectations in some areas? Which areas of the marketing can be turned to more cost-effective use?

Master plan

The plan to be all-inclusive

A marketing plan makes a set of recommendations. Upon approval, it becomes the final marketing plan or 'master plan'. When completed, a written master marketing plan must incorporate all marketing activities, and all of these marketing activities must subscribe to a common corporate objective. It must be a living, working document which is referred to daily.

Surviving in business is mostly a matter of sticking to the basics of business—that is making sure that more comes in than goes out. Having a working document that reflects this reality, and referring to it daily, is reflected in an old joke about a highly successful accountant who eventually became a multimillionaire. His staff observed over the years that this man had the habit of beginning each day by furtively unlocking the top drawer of his desk and carefully scrutinising a piece of paper. Everyone considered it to be the secret of his success. When the old accountant died, his ambitious assistant forced open the drawer to obtain the secret and make a fortune for himself. The document in the drawer which the assistant read with shaking hands and disbelief simply said: 'Debits left, credits right'!

The need for separate product plans

Each product in the mix should be dealt with separately and have its own plan. This is because each profit-earning entity requires its own 'subplan'—a situation analysis that contains its own marketing objective, its own target markets, its own budget, its own strategies for the elements of the marketing mix, and its own detailed set of operational tactics. These separate 'subplans' can be contained in the master document or can be individually documented. In the case of a large hotel, there should be a master plan for the whole hotel, and separate 'subplans' for marketing the restaurants, bars, seminars and conventions, groups, tour wholesalers, and so on—for every line in the product mix. New products launched or introduced during the planning period should have their own plans too.

Advertising, sales promotions, and selling plans are subsidiary plans. These follow the same format and should also fulfil the master plan.

Thus, a marketing plan for a large property with a complexity of product lines can be an extensive document. A different set of strategies is required for each of the following:

◆ the property as a complete entity;
◆ each product line and item; and
◆ each target market.

If there is a change of company policy or philosophy, the document has to be recast to incorporate the change in strategic direction.

Fundamentals of planning

When an opportunity arises, or when change becomes necessary, the initial step is to review the company's mission statement and to orientate it with existing circumstances. Too often, management forgets the business that it is in. Because marketing is the process of developing products and services to satisfy people's needs and wants, and arranging for them to be sold at a profit, the question must be asked: 'Is the business doing this according to its original mission?'. Hospitality is concerned with the experiences of people, and therefore hospitality marketing is essentially about understanding people. Before proceeding, does management know enough about the current state of mind of its customers, potential customers, staff, and the myriad intermediaries who influence the purchase decisions?

The next significant question to be asked is: 'Does the change contemplated fit with the corporate objectives?'. If it does not, a consultative process is necessary to assess the project and the corporate objectives—with a view to abandoning the project or realigning the corporate objectives. Business history is littered with examples of failures and near failures that resulted from marketing moves that diverged from the corporate brief. Objectives are the engine of achievement.

When products fail, or new ventures do not quite work out, a common cause is that the original idea came from someone—perhaps a senior executive—who had a bright idea and then arrogantly implemented it without proper planning procedures, and against the advice of timorous employees who were hesitant to go against the wishes of their superior. In the planning process, all information should be carefully considered. Market analysis is the beginning of the planning process. Its job is to gather all the information together and arrange it in a clear manner so that planning decisions can be made. There can never be enough appropriate information.

Once all the information is assembled it has to be analysed for problems and opportunities. Almost invariably, the analysis highlights the need for change to products or markets. These include:

◆ a market opportunity;
◆ a product line or item opportunity;
◆ a product line or item that has to be changed, modified or improved; or
◆ a repositioning of the establishment's image.

(See Chapter 20, 'Growth Strategies' for more on these matters.)

Let us assume that an hotel has a problem with one of its restaurants—which means that a product item has to be changed. Furthermore, let us assume that research suggests that a new Thai food theme restaurant might be popular. Using this example, let us now review the situation using a number of check points to assess the problems and opportunities.

◆ Is there a need for the product that the establishment intends to market? (Thai food has become very popular and is a growth area in the market.)

◆ Is there an idea for the product that will give it a sustainable competitive advantage? (There is an increasing number of Thai restaurants. What is to be special about this one?)

◆ Is there a market large enough to justify the investment? (Is there really a market for another Thai restaurant? A primary cause of failure or frustration in business is the discovery that the market someone thought worthwhile was either non-existent or too small to make the enterprise viable.)

◆ Is the market accessible? Is it physically close, and can the establishment communicate with the market relatively easily? (For example, in the case of a resort, apart from the hotel guests, the area might not have enough local population to support the required sales. In contrast, if the hotel is in the main city area, advertising and promotion will be simpler.)

◆ Are there sufficient production means—the facilities for making or preparing the product or service? (Who has the skills to cook and prepare Thai food? What additional equipment is required? What is necessary in the way of décor and presentation?)

◆ Does the establishment have the ability to maintain the service and the production standards? (The place could be vulnerable if it achieves rapid success. Continuity of supplies and availability of staff with the right credentials need to be considered.)

◆ Is there sufficient money to develop the project properly and follow it through? (The place has to 'look the part and play the part' to be successful. In a competitive environment, a half-hearted investment in furbishing, staff, and equipment could spoil the whole concept.)

◆ Is there enough knowledge about the people who comprise the market? (The expectations of the devotees of Thai food have to be understood.)

◆ Has a feasibility study been completed? (The costs of setting up have to be weighed against the forecast income and profit.)

◆ Does management have the experience to control the project successfully? (Who has run or worked a Thai restaurant before? The skill and expertise have to be evident to the customers from the beginning.)

◆ Does management have the marketing budget to promote it? (Selling, promotion, and public relations are expensive exercises. Will the costs justify the results?)

◆ Does it make sense to do it? (Would a Thai restaurant 'fit' with the overall positioning of the establishment and the customer mix?)

◆ How much business (in terms of sales, market share, or profit) is possible from the new development? What are the marketing objectives that will drive the endeavour? (When writing down the marketing objectives, measurable results have to be decided and a time frame allocated.)

◆ Which segments of people should be targeted to form the customer mix? (The answer to this question should come from the market analysis.)

◆ What will be the product strategies? What will happen to and for the customers? (Decisions have to be made regarding the service style, the menu, meal portions, plate presentation, and so on.)

◆ How will the place look? (The décor, the music, and the general ambience have to appeal to the target market.)

◆ What are the price strategies? (The price will determine the customers' perceptions of service and meal standards.)

◆ How will the product be positioned in the minds of the customers? (Promotion is necessary to communicate the place to the potential customers using a mix of advertising, direct contact, sales, promotions, and publicity. What will the message be?)

Writing a marketing plan

Once a project passes all the checks, the planner can proceed to prepare the plan in the form of a written document—a marketing report.

A marketing document must take the reader from a state of ignorance through awareness to understanding. Even if most of the readers are conversant with the subject and have a reasonable knowledge of its purpose and content, there will be others who do not have such knowledge. The document must therefore present the rationale behind the conclusions and provide evidence and logic for its recommendations. The writer must provide the background to the recommendations and the reasons for each step. The reader must not left be wondering how the writer reached certain conclusions.

There is a difference between facts and observations based upon those facts. In the main, the writer should present facts, make observations about the facts, and then draw conclusions in a logical sequence.

Order of presentation

The contents of the report should be presented in the following order.

1. Introduction

Begin with an introduction that explains the purpose of the document—what it is about and what it intends to explain.

2. Table of contents

Provide a table of contents so that readers can refer to points of interest.

3. Executive summary

Include an executive summary. This should be early in the document. This is for some readers who are impatient and want the conclusions immediately, leaving the detailed argument to be more closely scrutinised by others. Alternatively, some people are not necessarily impatient, but desire an executive summary to help them 'navigate' their way through the document without becoming 'lost' in detail.

4. Background history

Recite the history or background behind the organisation or product.

5. Market analysis

Present the market analysis information and quote its sources. The topics that are covered by market analysis might be as follows:

- how the product fits into the operation as a line or item;
- the product's positioning (the public's perceptions of the property);
- sales history;
- market share information;
- product trends;
- profile of the market segments of the product's customer mix;
- competitive activity;
- product assessment—comparisons of performance strengths and weaknesses with the market as a whole and with individual competitors;
- marketing activities and the results of previous strategies affecting the product's selling, pricing, and promotion;
- internal factors affecting the product;
- external factors affecting the product;
- market and marketing research data;
- internal observations by staff;
- external observations—informed opinions from the industry and trade sources.

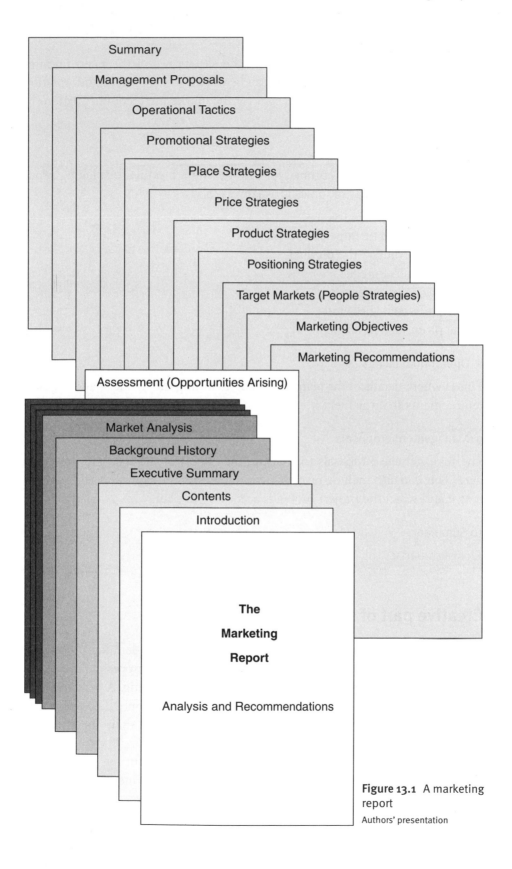

Summary

Management Proposals

Operational Tactics

Promotional Strategies

Place Strategies

Price Strategies

Product Strategies

Positioning Strategies

Target Markets (People Strategies)

Marketing Objectives

Marketing Recommendations

Assessment (Opportunities Arising)

Market Analysis

Background History

Executive Summary

Contents

Introduction

The

Marketing

Report

Analysis and Recommendations

Figure 13.1 A marketing report

Authors' presentation

6. Assessment

The assessment provides an analysis of the situation and the main findings from the analysis. Some conclusions can be drawn—based on the information gathered—and introducing the reasons for the marketing recommendations to follow.

7. Marketing recommendations

This is where the plan is outlined for introducing a product, or making product changes. The order of topics is usually as follows:

◆ the marketing objectives;
◆ the markets to be targeted (people);
◆ the positioning of the product;
◆ the product strategies;
◆ the pricing strategies;
◆ the place strategies; and
◆ the promotion strategies.

8. Operational tactics

This is where details of the plan are stated, including the financial and physical requirements to implement it.

9. Management proposals

The management proposals to measure the effects of the plan are presented here. This can also include proposals for the future of the property or its products if and when the project proceeds according to plan.

10 Summary

This summarises the conclusions.

Creative part of marketing

Many decisions are required in marketing planning. The planning procedures outlined in this chapter have been designed to assist this process.

There is a definite place for creative thinking in marketing. A person who is capable of 'lateral thinking'—of grabbing a 'great idea' from the cosmos—can often run away with a wild success. However, more often than not, tried and proven formulae in business bring success.

Some people claim that they proceed by 'gut' feeling. But the so-called 'gut' feeling' is actually an analysis in itself. Such people have mentally scanned a reference area of experience gained from the marketplace, and have, in effect, done the marketing planning in their heads. A 'gut feeling' is an analysis done without writing down and revealing the process.

A person who 'shoots from the hip' without proper planning is a person who places the organisation at risk.

Then there are those in management who manage by inactivity—failing to recognise the imperatives for change, and ultimately being forced to react rather than planning to act when the opportunities arise.

The best operator is the one who has a competent mixture of pragmatism and creativity and who plans carefully, justifying each step in the process. Such people always please shareholders and bank managers.

Questions for discussion or revision

1   What are the main reasons for having a marketing plan?
2   List the various aspects of an organisation that need to be considered in the planning process.
3   Who should have access to the marketing plan in a hospitality establishment and why do they need to refer to it?

Chapter 14

Marketing Audits and Marketing Information Systems

======= Aims of this chapter =======

The aims of this chapter are:
- to explain how to dissect and analyse a marketing situation;
- to explain the need for information systems for effective control; and
- to describe how to set up a marketing information system (MKIS).

Managing with hope instead of facts

The approach to a marketing audit is similar to that involved in doing a market analysis, but the intention is different. A marketing audit is a critical, 'outside–in' investigation which is aimed at establishing an organisation's exact market position and examining the effectiveness of its strategies and operational procedures. An efficient marketing audit requires the approach of a company auditor, or a detective. The auditor's task is to look for facts, and to ascertain reasons for a company's market position—that is, the performance of its products in the marketplace. And a good auditor should consider possible solutions, or alternatives, as the audit proceeds.

A marketing audit process is a form of appraisal used to understand an organisation. It is an appropriate process to use in the following circumstances:

- if you are thinking of purchasing a business;
- if you are entering an industry you know little about;

- if you are a newly appointed outside consultant;
- if you want to introduce a new product; or
- as part of an annual review before planning begins.

Marketing audit procedures

The following procedures are recognised marketing audit methods used by many companies and documented by various marketing authorities.

Macro-environment

The Koen brothers (see the case study, below) begin by carefully examining the marketing environment in which the business operates. In each case they look

---

CASE STUDY

Managing with facts, not hopes

The Koen brothers are very experienced hotel and restaurant operators.[1] Over the years they have excelled in taking over failing properties which they have then built into thriving businesses.

The Koen brothers have developed and refined a format for assessing properties as a test of their suitability for improvement. They leave nothing to chance because they know there are sometimes millions of dollars at stake. They do not like making mistakes, although they admit to an occasional blunder with a property that did not prosper as well as they would have liked.

The key to success is meticulous attention to a detailed analysis. The Koen brothers do not take on any failing enterprise until they have fully assessed the current situation, the reasons for the enterprise having reached that situation, and the likelihood of a successful resuscitation of the business. But, as Philip Koen, the elder brother states: 'If the company under examination by us had done its own independent audit and reacted to what it had found, it might not have been in the position of being forced to sell. There is nothing very smart about what we do. A lot of managers could do the same. The trouble begins with too many operators managing with hope instead of managing with facts.'

for market factors likely to have affected the operation of the property in the immediate past, and factors likely to affect it in the near future. The aspects they check are considered below.

Markets

Are the markets for hospitality growing, contracting, or altering in some way? Are there new market segments emerging and others dispersing?

Demographic

Where is the property situated and what major changes have occurred in building development or population shifts?

Economic

What are the economic conditions of the country and the region? What effect is the economy having on the standard of living and people's discretionary income and their attitudes to hospitality (especially holiday travel, business travel, and entertaining)?

Physical environment

Are there conservation plans likely to affect the property?

Technological

Have there been or are there going to be any advances in technology that will affect the way the property is operating? (Updated computer technology, for example, is often required to improve the way in which a place does things.)

Political

What is the government doing or planning that could affect the property? (Governments are always doing something with regulations and legislation that cause change to a business and the way in which it operates.)

Cultural

What changes are occurring to people's lifestyles? How have their attitudes to hospitality changed?

Micro-environment: the market factors

Factors to be considered under this heading include the following.

The state of the property

Where is it located and how does the property's position affect the perceptions of potential customers? What initial physical impression does the property make? What does its appearance convey to the customers? What expectations does the property arouse for the casual observer? What is the condition of the property externally and internally? What are the physical attributes of the place in terms of size, customer capacity, and the standard and quality of its equipment?

Customer mix

Which market segments have the property targeted as its customer mix? Which segments dominate? What types of people are not currently attracted to the property?

Product mix

What product lines and product items does the property have? Which ones are showing high usage and good returns, and which ones are languishing?

Competition

Who are the main competitors? How are they performing in comparison with the property? Who has gained which proportions of the various segments?

Agents and tour wholesaler activities

How do travel agents and tour wholesalers regard the property? How much business is generated through them? What type of business is it?

Outside suppliers

What is the attitude of suppliers to the property? How efficient are they, and how costly are their supplies? What deals are being done? What is the situation regarding future supplies? How much credit is being offered and what are the trading terms? How much money is owed by the property?

Corporate relations

What does the business community think of the property? Does the place have a high or low profile? What is the state of relations with banks, insurers, media, and the public in general?

Strategic planning

Is there a written business mission statement? What does it say? How closely has it been followed? Is it still viable?

Corporate goals and strategies

What have been the short-term and long-term corporate strategies, and how has management set about achieving them?

Marketing objectives

What have been the marketing objectives over the period of the property's existence? Have they been achieved? What is management's explanation for any shortfalls?

Market position

What is the property's actual position with regard to market shares, sales, and profits?

People strategies

Which markets has the property chased for each of its product lines (or outlets) and what share of those markets has it secured?

Product strategies

What have been the strategies of the property for achieving market penetration and growth for each product line and item over the period? How do the results reflect the success of these strategies?

Service strategies

What strategies are in place that are designed to provide a consistent, measurable, and effective series of experiences that happen to and for every customer? How are these strategies measured and managed?

Product positioning

How has management endeavoured to position the property and its products? Are the perceptions of customers in line with the objectives of the positioning strategies?

Promotion strategies

What advertising and promotional strategies has the property pursued, and with what degree of success? What is the annual budget for promotion and how is it expended? Are the effects of promotional spending being measured against the budget?

Pricing strategies

How has the property priced its various products? Has it adjusted to market realities, practised a uniform pricing policy, and adopted a flexible pricing strategy? Has it discounted extensively to gain business and remain competitive? Are the property's various products perceived by the customers to represent value?

The organisational structure

How has management structured itself?. How has authority and responsibility been distributed? Who does what? How good is the management standard overall, and which officers are performing to an optimum level? How are they monitored?

Lines of communication

How do the managers communicate with each other vertically and horizontally? What communication systems and meeting procedures are in place? How good is the functional efficiency of management? In other words, is management effective in achieving the marketing goals?

Company rules and policies

What are the company policies regarding customers and staff?. What is the basis for the policies? How are the rules and policies implemented? Who supervises them? How do customers and staff react to them?

Human resource management

What is management's attitude to staff? How do staff members regard management? How does management interact with the staff?. What training is provided, and how is it provided? What is the quality of relationships between management and unions? How good are the occupational health & safety measures? What are the staff amenities and privileges?

Marketing systems

Does management have a way of gathering and assessing market and marketing information? Which sources are used and what is done with the information gathered?

Market and marketing research

How much research is conducted by management and how often? To what extent is management guided by the attitudes of its customers as revealed in research? What sources are used by management to access data? To what extent does management refer to the staff for input?

Marketing planning system

How is marketing planning organised and how often is it updated? How are sales forecast for budgeting purposes? Does everyone work with a coordinated marketing plan, or is growth and market penetration opportunist and haphazard?

Marketing control system

Are marketing activities checked progressively by management? Is a sales analysis conducted regularly? Are quotas set? If so, on what basis? Are there strategic, profit, and tactical operations controls in place, and how are they monitored? For example, is there a system for tracking customer attitudes?

New product development, future planning

How does management decide on improvements and changes to products, or plan new products? Does management plan for change or is it simply being reactive to circumstances and opportunity?

Marketing profitability

How does management analyse the property's cost-effectiveness and profitability? Are the following regular checking procedures in place?

◆ return on investment;
◆ cash flows;
◆ profit and loss account by each product line and item;
◆ market share comparisons;
◆ profit margin contributions by products;
◆ cost-effectiveness analysis of products and staff;
◆ probability analysis.

Marketing functions

How well does the property perform?

The day-to-day functioning of the property

The day-to-day functioning of the property is a 'two-way' check of:

◆ the staff members and their operational procedures; and
◆ the reactions by customers.

Staff members and their operational procedures

This refers to staff members' attitudes to customers and their ability to provide service, the service strategies that they follow, the service systems in place, the standards of the equipment they use, and the overall efficiency levels achieved.

Reactions by customers

This refers to the reactions by customers resulting from their experiences of services rendered by staff members, and the level of satisfaction they have with each of the products.

Information about these two aspects of the day-to-day functioning of the property can be gained by talking to staff and a random selection of customers. From these interviews, management seeks to determine:

◆ staff and customer awareness of the property's products, attributes, and benefits;
◆ the effectiveness of service strategies and their ability to achieve the sum total of experiences that will satisfy and retain a high percentage of custom;
◆ attitudes to prices and whether there is a perception of value.

Further information about the property's ability to function effectively is gained by outside interviews and evidence. These aim to ascertain:

◆ knowledge of the property among tour wholesalers and travel agencies;
◆ effectiveness of the agents in selling the property;
◆ advertising effectiveness and the standard and presentation quality of 'collateral material'—brochures, fact sheets, folders, merchandising aids, the design and operation of the website;
◆ sales promotions and their effectiveness in increasing new business;
◆ publicity, and the frequency of the property's appearance in local and mass media (newspapers, television, radio); general awareness of the property;

Financial factors are an essential part of the marketing audit. Marketing reflects the property's condition as measured by customer numbers, cash flow, profit, and debt. It is not possible to separate the financial concerns from the marketing concerns when doing an audit. The two are intertwined because the ultimate aim of marketing is to achieve a profitable result for the investors.

A prospering property almost invariably has strong forecasting and control measures in place to ensure that it does not stray too far from its corporate objectives and its marketing planning. The 'outside-in' view provided by a marketing audit is a valuable tool to be used in addition to management control procedures—because it tends to focus on matters that might otherwise be overlooked from within the organisation.

Marketing information system (MKIS)

The purpose of a well designed marketing information system (MKIS) is to help management to make effective decisions. Essentially, an MKIS is a continuous process of gathering, aggregating, assessing, and distributing information to marketing managers to enable considered conclusions on the efficacy or otherwise of marketing policies, strategies, and tactics. The MKIS contributes substantially to the building of a successful operation and, more importantly, to the maintenance of strong growth through most economic conditions.

Why use the MKIS? A managing director of a leading hotel chain summed up the use of the MKIS and why it is important:[2]

> Every day I check on how we are going, right across every property. I need this information because I don't believe I can be an effective manager without it. I can act quickly to fix things before they go too far off track. I get concise figures and reports daily, backed up on a weekly, monthly, and more extensive survey results half-yearly.

MKIS process

The components of an MKIS provide a regular supply of information, or data flow, for the people involved in the following aspects of the marketing function:

◆ planning;
◆ executing; and
◆ controlling.

There are three types of marketing control that good management will wish to monitor through an MKIS:

◆ strategic control—to examine whether the planning and strategies that have been put into place are achieving the marketing objectives;
◆ tactical control—to examine the operational procedures and day-to-day running of the place to find out if the staff and the systems are working efficiently and effectively;
◆ profitability control—to ensure progress towards an acceptable overall profit result by determining whether the organisation is making or losing money by examining the profit contributions and the costs of each product line and item.

These will be considered in more detail below (see pages 189–92).

An MKIS therefore has to provide data from many different sources, and the type of data has to be defined.

A large property such as a five-star or six-star hotel obviously needs a large amount of information—far more than that required by a 100-seat restaurant or a small suburban public hotel. But smaller size does not diminish the importance of collecting relevant information. The owner of a 'pub' might argue that he or she and the spouse run the bar and the dining-room, and that a relative looks after the few rooming guests they have. In this scenario, the members of the family might argue that they store the required information in their heads. The trouble with this is that the human mind is prone to selective memory, and what they think is happening is often far removed from what the customers know is happening.

The trap for a small operator is complacency and the inaccurate reading of the customers' requirements. An MKIS for a small place does not have to be elaborate, but it should exist in some form for the owners' self-protection. Loss is far more painful for the 'little person' than it is for investors in a big property.

We now turn to each of the three major components of the MKIS process—strategic control, tactical control, and profitability control.

Strategic control

Strategies for people, positioning, product, price, place, and promotion are not merely long-term concepts. To review its ability to 'keep the customers rolling in', an establishment has to keep up-to-date records. Information is required as follows:

◆ internal information;
◆ external information; and
◆ a marketing research system.

Each of these is discussed below.

Internal

Internal information is obtained from:

◆ sales analysis;
◆ advance bookings;
◆ number of enquiries;
◆ market and customer mix information; and
◆ customer-attitude tracking.

External

External information is obtained from:

◆ market share comparisons;
◆ competitive action information;
◆ suppliers' information;
◆ channels of distribution information (especially agents); and
◆ awareness and positioning information.

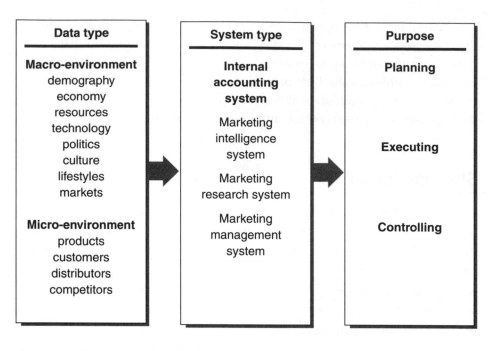

Figure 14.1 The marketing information system
Authors' presentation

The information needed for strategic control can come from the following sources:

◆ internal accounting and sales analysis;
◆ marketing management feedback—comments from supervisors and staff;
◆ market and marketing research; and
◆ tracking of customer attitudes.

Internal information should be easy to obtain with a sound record-keeping system, set up with any of the common computerised accounting packages, together with reporting procedures from each product line manager. The external information is more difficult to obtain. Market share comparisons should be an industry task—because everyone benefits from sharing such information. However, some operations are not always cooperative, and others tell lies to impress. Simple observation can often overcome the difficulties. Sitting in a property at random times over a few days usually provides an experienced operator with a sound impression of the performance of a place.

Marketing research system

A marketing research system is one of the most critical tools of an MKIS because it provides advance warning of change from the source of all business—the customers themselves. In short, it is a check on:

◆ customer attitudes, customer motivations, and early warning of changing attitudes;
◆ advertising, sales, and reactions to promotions;
◆ implications of new products or changes in sales patterns;
◆ market awareness and positioning information; and
◆ external market intelligence.

Marketing research in any organisation should be conducted every six months. However, a faster use of customer reactions can be achieved by *customer-attitude tracking*. There are several ways of doing this:

◆ complaints and suggestion systems that record, analyse, and respond to customers' complaints (written and oral);
◆ customer panels—having a group of selected customers who have agreed (usually for a concession or consideration) to report regularly by phone or mail questionnaire; these customers are sometimes referred to as 'mystery shoppers';
◆ customer survey—mailed questionnaires or personal interviews conducted regularly to evaluate product performances; and
◆ observation—a simple, watching brief by a trained person of what customers do, say, and think.

Tactical control

The tactical operations of a place are the day-to-day activities of the service systems. They are the lifeblood of customer satisfaction. A tactical control system is implemented by having a regular reporting system supervised and provided by product line managers. Their task is to measure productivity and make performance evaluations of:

◆ service staff and services;
◆ salespeople;
◆ agents;
◆ suppliers;
◆ outside service providers; and
◆ equipment.

The information can be subjective—which is better than nothing. However, the information is best gathered by having a series of competency-based statements with required outcomes. Each outcome is then measured on a graduated scale from one to five. Over a period, a norm is established and results are compared with that norm. An unsatisfactory result is when there is a progressive tendency for results to fall below the norm. Ideally, the results should demonstrate a growing trend towards exceeding the norms.

Profitability control

Profitability control is achieved by having an accountant or financial manager draw up a reporting system that analyses expense-to-sales ratios of every product by:

◆ territory;
◆ market segment; and
◆ client or corporate group.

This information normally comes from internal records that provide:

◆ sales figures and analysis;
◆ costs;
◆ stock inventories;
◆ cash flows; and
◆ accounts receivable and payable.

Marketing intelligence

The purpose of marketing intelligence is to provide management with information concerning:

◆ developments in the market environment;
◆ identification of social and cultural trends and opportunities;
◆ new laws;
◆ trade information; and
◆ technological changes.

The information sources for marketing intelligence are many and varied. They include trade reports, magazines, employees, customers' comments, suppliers' comments, agents' reports and comments, observation of competitive activity, published reports, industry conferences, staff movements, tourism reports, travel information, and so on.

Some groups in the hospitality industry exchange information—either through an industry association, or by arrangement. There are also trade intelligence suppliers, and the gathering of this assortment of information can be done by a clipping service, or a well-researched newsletter. Good management keeps itself up to date with developments in the industry. Copying an idea that has been a success in a similar situation elsewhere makes good sense. Conversely, avoiding a problem that has occurred somewhere else also makes good sense.

Setting up an MKIS

An MKIS provides the information, management makes planning decisions based on that information, the planning is then implemented, and the MKIS records the reactions of markets. All information supplied by an MKIS must be progressively measured and compared. It should be quantitative (numbers and percentages), qualitative (behavioural and attitudinal), evaluative (judgmental and opinionated), and exploratory (sounding out information sources).

The trend today is towards small, focused reports. Otherwise, management can be overwhelmed and confused by lengthy volumes of data. To avoid managers drowning in data, the amount of information has to be controlled. Therefore, in a large organisation, each manager needs to be asked a series of questions.

◆ What types of decisions are you required to make?
◆ What information do you need to make those decisions?
◆ How and when do you need this information?
◆ In what form do you want this information?
◆ How detailed does the information have to be?

To make it work, a marketing management system has to provide:

◆ centralised reporting procedures;
◆ a means of dissemination of information obtained to all concerned;
◆ a regular and intelligent evaluation of the information; and
◆ a decision-making methodology.

There have to be reasons for gathering the information, and good use has to be made of it. By itself, information has no worth—its value comes from how it is used. Its primary use is to take advantage of situations and to find solutions to problems. Progressive comparisons are essential. The information for an MKIS should be delivered in a simple, easy-to-read, and digestible form on a daily or weekly basis so that management can maintain an ongoing graph or grid. Management is then placed in a position to be able to:

◆ compare progressive results with goals;
◆ conduct performance measurement;
◆ do a performance diagnosis; and
◆ take corrective action if needed.

Solutions and decisions

The two primary concerns for management are sales and profit. Although the two are closely related, they are different, and the causes of problems in sales and profits need careful analysis. An MKIS is designed to reveal the situation and the causes of the situation. Then solutions are needed.

When sales are down

When sales are down, the natural solution is an intensified sales effort—but this is not as easy as turning on a tap. An increase in sales can be achieved by the following corrective measures, or a combination of them.

An improved sales effort

An improved sales effort could entail:

◆ an increase in the number of calls to clients and prospective clients;
◆ putting on more sales representatives;
◆ appointing more agents;
◆ extending into new territories;
◆ targeting different customer groups;
◆ eliminating wasteful sales calls;
◆ concentrating on more profitable customer groups;
◆ providing sales incentives and motivations; and
◆ providing more training, or making staff changes.

Making product improvements

Making product improvements could mean adding new or different facilities to attract more of the same types of customers or entirely new types. (See Chapter 20, 'Growth Strategies', page 257, for more on this.) Increasing the number of service strategies, or expanding existing specific service strategies, is another way of increasing sales. Add-on services or benefits is another.

Improved advertising or promotions

An altered image can reposition the property and generate new customer interest. Spending more on advertising is a popular means of increasing sales, especially if research reveals that there are many people unaware of the property or uncertain about what it offers. Developing sales promotions is an excellent means of drawing attention to a property and exciting people into making a purchase—often attracting them away from their previously favoured establishments.

Pricing changes

Most markets are price-driven, unless there is an exclusive benefit advantage for the customers (See Chapter 21, 'Pricing Strategies', page 265, for more on this.) Add-on value, discounts, special privileges, negotiated deals, and price-geared options all attract prospective customers who are seeking value for money.

When profits are down

When times are tough, everyone complains about the lack of profit. In the hospitality industry, it is natural for operators to look at (i) increasing sales and prices, or (ii) trimming expenses.

Areas that need to be examined are considered below.

Increasing sales and prices

Increase prices selectively

Price increases must be selective, and carefully considered. This means raising prices where there are justifiable reasons in the minds of customers.

Increase sales

Increasing sales is usually the solution to most profit problems. Additional sales that increase the variable costs (while fixed expenses remain the same) improve profit margins quite dramatically. For example, a busy bar with a rapid turnover of liquor stocks means the bar attendants are working to capacity. Bar attendants are a fixed expense, liquor costs vary according to the number of customers.

There is always potential for selling additional products to a pre-existing regular customer group. But all too often this idea is forgotten, and nothing new is introduced. An hotel or a motel becomes just another place to eat and sleep. There is no point in change for change's sake, but there are definite reasons for making the best use of the property and the existing customer base by adding on to existing products, even on a trial basis.

Trimming expenses

Unfortunately, most attempts at trimming expenses lead to reducing services and customer comforts. This, in turn, can have drastic effects on sales. In the end, a reduction in services frequently achieves the opposite of the desired effect. In the short term, profitability seems to improve—because, on paper, the ratio of expenses to income decreases. However, as sales decline, the total profit gained can actually reduce. Therefore, attempts to trim expenses should be aimed at eliminating waste, rorts, and expensive systems. Customer benefits should not be cut.

The following cost-cutting measures are often considered.

Reduce staff

If such reductions do not affect customer comforts, there is sometimes room for staff reductions in ancillary services. If these can be more cheaply performed by hiring contract services outside the organisation, this should be considered. Valet services or laundry services might come into this category.

Improve service efficiencies

The use of labour-saving systems—following a careful examination (by time-and-motion studies) of labour-intensive activities—can usually lead to services being provided more easily or quickly to customers. Sometimes the solution will be a new machine or new equipment—such as a computer reservations program for front-office procedures, or a stock-control reordering program.

Eliminate unprofitable lines

There is a general acceptance in the hospitality industry that certain services are expected by customers—almost as a matter of tradition. But every property has product lines that provide a dubious return for the money invested. A check with customers, or a check of the actual usage of such facilities, often reveals that few customers would be lost if these products were not there. For example, on most menus and wine lists in restaurants there are usually items that cost money to maintain, but would not be missed by many customers if they were not there.

Take on more profitable lines

Cost-cutting can also be achieved by making better use of space that is used for unprofitable lines. This space can often can often be better utilised by replacing unprofitable lines with new products or services that can attract more use by existing and new customers. For example, a property might have a large space that is used only occasionally for functions. Such a space might be better utilised as a games room.

Sell old stocks

A storeroom is the best place to start in a search for old stock that might be disposed of. Old 'treasures' can usually be found—furniture, equipment, stock, redundant fixtures and fittings, and a host of stuff that has been designated as material that 'might come in handy one day'. Seldom does that day arrive. It is best to quit it and realise its value.

Reduce spoilage and eliminate waste

Most properties keep a watchful eye on spoilage and waste, but it is amazing how often an outsider can observe procedures and activities that have become the accepted way of doing things, but which, in fact, cost unnecessary time and money.

Stop pursuing the wrong customers

Often managers have a delusion that the market contains 'untapped' people with lots of money. In pursuit of these supposed potential customers, management builds and redecorates, provides services, and creates expensive advertising brochures and other sales material to attract these people. In fact, these people either do not exist or have little interest in ever patronising the place. Nevertheless, many properties persist with this futile and expensive exercise of unrequited pretension. Management should remember that the majority of customers are average people with basic interests and requirements, and a limited budget to spend on these things. The real majority is always worth pursuing, rather than the unattainable minority.

Questions for discussion or revision

1 In which circumstances should a marketing audit be used, as opposed to a marketing analysis? Explain the difference between these concepts.
2 What is the difference between information obtained from the macro-environment and that obtained from the task environment?
3 There are four primary marketing information systems. Name each one and briefly explain its purpose.
4 How does management make use of the information it obtains from an MKIS in the routine day-to-day management of the business?

Marketing Research

Theory

Research is the systematic gathering of qualified information to establish facts. Marketing research has one purpose—to remove from business decisions as much of the guesswork and assumption as possible.

There is nothing more dangerous in business than an assumption or a guess. It is true that history records the brilliant successes of those who 'made it' in a venture by backing their judgment or using intuition—and guessing correctly. Unfortunately, history mentions only the small number of successes. History seldom talks of the huge number of of failures.

A small operator in the hospitality industry might shrug and say that its small size means that it cannot afford research, and does not need it. This is nonsense! A survey made up of a few well-chosen questions and a small random sample of twenty customers is often sufficient to stave off a disastrous decision. Such a survey costs nothing. For a few dollars, a book or an industry magazine can provide vital clues to profitable opportunities. Without research a business is being run on ignorance.

Research must be done, and the results of that research must be taken seriously. Even the largest of companies have been guilty of not doing research, or of defying research that provided an answer different from the answer that management wanted. Consider the true stories in the case study 'Ignoring research at your peril' (below).

CASE STUDY

Ignoring research at your peril

Consider the following true stories of the disasters that can occur if research is not done, or if the results of research are not taken seriously.

- A beer was launched for an international market, despite the fact that research had said that the international market did not want it. The research was right and the company lost millions.
- A cigarette brand was marketed for women, despite research suggesting that it would not work. It did not work.
- A car was designed for 'everyone', despite research saying that no one would want it. They did not want it.
- A restaurant went through sixteen different name changes, expensive refurbishing, and several owners, but none of the owners ever asked a single customer in the market what the customers would like, and nor did they bother to research the market to see what was working and what was not. One owner went to New York, Paris, and London and came back full of wonderful ideas that he tried. Each was a flop. He blamed the customers for their lack of interest in his brilliant concepts!
- An airline threw away its first-class section and 'upgraded' the economy and discount passengers into so-called 'Premier Club' and 'Australian Club' sections. Despite the fancy names, the real effect of the changes was to force everyone to fly in cramped seats and eat cold meals. Millions of dollars were spent on promoting the changes to increasingly sceptical passengers. Three months later the first-class section was back and everyone was eating hot meals again. What had gone wrong? Management said that nothing had gone wrong—management had simply changed its mind on the changes. However, it is likely that before it made the changes management had not asked its customers the right questions, or perhaps had not asked its customers any questions at all.

Market research is finding out what is happening, and finding out why it is happening. Because they are in direct contact with their customers on a daily basis, many managers and members of staff believe that have a good idea of customer attitudes. Moreover, many believe that this sort of generalised observation technique, backed by data such as unit sales figures, gives them a fairly accurate picture of how the operation is going. Perhaps this is true in some cases. But many members of staff and management are so busy doing their jobs that they go through the motions of asking guests about their stay or experience. 'And how was everything?' they ask with a smile as they make up the account. 'Did you enjoy your stay? Oh, that's good. See you next time!' When staff members are busy they are not really interested in the answers. Besides, at check-out, the guests are in a hurry and are not interested in any real discussions. Usually the guests' comments are not recorded, accumulated, and analysed in any way—leaving management reliant on asking staff members for 'impressions'. These, in turn, are often unreliable. Some members of staff have not really paid much attention, and some are merely expressing a personal prejudice. Some members of staff have personal ideas on how the establishment should be managed and these staff members might selectively report real or imagined customer attitudes to provide 'evidence' for their opinions.

Much market research involves the progressive collection of data from existing resources. A well-organised MKIS, for example, ensures that this information is collected, sorted, and distributed on a regular basis. This is sometimes referred to as 'desk research'—information that comes across the desk or can be accessed from computer records, a private library, or an industry library.

Data can be primary or secondary. *Primary* data are original data gathered for a specific project. *Secondary* data have already been gathered for another purpose or general usage, These data come from sources such as government statistics, various associations (industry, trade, professional, and business), private research agencies, higher education institutions, and so on.

Hotels have a large amount of information at their disposal, especially since the introduction of computerised booking systems which management is able to use to make marketing decisions. For example, menu design at a restaurant can be directed by an analysis of sales to determine the guests' preferred dishes. Accommodation analysis can indicate which packages are most popular, and who is purchasing them. The geographic origins of guests can be tracked. The types and number of sales of all products can be analysed by a centralised computer network when it is programmed to collect helpful data from the various sale points. For example, the data of an operation might reveal that its guests seldom use the establishment's dining-rooms, and that most of its customers come from the local population. Similarly, data might reveal that the gymnasium, pool, spa, and sauna are mostly used by outsiders. This sort of information has made many property investors wonder why they install and maintain such a wide range of expensive facilities for guests who seldom use them.

Compiling a computerised database

A database is a collection of information organised and presented to serve a defined purpose. A telephone book is a database. Most hospitality databases once consisted of guest cards that contained written information on each guest. Now most guest records are computerised, and these records constitute a database management system that allows the users to access the information quickly and efficiently, and in a number of different formats. With a planned data-retrieval program, management can use the computer system to build a database of customers for email, direct mail, and telemarketing contacts. Thus, it is possible to create a sales promotion and then ask the system to choose those customers who would be the best prospects for the promotion. The same system can be used to address letters and envelopes from its files.

However, at the time of purchasing the system, management must decide which information it wants, and must program the system accordingly. Otherwise, many of the potential advantages of having the system are lost. Most systems are used by financial people for accounting purposes, with the needs of marketing being a secondary consideration, or overlooked completely.

Once the systems are in place to retrieve the desired data, maintaining the flow is a relatively inexpensive process. Field research is more expensive because it involves the preparing of a questionnaire, coding it for keying into a computer, organising researchers to interview respondents, finding appropriate respondents, conducting the interviews (in person, by email, by mail, or by phone), collating the information, cross-tabulating it, and then analysing the results.

Marketing research surveys

Marketing research surveys are usually conducted sporadically on a 'need-to-know' basis. However, a good MKIS provides for field research to be conducted annually so that data can be progressively monitored for indications of changing market behaviour. It is an 'early warning system' of trends and attitudes. Whereas sales analysis is historical, research will often uncover what is in people's minds before the purchase decisions are made.

Marketing research takes several forms and is not the forbidding monster that some people believe—although motivational and psychological research can be complex and best left to the experts. The most difficult aspect of marketing research is not so much the gathering and interpreting of the data. More often, the problem is getting management to act upon it. Management often does not want to believe the answers—preferring to persist with its delusions about how things are, instead of listening to what the market is saying. Important decisions should be made on the basis of fact—not guesses or assumptions. Hence, marketing research is a key factor in the marketing process because, in the formulation of strategies, questions can be answered only by marketing research of some type.

On the basis of research, marketing mix strategies are formulated. For example, a decision on which market segments to target ('people strategies') can come only from a proper understanding of the market of a given city or region, and the people who comprise that market. Product mix strategies follow logically from the decisions on the best market segments to target. Pricing strategies flow on from the people strategies, as will product and positioning strategy decisions. Then follow promotion strategies.

Customer mix research aims to find out which groups of people make up the market and what percentage of each group uses the facilities most often. In addition, this type of research establishes from where the customers are coming, and their reasons for travel. This research is designed to answer questions such as the following.

◆ Where does most of the lodging business come from? Which towns, cities, countries, or states do they come from?
◆ How do they arrive? Do they arrive by plane, car, train, or ship?
◆ What are the reasons for each segment choosing to travel? Is it business, meetings, seminars, holidays, or personal?
◆ When do they come?
◆ What types of people are they? What are their social, economic, cultural, and national characteristics?
◆ How much does each type spend, and on which products?
◆ How is the market shared among the various operators?

Marketing research is thus necessary to guide the marketing mix decisions and the day-to-day operations of a property. But it is also required for discovering *opinions* on the property. 'Attitude research' attempts to find out the attitudes of each of the customer-mix groups towards the property and its products, compared with attitudes towards the competition. This research is designed to answer questions such as the following.

◆ What attitudes, preferences, and criticisms do potential customers have about the property and its various products?
◆ How well are the service systems working?
◆ How good is the staff in implementing the service strategies?
◆ Why do some groups choose the property and others do not?
◆ Which promotions and advertising appeal and which do not?

1

What types of people use the property now?

Where do they come from?

Why did they choose this property?

2

What types of people are not coming to the property?

Where are they going now?

Why are they going there?

What is the property doing or not doing that makes them stay?

3

What types of people can the property get that it is not getting now?

Why does this property have to do to get them?

Figure 15.1 Three groups of questions to be answered by marketing research
Authors' presentation

Six stages of a research study

1. Define the problem or opportunity

What information is needed? Some research is ill-directed and lacking in purpose. It can ask the wrong questions or miss out on vital ones, and this sometimes becomes apparent only after the study is completed and the money is spent. The problem should therefore be carefully defined before undertaking the research.

2. Establish the research objectives

Who should be asked the questions? What questions should be asked? What will be the size and nature of the sample? How should the questionnaire be constructed? The answers to these questions depend on accurately establishing the objectives of the research.

3. Develop the research plan

A plan must be developed that will obtain the required information. This means that the sample must be decided—including its size and location. From this, the survey method that will best gather the required information must be decided. If this is to be a questionnaire, this should be prepared.

4. Implement the research

Activate the research—by sending the operatives into the field, or by mailing the questionnaires, or by making the telephone calls.

5. Collect and analyse the data

Once all the questionnaires have been completed, the next stage is to put the data into a computer and to sort them into measurable quotas for cross-referencing and analysis.

6. Interpret the information and recommend a course of action

What does the information mean? Information for its own sake has no purpose. Without proper interpretation and recommendations, information can be misleading, and wrong conclusions can be drawn.

Field surveys

A field survey involves interviewing and asking questions of a number of people who are representative of the market. It is one of the most common means of performing marketing research. Others are observation, experimentation, and group discussion. Each has a reason for its use.

Nearly all research begins with a hypothesis—that is a proposal or consideration that something might be so. Then the research sets out to prove or disprove the hypothesis. In classical scientific method, the researcher sets out to *disprove* the hypothesis (even if the researcher personally believes that the hypothesis is likely to be true). By deliberately setting out to disprove the hypothesis, the researcher is more likely to obtain meaningful and reliable results—because the personal bias of the researcher is less likely to influence the conclusions. If the hypothesis 'stands up' despite these efforts to disprove it, it is more likely to be a valid hypothesis. Therefore, retain an open mind.

Beware of trying to find out more than is required. Keep the study simple. However, despite the desire to keep things simple, always pay attention to relevant demographics. The age, sex, income, place of origin, and other characteristics of the respondents can markedly affect the significance of the results.

The main use of a field survey is to interview a broad sample of the whole market. It seeks information from potential customers, customers of other establishments, and the general public. A field survey is not restricted to guests of the establishment. Field surveys using a carefully planned questionnaire can be conducted by email, mail, media, telephone, or face to face.

A mailed survey is the least effective because, even with a reply-paid envelope and a very easy questionnaire, most people do not have the time to answer or cannot be bothered. Those who do answer are usually a particular type of person—unrepresentative of the whole sample—and this places a bias on the results. A survey questionnaire placed in a magazine has similar shortcomings.

An email survey is more effective than mail, because addressees can readily and quickly reply. However, as a survey group, people reached by email might not be representative (because the sample will obviously be restricted to people who use email frequently). This might not matter in certain targeted groups. For example, a survey of businesspeople will probably be fairly represented by email survey because email usage is common in this group. However, if a hotel is seeking a survey of holidaytakers in general, an email survey might not fairly represent all private households.

A telephone survey is relatively inexpensive and more people can be interviewed in a given period of time. It is best used when the questionnaire is short and the questions require a minimum of explanation. There is some sample bias because not everyone has a telephone and some have unlisted numbers. Telephone surveys are useful for testing public perceptions of a property and its products, for following-up guests and getting a reaction to their experience, and for checking on the appeals of promotions and advertising.

A personal interview is the best form of field survey. Reactions can be gauged by the interviewer—such as shrugs or facial expressions that might be indicative of the need to probe further in some instances. Longer question-naires are also possible with a personal interview, although much depends on where the interview is conducted. Home interviews are best, but interviews on street corners are less than ideal.

Guest-room or front-desk questionnaires

A guest-room or front-desk questionnaire is the most common means used by establishments to test the attitudes and satisfaction levels of guests. Participation is voluntary, of course, and this can result in the answers not being representa-tive of all guests. Most people who respond are either very happy with their experience, or very displeased with it. Such surveys can therefore be inaccurate, and can provide a misleading appreciation of overall levels of satisfaction. However, serious problems can be revealed. In addition, such questionnaires do provide an opportunity for a disgruntled guest to obtain a satisfying response.

A telephone call to guests a few days after their stay by an independent researcher can be more revealing. People are then away from the property and they might feel that they can be more honest with someone who is not an hotel employee.

Focus groups

The focus-group research method, or pilot study, is an economical method of uncovering information—especially where attitudes need to be qualified rather than quantified in numbers or percentages. A focus group involves gathering together a group of people—usually eight to twelve in number, sometimes selected with demographic or psychographic characteristics broadly in common—to discuss a topic which is of interest to the researchers.

Focus groups are essentially exploratory in nature. As focus group partici-pants give their comments, researchers observe and listen to the discussion and note the interactions of participants. With four or five group discussions, an understanding of certain emotions, opinions, and attitudes can be ascer-tained. Such understanding helps in the formulation of products, positioning strategies, advertising, and promotion themes.

Focus groups are also very useful in giving direction to field surveys by sometimes revealing surprising attitudes that need to be quantified to establish their extent.

Observation research

The simplest form of market research is to watch and record what people do—either in your own establishment or in that of the competition. A traffic count, staff attitudes, and customer reactions can be gauged by observation, especially if the observer is not biased and is watching what is happening, and not seeing what the observer wants to see. See the case study 'Observation research tells all', below.

CASE STUDY

Observation research tells all

A bistro that had been doing good business for nearly two years slowly lost its business for no apparent reason. An independent observer was asked to sit in the place on and off for several days. The observer soon discovered the reasons for customer dissatisfaction.

The front door screeched every time it was opened, and the servery doors, which were in continual use, squeaked back and forth and put everyone's teeth on edge. If that was not enough, staff members were in the habit of shouting their orders into the kitchen to save time.

When questioned about this by the observer, the operators said the screeching front door alerted then to the fact that a customer was entering or leaving. They argued that this was a good system. If the waiters were out the back they could rush back to the room and greet the new customer, or chase one who had not paid! As for the squeaking servery doors, this was considered to be a good idea also—because it signalled to the kitchen to put up the completed orders for an incoming waiter.

The independent observer carefully pointed out that the screeches and squeaks were extremely aggravating for the customers. Moreover, not only did the screeches and squeaks alert the staff, but also the customers! All eyes went to the screeching door every time someone came in—much to the embarrassment of the newcomer. And when the servery doors squeaked, all eyes turned in that direction—each table hoping that this signalled their order arriving. On top of all this aggravation was the bedlam created by the waiters' shouts to the kitchen.

For the customers, the whole experience had become disconcerting and unnerving. A few drops of oil and a new way of getting the orders to the kitchen rescued a failing business!

Sampling

Research draws conclusions about large groups by questioning or observing small groups. For the results to have meaning, the research sample must be representative of the whole. The underlying principles of sampling and research for marketing are the same as for any scientific discipline, and are based on the laws of probability: if the sample is true of the whole, the results will apply to the whole with an error factor that increases or decreases proportionate to the size of the sample.

The total market population must be defined before sampling begins. Does it consist of users, purchasers, or influencers? Are they male, female, old, young, married, left-handed, and so on? To select a probability frame, each population element must have an equal chance of selection.

Accurate sampling is crucial for obtaining accurate answers to research questions. Some of the main sampling techniques used by marketing research agencies are discussed below.

Probability sampling

Probability sampling can take several forms.

Simple random sample

A simple random sample can be used when every member of the population has a known and equal chance of selection. An example of a simple random sample is to choose the tenth name of the second column of every page in the telephone directory. This process of selection can be repeated until the required sample number is achieved. This technique yields a representative sample of the population without undue bias. There is an inbuilt bias if the majority of people do not have telephones. However, in Australia, approximately 95% of homes have telephones, and this makes the bias small, and tolerable.

Stratified random sample

A stratified random sample involves people representing the population as divided into mutually exclusive groups—age, sex, income, and so on. From these, random samples are drawn.

Cluster sample

A cluster (area) sample involves people representing the population being divided into mutually exclusive groups by geographical area from which samples are drawn.

Non-probability sampling

Non-probability sampling can also take several forms.

Convenient sample

A convenient sample refers to the selection of members of the population who are easiest to access.

Judgment sample

A judgment sample refers to people being selected on the basis that they represent good prospects for information.

Quota sample

A quota sample involves researchers finding and interviewing a prescribed number of people in each of several categories. For an amateur researcher, this form of sampling is the best. Although the information might have a bias, it could be reliable enough for broad decision-making. Most decisions in business do not hinge on minute percentage differences, but on majority indications of attitudes and behaviour.

Questionnaire design

If management wants real information upon which to make decisions, research must be done in a planned way with clearcut objectives as outlined earlier in the six stages of research (page 204). This is best done by a competent marketing research firm. Conducting personal interviews (face-to-face or telephone) are best done by experienced interviewers who do not work for the establishment.

However, conducting a survey is not a great mystery, and an operator can gather useful information doing his or her own. To do this, some understanding of questionnaires is required.

Basically, a questionnaire is a series of questions designed to obtain answers that reveal the opinions, preferences, or thoughts of the people being questioned. To be effective, every question in a survey must be relevant, concise, and easy for the respondent to understand.

In addition, the questionnaire should have a means of identifying the respondents by some form of demographic reference. In other words, what types of people are making these statements? There should be some way of identifying whether they are people, younger people, young, wealthy, poor, and so on.

There are many traps in the construction of a questionnaire. Two common errors are: (i) are asking an ambiguous question; and (ii) asking a leading question that prompts the respondent towards a certain answer. For example, an ambiguous question is: 'Do you dine out frequently?'. There are two ambiguities in this question:

◆ How often is 'frequently'? For some people this might mean once a month. For others it might mean once a week.

◆ What exactly is meant by 'dine out'? Does this include meals at the home of friends or relatives?

The purpose of the question could be achieved by posing it in association with certain alternative responses. If two alternatives are offered, this is referred to as *dichotomous*. If three or more alternative responses are offered, this is called *multiple choice*.

For example, the question could be posed in a multiple choice format as follows:

'How often do you eat in a restaurant, café, or hotel? Never? Once or twice a year? About once per month on average? About once per week on average? More than once a week? (Please choose the alternative closest to your own experience.)'

Most questions are classified as being 'closed' questions—meaning that the respondent is forced into a committed response. In contrast, an 'open-ended' question means that the respondent can answer in an unlimited number of ways. A closed question can be converted to an open-ended question by adding the alternative 'other' to a list of alternatives (and leaving room for the respondent's answer to be written in). Another form of open-ended question is a totally unstructured question that invites comment. An example is: 'What is your opinion of the food at this restaurant?'. Closed questions are better for research because they prompt a definite answer, and because the responses are easy to enter into a computer for analysis. Open-ended questions are best used when the question is exploratory—when there is some uncertainty about the extent and nature of the responses.

If it is necessary to find out the strength of people's thoughts, opinions, or beliefs, the Likert scale (or *graduated response technique*) is helpful. With graduated response questions, the researcher gives the respondent a scale of choices to measure the extent of his or her answer. For example, a scale of 0–5 might be offered with the respondent being asked to choose one of the alternatives 0, 1, 2, 3, 4, 5—in which 0 represents 'never' and 5 represents 'always'. Using six alternatives makes it less likely that people will simply tick or mark the middle response to the question. (Taking the 'easy option' and choosing the middle alternative is frequently done if people are given this opportunity.)

Another way to use a graduated response technique is to use words (rather than numbers). For example, the respondent might be asked to choose one alternative from the following list: 'never', 'seldom', 'sometimes', 'often', 'very often', 'always'. Note that six alternatives are again offered—to decrease the tendency of people to choose the middle alternative.

When seeking people's attitudes on a subject the researcher must be aware that some people have difficulty finding the right words to describe their feelings. To allow for this, a useful technique is to use a *semantic differential question*. This measures the intensity of feelings towards a word or phrase. For example, the person might be asked: 'How did you feel about dining at that particular restaurant?'. The person is then asked to choose from a scale of 1, 2, 3 ,4, 5, 6— in which '1' represents 'comfortable' and '6' represents 'uncomfortable'.

Alternatively, the attitude of a respondent might be gauged by an open-ended type of question known as *word association*. This involves asking the respondents for a phrase or word to gauge their reactions. The respondent might be asked: 'What is the word or phrase that comes to mind when I mention the following holiday destinations?'.

Developing a questionnaire is a bit like being a detective. It certainly requires the gift of understanding people. A good test of how a question is likely to be received is to ask yourself: 'If I were that person, how would I respond to that question?'. It is vital to pretest a questionnaire with a pilot study before putting it to the entire sample of people you have chosen. Some questions can evoke a response quite different from the one intended.

Other suggestions include the following.

◆ Do not stretch people's memories too far. It is difficult for many people to remember what they were doing this time last year.

◆ Lead from easy questions to more difficult ones.

◆ Do not ask very personal questions. For example, people do not like being asked their income.

◆ Some people try to give answers that impress. They might try to appear to be more honourable or more wealthy than they are. They might try to give the impression of being younger, better educated, or well connected. They might also try to avoid negative connotations. They might try to avoid being bigoted, silly, insular, racist, or sexist. It is therefore important to avoid questions that give respondents too much scope for exaggeration.

◆ Researchers have to use charm and care to make people feel relaxed and confident about answering the questions. People might need reassurance that the information they give will not be used for other purposes.

Analysing the data

When the survey is completed, the answers can be added together and the results expressed in raw figures or percentages. They might also be presented as bar graphs or pie charts to allow for easy comparison. For an extensive survey, the data should be entered into a computer using a program designed to cross-analyse the results.

In analysis, the demographics of the people answering have to be cross-referenced against the results to determine significances. For example, a survey of a restaurant's customers (to determine their levels of satisfaction with service) might reveal that 30% of people considered the service to be too quick. Such a result could lead the management to slow down the service. However, cross-referencing the results against demographics might reveal that the 30% of respondents who answered in this way were mainly retired people. It might well be that the employed customers want the service to remain as it is—or perhaps be even quicker.

Survey results are always interesting. Sometimes they are predictable, but there are often enough surprises to make marketing research not only one of the most profitable marketing tools but also one of the most fascinating. See the case study 'Things are not always what they seem', below.

CASE STUDY

Things are not always what they seem

Market research can be fascinating, and unexpectedly illuminating. For example, an airline commissioned a survey of air travellers. Like many operators in the hospitality industry, the airline's close contact with its customers led it to think it knew and understood them. At the time, the airline believed that most of its customers were businesspeople.

The survey confirmed that 75% of all flights taken were for business reasons. But this counted the number of flights; it did not count the individuals involved. The surprising result was that only 25% of the airline's customers were businesspeople. That is, 75% of their customers were flying for non-business reasons. This resulted in the airline altering its focus somewhat. Although it still had to cater for the business market (75% of all flights), it was apparent that it could not ignore 75% of its passengers. It therefore promoted other reasons for flying—such as holiday travel.

Establishing the database and model banks

Marketing research firms utilise some sophisticated methodologies for analysis—such as regression analysis, correlation analysis, factor analysis, and cluster analysis. These are used to determine significant differences among groups in terms of their attitudes, beliefs, and behavioural patterns.

There are also 'model banks' available for comparative analysis—each one having a 'control' or 'norm'. These model banks are the result of long-term industry experience in forming the basis of the models. These include:

◆ hotel services model;
◆ pricing model;
◆ site-selection model;
◆ management model; and
◆ budgeting model.

Beware of presumptions or predictions based on trends. Research does not replace common sense and sound judgment. Research is a tool for providing information upon which decisions can be based.

Questions for discussion or revision

1 When preparing a survey, why is it important to have research objectives and a hypothesis?
2 What is the underlying principle of all forms of sampling that makes it possible to conduct field surveys with a reasonable degree of certainty that the results will be usable?
3 What are the most frequently used methodologies applied in marketing research?

Chapter 16

Sustainable Competitive Advantage

Aims of this chapter

The aims of this chapter are:
- to explain the concept of competition;
- to describe how to achieve a sustainable competitive advantage (SCA); and
- to explain the importance of doing more than the competition.

Theory

Marketing is obsessed with competition. The terminology of the subject, and the statements by the grim-faced, determined people of the business, abound with examples of a preoccupation with beating the opposition. And yet, as Edward de Bono contends in his book, *Sur/Petition*,[1] the notion of competition is a dangerous and seductive trap that limits and restricts business thinking.

Competition is about getting sales ahead of rival organisations. It reaches its heights in the concepts of warfare extolled by Ries and Trout in their book, *Marketing Warfare*,[2] with terms such as 'defence', 'attack', 'flank', and 'guerrilla' being used in their considerations of marketing. They contend that marketing is a battle waged in the consumers' minds. This 'kill or die' philosophy of modern marketing results in desperate struggles for sales ascendancy as exemplified by the fight between Coke and Pepsi for the cola market.

It is sometimes asserted that 'if you cannot compete you cannot survive'. There is undoubted truth in such a contention. However, what does it mean to compete? Edward de Bono has this to say:[3]

> *Competition is essential for survival, but traditional strategic competition is no longer enough . . . The word 'competition' comes from the Latin,[4] and means 'seeking together', or 'choosing to run in the same race'. Success involves going beyond competition to a new level—to 'sur/petition', or 'seeking above'. Instead of choosing to run in the same race, competitors choose to run their own race, in which they are the only competitor. Sur/petition can be achieved through integrated value, concept research and development, and creativity . . . There can be no doubt that creativity is the most important human resource of all. Creativity provides the value that is the whole purpose of any business. Without creativity, there would be no progress, and we would all be forever repeating the same patterns.*

It is more logical to avoid direct competition and, instead of running in the same race, to run your own race. If you want the prizes of success, the strategy is not to play the same game as the competition. De Bono's concept of 'sur/petition' means surpassing the competition by being obviously different—that is, to have a sustainable competitive advantage that does not draw an equal comparison. Consider the following examples.

'Living Benefits' assurance is an example of what de Bono calls 'integrated value'—the provision of something that is above competition and offers a value monopoly.[5] With traditional life assurance, the benefits are paid out after death to the beneficiaries. 'Living Benefits' assurance, developed by Prudential, pays out 75% of the benefits to the policy holder immediately if the policy holder is diagnosed as having a potentially fatal disease. This means the benefits of the policy are available when they are most needed, during life. This concept of insurance has been copied since by rival companies. However, for a while, Prudential held a clear market lead.

As another example, when Nestlé's Nescafé instant coffee was introduced it competed directly with the then accepted ways of making coffee from ground coffee beans. Today, Nescafé and its many imitators in the instant coffee market are regarded by the consumer as being a separate sort of product. Nestlé has approximately 75% of the instant coffee market and no longer competes with markets involving coffee beans or ground coffee.

The key to success in sur/petition is not technology so much as *concepts* that appeal to a specific group of customers. Concepts create the added value that provides a valid sustainable competitive advantage (SCA) for the customer to consider. Cost-cutting, quality control, service, competence, and efficiency do not, by themselves, create business. A product that is of no use will not sell to anyone—no matter how cheap, well-made, and highly efficient it might be.

CASE STUDY

Who is the competition?

As a good example of sur/petition, consider the *Crystal Harmony*. A US$200 million, 48 621-gross-ton cruise ship, *Crystal Harmony* is a five-and-a-half-star floating palace with berths for 960 rich passengers. In 1992, participants in a *Los Angeles Times* survey named *Crystal Harmony* the world's most popular cruise ship.[6] Its nearest alternative is the Royal Viking Group. However, that group does not really compete for the same passengers. There are differences in pricing policies, variable routes, and the types of passengers.

It seems that the owner of the *Crystal Harmony*, the NYK Line, is not necessarily competing with other cruise liners. Rather, the competition is élite leisure vacations in general. *Crystal Harmony* claims, by being quite exceptional, to be competing against such élite leisure holidays, rather than against other cruise ships.

But even within the cruise ship market itself, there is still room for a distinctive difference to offer a distinct position within an increasingly crowded market. In 2000, an estimated 7 million people took ocean cruises and 2 million took river cruises. A total of 54 cruise ships were being built to come into service before 2004.[7] So, how does a cruise ship establish a distinctive difference without necessarily being a floating palace? Another cruise ship is the *Radisson Diamond*, built and operated by the Radisson Hotels International group. The *Radisson Diamond* is a catamaran—a twin-hulled ship that will not roll and pitch. Its market difference is that it will reduce seasickness among its 354 passengers.[8]

Competitive strategies work only when there is a high demand for a product and when competing offerings are substantially similar.

Being competitive should not mean being 'the same, but better'. Being competitive should mean being 'recognisably different, and better'. Many businesses, especially in the hospitality industry, are essentially identical. The propositions of the contenders for the customers' dollars are really 'me-too' strategies. To offer a difference, and thus obtain a comparative advantage, an establishment needs to offer an 'only me' proposition.

The term 'niche strategy' refers to the concept of finding a specialised market, concentrating on it, and being able to dominate it. Niche ventures can do very well in certain climates. For example, backpacker hostels tend to increase their occupancy and their income in difficult financial times.

Environmental scanning

There is a technique called 'environmental scanning' (not to be confused with *environmental impact studies*) which is intended as a brief overview of the competition. Environmental scanning involves seeking information on competitors—who they are, what they are doing, what their plans are, and how their plans will affect our plans.[9] The concept includes that of competitor intelligence. An emphasis upon competitor analysis enables us to anticipate competitors' actions, rather than having to react to them.

Environmental scanning can usefully serve as a summary, or as an initial analysis of the local market, with a view to deciding whether there might be an opening in the market and whether a new proposal is possible. It cannot take the place of a full and detailed study.

If management can make a reasoned decision that the project is at least possible, the process can be advanced to the next stage—the project evaluation itself. This includes a formal analysis of the market, an assessment of supply and demand, consideration of the financial feasibility of the project, and an implementation of strategies.

Phantom opponents

Who is the real competition? In many instances, owners of hospitality establishments are fighting 'phantom' opponents. They think that other operators who are doing similar things must be the enemy. This is not always true.

A five-star hotel with a fine-dining restaurant might believe that it is competing with other five-star hotels offering similar fine-dining restaurants. However, how many people ask their partners: 'Which five-star hotel with a fine-dining hotel restaurant shall we go to tonight?'. No one asks this sort of question. The selection of a place to eat does not work this way in the real world of customers.

Deciding who comprises the competition requires careful thought about the target market. The competition is not always other establishments that you might think are in the same category as your own. Many owners receive an unpleasant surprise when surveys reveal that some respondents never think of their place when asked to list the names of places in their category. How did they miss out? 'Surely everyone knows,' they wail, 'that we are one of the best fine-dining restaurants in town?'

The explanation is fairly simple. Customers have their own methods of labelling and categorising places and products. And these methods do not group eateries (or anything else for that matter) into convenient lists that match business directory lists. When there is no direct conflict in the minds of customers, there is also no competition in their minds. Therefore, by avoiding conflict or confusion with another product, you are creating a separate and unique category for your own product in the minds of customers. You are achieving an identifiable difference. Ideally, this identifiable difference should equate to a recognisable advantage for the customer. This provides the customers with a reason for labelling it and categorising it in a unique category in their own estimation.

For example, a restaurant called 'Tops', which sits on top of a hill—with the stars above and the brilliant lights of the city below—will not be confused with a restaurant situated on the plains. Moreover, 'Tops' is not necessarily competing with another restaurant on a hill. The views are never the same. If, in addition, 'Tops' has a dreamy, romantic cocktail bar with an attractive and cheerful cocktail barperson, this is another reason for 'Tops' to occupy a special place in the minds of many people. Taken together, the unique features of 'Tops' constitute a value monopoly.

In times of recession, the real 'competition' for many places is a shortage of discretionary spending power by most customers. In these circumstances, a hospitality establishment is not losing customers to the competition posed by other establishments. Rather, it is losing customers to the common enemy of budgetary restraint. To maintain the same growth pattern that the place has enjoyed in the past, an establishment needs to go out and find entirely new customers.

Cure for boredom and apathy

If an hotel is not doing anything exciting, it will be losing business to apathy. This is the case with some hotels in country towns or suburbs where there is a virtual monopoly by location. The owners stop trying because they believe that they 'have it made'. In this situation, the people do not go elsewhere; they just do not go anywhere.

The cure for apathy is something new, as opposed to something drastically different. For example, there was a highly successful restaurant that gained a large following by serving a free entrée when the customer sat down, and a free salad while waiting for a delicious main course. Ten years later the routine was the same. Even the waiting staff appeared to have an expression on their faces that suggested: 'Here we go again'. There was still a loyal band of clients in attendance, but the majority had moved on to new experiences. This restaurant was not defeated by any competitor. It had defeated itself by its laziness.

A small change or improvement—an exciting innovative way of providing a service—stimulates the management, the staff and, most importantly, the customers. Innovation should not be confused with wholesale change. It is a matter of maintaining standards while trying a new way of doing something. Drastic change is like starting again.

A new restaurant that features dishes from another country might be competing with the natural reluctance of many people to try something they do not understand because they consider it to be 'alien'. Chinese restaurants in Australia had this problem for decades until 'going Chinese' became 'all the rage'. Later, Vietnamese, Japanese, and Thai venues similarly became more popular. It might seem that these newcomers provided spirited competition to the existing Chinese restaurants, but the real enemy for many Chinese restaurants was customer boredom with Chinese cuisine as it was being presented. It became apparent that it was not good enough for them to offer the same 'Australianised' Chinese dishes that they had served in the past—served in the same way with the same pseudo-Chinese décor that had persisted for twenty years or so.

A good manager should regard every day as being like the first day of the business. Every day, the manager should want to do things better. The manager keeps the things that are good, but strives to do them better. Meanwhile, the manager tries to think of new things that have never been done before. For example, Michael Hurst of '15th Street Fisheries' has a dish called 'The Flying Fish'. This is a flying fish caught commonly in the ocean but, to make it really special for the customer, the waiters bring it to the table suspended from a helium balloon.[10] Innovations such as this give a restaurant a value monopoly.

Key to profitability

If customers have nothing to choose among a cluster of similar types and styles of establishments, the only comparative advantage for the customer is price. Lowest price becomes the basic selection criterion, with discounting or add-on-values as additional factors in the decision. In this scenario, an attitude of 'sales-mindedness' can predominate—rather than an attitude of customer-mindedness'.

The key to profitability is to seek a sustainable competitive advantage (SCA). An SCA must, by its very name, be sustained. It must also be different—once others do the same it is no longer a competitive advantage. Many places strive to provide whatever the customers want, but the ones with the competitive edge do what the customers do not always expect. They go the extra bit, provide the added value, and offer the memorable service to entice the customers back. In striving for this, it is not what you do but the way that you do it that counts with customers. An additional service becomes a 'gimmick' unless it is delivered with enthusiasm and genuine interest.

As noted above, a value monopoly is essentially represented by the personalised service you offer. It means special things that make customers feel special. It is customer-orientated marketing—concentrating on the customer as if every customer is worth a thousand dollars because the word-of-mouth value of one really happy customer can be multiplied many times. 'Special things for special people' is a useful slogan to keep in mind. This might extend to having special crockery for some customers. The cost at the time might not warrant this sort of gesture, but this is not the point. The customers with their special crockery bring in a steady stream of new customers who could not be bought with advertising. Similarly, some hotels have special glasses for customers with their names on them. No one else can use a named glass. Another hotel sends birthday wishes to their customers every year. Another sends anniversary congratulations a year after a honeymoon or wedding anniversary.

At some large hotels, the manager invites new guests to a private reception to meet other guests and mingle with the staff. There are many variants on this approach—such as the 'Captain's Table' for single guests, so that they will not be left alone in strange surroundings. The imperative of concepts such as these is to make sure the reception or the table is hosted by someone with personality who is a natural catalyst and who can bring people together and make them feel relaxed and convivial. It will not work as well if the customers believe that the management and staff are just going through the motions. Indeed, any establishment that wants to introduce ideas such as these must remember that the person who does them, and the way in which they are done, are crucial. A rival hotel can copy the idea, but if the personality of your catalyst is unique it is unlikely that the rival will attract any of your customers.

Run your own race

A guest history system assists the customising of guest services. It requires maintaining a database on a computer and takes a lot of extra work. But the results for the customer can be quite startling. Everyone likes to feel special. Guest histories make it possible for front-desk staff to greet people personally and to provide services with knowledge of the guests' preferences. They also make it easier for the hotel to solicit repeat business.

An added benefit of guest histories is that the stored data can be cross-referenced to generate profiles of customer clusters—groups of people who have things in common. Often, these clusters reveal group preferences, enabling the property to amend products and facilities accordingly. Some places form clubs with special privileges for members. Usually these clubs are for corporate and regular business travellers, but clubs can also be formed for sporting people and fitness enthusiasts.

Recognition of the customer as an individual, rather than as a 'sale' to be processed, is the essential secret of a successful establishment. It must think of its guests as individuals, and treat them as individuals, using their names whenever possible. This, in turn, impresses the individual guests, who are likely to develop a view of the establishment as being the only place to consider.

Many owners of establishments perceive themselves as being 'custodians' of their business. They ensure that everything stays the same. There is no interest and no excitement. How can you be enthusiastic if you are not engaged in an ongoing process of building the business? McDonald's is not the same as it was twenty years ago. Indeed, it is not the same as it was last year. Every year they do something a little different, and a little better. This ongoing process of building the business keeps them alive and competitive.

A business in the doldrums is a business that is run by uninterested management. It is a business that has become boring for management and customers alike. It does not require a great deal of imagination to make some improvements to a place. Essentially, it requires an attitude in which management thinks for and on behalf of the customer. Instead of thinking 'I am doing this because it is my job', management thinks 'I am doing this because I am thinking of the customer and what the customer would like'. When everyone in an establishment thinks like this, and when everyone has the freedom to make individual contributions (rather than simply following a rigid system), there is a dramatic improvement to the business. An individual contribution can be a small gesture of kindness, as illustrated in the case study 'Hope you don't mind' (page 222).

CASE STUDY

'Hope you don't mind'

A guest at an hotel in Chicago left his shoes out to be cleaned. The shoes were returned, cleaned with a new pair of laces and a note.

'One of the laces was fraying so we replaced them. Hope you don't mind. No charge.'

It was not a one-off incident. The guest noticed a series of similar little gestures during his stay. He still talks about it.

And guess where he stays every time he goes to Chicago?

Questions for discussion or revision

1 Explain what is meant by the term 'value monopoly'.
2 What is meant by Edward de Bono's concept of 'sur/petition'? Does this concept fit into today's competitive business environment?
3 How does the concept of 'sur/petition' relate to the concept of 'positioning'?
4 What are the key strategies for achieving a sustainable competitive advantage?
5 What is a niche strategy?

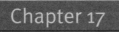

Chapter 17

Positioning

===== **Aims of this chapter** =====

The aims of this chapter are:
- to explain how to develop a competitive position;
- to explain the use of information feeds to create sustainable competitive advantage; and
- to describe some strategies to maintain sustainable competitive advantage.

Theory

Hospitality is basically about providing people with a place to sleep, eat, and drink. Some places offer an extensive range of additional facilities to make a stay at an hotel an experience in itself. The style of place can range from a 'doss-house' to a six-star hotel,[1] from a little corner coffee shop to a gourmet restaurant, from a country pub to a glamorous tourist resort, from a bed & breakfast stopover to an extensive motel, from a tavern to an exclusive club.

In many localities the customer has a wide choice of hospitality establishments. The customer's selection is based on how he or she feels about a particular place—an assessment of several attributes of the place based on knowledge and perception. One of these attributes is price, weighted by the decision-maker's perception of value. Such a *perception* is usually a stronger motivation for purchase than reality. When a significant number of people hold a similar perception about a property, that property has what is called a 'market position'.

Positioning takes place in people's minds. Two places can look the same and offer the same facilities but occupy quite different positions in the market. Positioning is what people feel or believe about a place. For some types of products (for example, beverages and food), positioning is often the only difference between competing products. Taste tests of various beers suggest that the majority of consumers cannot discern any real difference between brands. Similar findings are found on tests of various wines, or tests on various soft drinks. Some people insist that they can tell their favourite brand easily, only to be embarrassed when they are fooled by a blind tasting test. Based on this sort of knowledge, marketers who spend millions on brand promotion know exactly what they are doing—they are building a brand image that exists solely in the minds of the consumers.

Positioning is a marketing strategy. Its purpose is to provide an organisation with a sustainable competitive advantage (SCA) by creating differences, advantages, and benefits (DAB) that make people think about a place or a product in a certain way.

Some people describe a property by saying it has 'a good reputation'— which means that it has gained a positive place in people's minds as a result of sound positioning. It also means that many recommend the place. Different aspects of hospitality might be involved in this reputation. One place might have a reputation as the 'biggest', another as the 'smartest', and another as 'good value'. The key to reputation is perception—a property might claim '*We* are the best place in town', but positioning is achieved only when the customers say, '*You* are the best place in town!'

The name and reputation of an establishment is its essential asset. Upon this rock a customer base is built, and this represents the real worth of a business. Its buildings, fixtures, fittings, and furnishings, by themselves, do not create a business. Positioning does.

We all make judgments about things, unconsciously or consciously, and our judgment process is based on many factors including education, life experiences, lifestyle values, expectations, needs, and ability to pay. Because of these differences among people, a place cannot appeal to everyone. The wide range of people's preferences and needs explains the diversity of sleeping, eating, and drinking options in the hospitality industry.

Positioning can also apply to the customers. A customer's choice of place to stay might be influenced by that customer's own positioning needs. For example, a high-profile corporate executive might want to impress clients and business associates by staying at the most expensive, high-profile place available.

Another executive might want to indicate cost-consciousness by choosing a less flamboyant property.

Two factors are required to gain a position in people's minds. First, the place must be known. Secondly, it must be known for something that separates it from the competition. To be unknown is to be unloved.

Information feeds

Using information feeds

Positioning is achieved by 'information feeds'. These are communications that demonstrate what an organisation is, what it says, and what it does—communications that leave an impression in people's minds and so create a sustainable competitive advantage. The main information feeds are discussed below.

Physical presence

The physical presence of the place is determined by:

◆ where it is—its general regional location, its town, which street it is in, where it sits in that street, and the buildings or businesses that surround it; and

◆ how it looks from the outside—how it is signed, painted, and decorated.

These are all tangible factors that contribute to the imagery that helps create a position.

First impressions are said to be lasting. However, it should be noted that first impressions are not everything. For example, the ordinary house frontage of Melbourne's 'Walnut Tree' restaurant, which rose to pre-eminence in the 1960s, belied the opulence of the interior and the gourmet excellence of its cuisine. Conversely, the grandeur of some striking and highly publicised hotels cannot mask the disappointing overrated service within.

Nevertheless, despite these exceptions, it must be said that it is easier to achieve the desired market position by first looking the part.

Personal recommendation

Personal recommendation—the pass-on value of word-of-mouth advertising—is the strongest means of gaining a hold in the minds of customers. Most people listen to opinions of friends and acquaintances, and are considerably swayed by what they hear—both negative and positive opinions of a place. About 85% of customers come from pass-on recommendations, with the remaining 15% coming from other sources, including advertising. It is therefore very important that establishments place a huge emphasis on providing customers with a great experience so that they will go away with a memory of a good occasion and recommend the place to friends and acquaintances.

Publicity and the public opinion

A perception generated by publicity is another powerful means of creating a position for a property. A good review by a critic is useful, but publicity can also be generated by media reporting of events at the place, and people who attend it. This is why many large properties like to have visiting celebrities stay, even offering ridiculously cheap rates for the privilege.

Advertising

Advertising presents the best opportunity for a property to convey the position it wants to occupy in people's minds. What is said can be controlled and presented in the best possible way, and can be beamed at the target market that suits the property best. Positioning can be achieved by a phrase, a pictorial image, or memorable music. But deeds are different from words and images, and the property must always live up to what is said. Otherwise the advertising is nothing more than a very expensive and useless gesture that ultimately will fool no one.

Brochures

Brochures and other collateral material used to promote facilities represent another excellent means of conveying a property's position to would-be customers. The products and facilities they describe raise the hopes and anticipations of customers. They are indicators for guests and travel agents that comfort and service will be provided.

Interior design

The interior design layout, fittings, and décor follow from the first impressions created by the building exterior. Obviously management should ensure that one complements the other.

Staff

The attitudes, appearance, service performances, and attention to detail of the staff are extremely important in creating an impression of a property. The edifice might be crumbling, and the interior décor might be disappointing, but this will all be forgiven by customers who are treated to an outstanding service performance.

Prices and value

The prices and value offered are basic to the positioning of an establishment. Both management and customers use price and value to position a place in terms of its being 'expensive', 'moderate', or 'inexpensive'. But whatever, the price might suggest in terms of positioning, that price must represent value for money.

Ambience

The ambience of an establishment—the music, noise, smell, and general activity of the place—positions it as being comfortable, popular, busy, noisy, élitist, or whatever. Care is necessary with ambience to ensure that it conveys a perception that fits the desired positioning.

Slogans and symbols

The name of an establishment, and the slogans or symbols that are chosen to represent it, should sum up the desired position for a property. Designers frequently get carried away when designing a corporate logo, and can create symbols that are impossible to decipher. If a symbol or slogan is to work for the property it must create an image that fits with what the place actually is and does.

Take care with messages aimed at positioning the establishment. The basics of the hospitality industry are the ways in which members of the industry transform the mundane needs of eating and sleeping into pleasurably heightened experiences. The images of escape, excitement, glamour, romance, conviviality, and (perhaps) glitz, are all part of the positioning process.

Clientele

The people who patronise the place contribute to its positioning. An establishment attracts customer groups as a result of the strategic positioning provided by the information feeds discussed above. In turn, the clientele thus attracted becomes an information feed itself. Most people like to associate with others who are like themselves.

Problems with information feeds

Negative effects of information feeds

It should be noted that positioning not only attracts people, but also repels certain groups of customers. An expensive property, for example, dissuades a large percentage of would-be patrons who simply cannot afford to stay there. Conversely, a family-style restaurant will not appeal to a business luncheon group. An establishment cannot be all things to all people. It is important to target the markets that have a natural affinity with each other.

Need for consistency

Several information feeds are usually required, and these must be coherent and consistent. Because one information feed will not be sufficient to establish a marketable position, support is required by other information feeds, and the sum total of information feeds establishes a position for an establishment. A leading hotel, for example, will ensure that every information feed they use gives the impression of a place that is impressive and expensive, with every creature comfort catered for, and every service requirement pandered to. The same principle applies to other types of establishment. For each target market in the customer mix, the position adopted by the property in one information feed must be consistent with another.

Do not oversell or mislead

Good marketers build images, and they use facts to support the image. Good marketers are careful not to develop an image that cannot be sustained by facts.

When customers are seeking a specific attribute, they believe that the establishment will have the attributes that it claims to have. It is important not to oversell or mislead. A property that promotes its facilities as being of 'world-class standard' has to deliver a level of excellence that really is comparable with the best in the world. If it does not, it will suffer rejection by its customers. Moreover, it will develop a reputation for being unreliable with the truth—that is, not only a place below standard, but also a place not to be trusted. Although few people believe every bit of 'good news' in advertising, most people will believe every bit of 'bad news' that they hear.

Positioning strategies

To achieve the desired positioning in the market requires a strategy in the use of information feeds. This requires information from market research about the market's knowledge of, and attitudes towards, the establishment. The research should aim to discover the answers to the following questions:

- How is the establishment perceived by the market now?
- How many people can recall its name and know where it is?
- How many have used one or more of its facilities?
- How many of those who have used the facilities report favourably on their experience?
- How do the facilities rate in their minds by comparison with competing establishments?
- What is the market's opinion of the 'social standing' of the place?
- How many people know about its outstanding features ('primary attributes')?
- Do people think that the place offers value for money?
- Is its present positioning competitive enough to meet the corporate objectives?
- Is it attracting a large number of people from the targeted customer mix?

◆ Does the establishment have the right product mix for the target markets?
◆ Should the positioning of the establishment or any of its products or facilities be improved, modified, or changed?

The process

Successful marketers decide upon the position they want and fine-tune the market's perceptions to keep pace with altering market conditions, to match competitive strategies, and to change customer attitudes. For example, to improve its position against some strong challenges from new properties, Hyatt on Collins (Melbourne) upgraded itself to being a 'Grand Hyatt', claiming to be 'only one of ten Grand Hyatts in the world'. The positioning strategy was the adoption of a leadership stance. Fine-tuning a property's positioning is accomplished by using the information feeds to communicate the modifications and improvements decided upon. That is, Hyatt did not just talk about being a 'Grand Hyatt', it improved its product lines, refurbished the property, and sharpened its service strategies to deliver a 'commitment to excellence'. Its primary target market was the business market, and included special room rates for business clients and business meeting packages.

A good positioning strategy aims to achieve awareness through promotion, but the positioning strategy must be capable of fulfilment. Without awareness, credibility, and a sustainable competitive advantage, it is unlikely that a satisfactory position can be achieved for a property. Grand Hyatt is a good example of how it should be done.

The terms 'reputation', 'positioning', and 'image' are similar, but there are minor differences.

◆ *Positioning* is a strategy.
◆ *Reputation* is market opinion.
◆ *Image* is an emotive or pictorial perception that helps to position a product or an establishment. *Image association* is the use of descriptive terms that have emotive connotations, both positive and negative.

Difference, advantage, and use of imagery

Imagery is a created proposition that is persuasive or inspiring, and imagery certainly contributes to positioning. However, images alone are not enough to motivate a customer to buy. Apart from imagery, other psychological factors are involved—beliefs, feelings, knowledge, rational thought, and memory of actual experience.

An awareness of the interaction of various psychological factors was recognised long ago. More than two thousand years ago, a Greek philosopher, Aristotle, explained the three basics of persuasion as being *ethos* (credibility), *pathos* (feeling or emotional appeal), and *logos* (logic and reasoning). Aristotle also said: 'Know your audience [target market] first'.

Examples of market position

The various competitors in any market can be divided into:

◆ 'market leaders';
◆ 'market challengers';
◆ 'market followers'; and
◆ 'market specialists' (or 'niche marketers').

Although the average customer does not care much about these terms, he or she is affected by their implications. The terms matter a great deal to the properties involved in a particular market category, because they make a difference to how each property goes about marketing its services.

The *market leader* is the property that has achieved the best 'top-of-mind' rating by customers. It is the place most people first think of when they ask themselves where they should stay, or where they should go for a great steak, or where they could get good fast food, or where they should go to dance and have fun, and so on. Because market leaders are first to come to mind, they are usually the places that obtain the biggest share of the available business in their market category. The leaders' strategies have a broad appeal. They are positioned in people's minds with ideas such as their being 'big', 'popular', and 'value for money'. They will often be perceived as being 'confident' and 'extroverted'.

The *market challengers* are the ones that want to be where the leader is. They are therefore constantly chasing the same markets, and trying to create strategies that will shift the leader's customers over to them.

The *market followers* copy the leaders and challengers and offer a 'me-too' alternative for customers. They follow at a distance, never promoting very hard, and content to receive the 'spillover' from the strategies of others.

The *market specialists* (or *niche marketers*) achieve a position by targeting specific groups of customers who have been overlooked by the rest, and therefore not catered for. These include theme restaurants aimed at people of a particular nation, vegetarians, or artistic and cultural groups. Niche marketers adopt various strategies aimed at attracting one group by doing something special for that group.

Positioning statement

The *positioning statement* is a description of the position that an establishment wants to occupy in people's minds. It involves the use of concepts expressed in adjectival terms that have emotive meanings to people.

For example, a top-class hotel in Canberra might want to position itself as being 'an international hotel of traditional elegance at the centre of Australia's politics and history'. For the customer, these words are designed to produce emotional responses along the lines of: 'Yes, I could be dining in the same room as prime ministers, presidents, and ambassadors from any country in the world'. An hotel with less pretensions might simply want to be positioned as 'having the best steak and chips in town'. This is hard to ignore if the customer loves steak and chips! A roadside tavern might simply offer 'the last drink for the next 200 kilometres'. This is hard to go past on a long journey!

Other examples include Singapore Raffles Hotel which has positioned itself as 'the grand old dame of the East where the notables of the world have always preferred to stay'. The implication is that this is where you stay if you see yourself as being part of history, rubbing shoulders with famous people. An hotel next to a major city airport might position itself as being 'closer to the airport than any other hotel', and offer 'double-glazed windows'—to offset any misgivings about potential noise of the jet engines. In doing so, it capitalises on a positive image (proximity to the airport), but anticipates a potential negative image (being disturbed by awful noise).

Everyone makes experience comparisons. We describe things to other people—in much the same way as we talk about other people! These descriptions of places help other people to position an establishment. It also helps us to position the place in our minds as we describe things to other people. We are using what is called 'associative imagery'.

A property should not attempt a positioning strategy if it is incapable of fulfilling it. Instead, it should endeavour to adopt a positioning strategy that takes into consideration the realities of the following factors:

◆ market demand;
◆ competitive activity;
◆ economics of its target market;
◆ economics of its own corporate resources;
◆ targeted customer mix; and
◆ realisable product mix.

Advertising can do a property a grave disservice by overstating its benefits. The very nature of service makes it difficult for a customer to make a decision from the outside until that person has actually experienced it on the inside, and some marketers therefore argue that exaggerated advertising at least captures an enquiry or produces an experimental visit from customers. This argument is naive. Satisfaction must be provided. Referrals and the supporting evidence of satisfied customers give a place its real reputation and fix its position.

Successful operators promote differences that have real advantages for the customer. A price advantage is probably the most obvious advantage. Such an advantage is believable because it is provable. But it is also the easiest for competitors to match. Proximity to a facility or tourist attraction is also believable and provable—such as an hotel's claim to be 'the only five-star beach house on the Gold Coast'. Less believable and provable was a Singapore hotel's advertisement with the headline: 'Uncompromising service'.

DAB formula

As previously noted, positioning is a marketing strategy. Its purpose is to provide an organisation with a sustainable competitive advantage (SCA) by creating differences, advantages, and benefits (DAB) that make people think about a place or a product in a certain way.

The steps in strategic positioning are:

◆ target the customer mix you want;
◆ find out what they expect;
◆ decide if you have the resources to satisfy what they expect;
◆ develop the services and products to meet the market's requirements;
◆ decide on the key DABs that will give your organisation an SCA;
◆ develop a staff commitment to the positioning of the organisation; and
◆ build and sustain the strategic position with fact.

Each of these is considered below.

Target the customer mix you want

The targeted markets always drive the other aspects of the strategy. When you begin a marketing assignment, always first consider the people who will comprise your customer mix. If you have a clear idea of the groups of people you want to attract, it is easier to develop a positioning strategy, and the product, price, place, and promotion strategies to go with it.

Find out what they expect

This is a mandatory exercise—to research customer attitudes and uncover their needs, wants, likes and dislikes, what services they are not getting, and what services currently satisfy them.

Decide if you have the resources to satisfy what they expect

The product mix has to be in place or it has to be developed to meet the requirements of the targeted markets. This might require additional financing and personnel. More people might be needed, or different types of people to deliver the services.

Building or remodelling is expensive and is often the first resort of management when change is contemplated. It is a fond belief of managers everywhere that this must be so—as if the appearance of a place will automatically change how everyone feels about it. However, like a new hairstyle and a new clothes, change for the sake of change looks great to begin with, but ends up with the same person in the end.

Develop the services and products to meet the market's requirements

This is where all the service strategies come into effect—the procedures that will determine what will happen to and for the customers. The other positioning concepts are irrelevant unless this one fulfils what you are striving to achieve.

Decide on the key DABs that will give your organisation an SCA

The ultimate aim of the positioning strategy is deciding upon what you do to achieve a discernible advantage for the targeted customers. The DAB decision will probably arise from research into their needs and wants.

Develop a staff commitment to the positioning of the organisation

Make sure staff acknowledge and understand the modifications and improvements that are being introduced to implement the strategy. Use the information feeds to communicate the image to staff as well as to customers.

Build and sustain the strategic position with fact

The follow-through and maintenance of a positioning strategy is what will make it work in the longer term. Seldom does a strategy change a market situation overnight. Before a significant number of customers will react and favour the place with their custom, the positioning strategy must be sustained by fact over a long period to produce high awareness and conviction in the minds of customers.

Repositioning

For a variety of reasons, an establishment can develop a reputation that adversely affects its position in the market. Advertising and price-cutting do not always help. The solution in such circumstances is to change the positioning of the establishment. This involves a new marketing plan with specific attention to the key factors in positioning.

Questions for discussion or revision

1 Explain the distinctive features of the following terms: 'reputation'; 'image'; 'position'.
2 A particular hotel is considered to be a 'niche marketer'. What does this term mean?
3 Explain the DAB formula and its relevance to positioning.
4 Which tangible and intangible factors should be considered in the positioning of a restaurant?
5 If an hotel was considered 'old' by most people in the hospitality market, how could this be turned to advantage if it were refurbished and repositioned?

Chapter 18

Local Hotel Strategies

━━━━━━━━━━━━━━━━ Aims of this chapter ━━━━━━━━━━━━━━━━

The aims of this chapter are:
- to describe a range of strategies for increasing the customer base of a local hotel;
- to explain the important considerations in selecting appropriate strategies; and
- to explain how to choose the best possible outcome for customers.

Some background

> There is nothing which has yet been contrived by man, by which so much happiness is produced, as by a good tavern or inn.

> Samuel Johnson [1]

They might be called a 'local' (short for 'local hotel') or a 'pub' (short for 'public house'). Similar places might be called a 'tavern', an 'inn', or a 'guest house'. Whatever the name, the various terms describe places that are basically similar in concept. This type of operation is the most widespread and most used of all hospitality establishments. It is also the largest employer of people in the hospitality industry.

This chapter discusses these small, unpretentious establishments that service the hospitality requirements of the nearby residents of a suburb or a country town. In some cases they offer a few bedrooms for travellers, but they do not pretend to be star-rated properties for extended stays by businesspeople or holidaymakers. By and large, these establishments cater to the needs of local residents for a place to drink, eat, meet, and enjoy convivial recreation. In concept and cultural environment, small hotels are quite different from their larger glamorous cousins that cater for the sophisticated and wealthy travellers of the world.

In Australia, all hotels that serve liquor have to be licensed, and there are stringent regulations that stipulate how, when, and under which conditions liquor can be sold. Places without accommodation hold a tavern-style of licence. Those that provide accommodation have a full hotel licence. By an Act of Parliament passed in 1830, all hotels were compelled to have accommodation available and there was a heavy fine for anyone found guilty of refusing accommodation to a traveller. This Act was not repealed until comparatively recent times to allow for the needs of modern lifestyles. The number of licences that can be issued is controlled. In most regions, the residents and business owners of the locality have to be consulted and their approval obtained.

The hotel business in Australia has a long and colourful history dating back to its early colonial beginnings. Much of this history has to do with the growth of the colonies, and later the nation—a history that includes a series of mining 'booms' and 'busts', the expansion of road and rail transport, the development of rural and urban industries, and the resultant establishment of the country's towns, cities, and suburbs. And, wherever the people went, invariably a local hotel was one of the first substantial buildings to be erected. To understand the building shapes, architectural styles, and room layouts of the many local hotels of varying vintages that populate the urban and country landscapes, one has to appreciate this colourful past, and the hospitality needs of the people.

Part of this story of Australian hotels also has to do with liquor controls arising from community concerns with drinking, alcoholism, and crime. At times there were severe restrictions on drinking hours and, at one stage, a withdrawal of many licences. For example, In a 1907 referendum, 65 of a total of 95 electorates voted for a reduction in licences, and hundreds of licensed hotels and wine bars were deprived of a livelihood.

Before such restrictions, the industry flourished. In 1810 it was calculated that there were 82 people for every hotel in Victoria! In Bendigo, Victoria, at the height of the 'Gold Rush', there were 1700 outlets serving approximately 65 000 men, women, and children!

The hotel business has always been associated with alcohol—apart from a relatively small number of unlicensed guest houses that cater for a temperate, family, and elderly customer base. Indeed, until recent times, the size and value of a public hotel was solely related to the amount of beer it sold. Hotels were thus rated as a '12-keg hotel' or a '70-keg hotel'—indicating the average amount of beer sold every week. Customer satisfaction with the 'frills' of hospitality was not really an issue! Even today, the value of a licence, and the excise duty paid by the licensee, are still related to the sales of alcoholic beverages.

These days, the worth of an hotel is not evaluated solely by the amount of liquor consumed. A degree of sophistication has emerged in the management of such hotels and the services provided to its patrons. Hotels are more inclined to concentrate on meals and spaces for relaxation, recreation, and entertainment for the whole family—rather than offer little more than male drinking troughs, as used to be the case. The trend now is definitely towards the 'European style' of establishment—a place that is the centre of the community, and one that offers a wider selection of activities. The places that have embraced this concept have prospered, and the cash registers are busier. The needs of established customers have changed, and there are different customers entering the market.

Outcomes for the customers

The outcomes for the customers constitute the critical marketing consideration. Building a business is about building a customer base by providing a broad range of facilities and interests for the local community. Because the majority of patrons come from an area near the establishment, the hotel has to be regarded by the patrons as being 'their' place. Involvement is the critical issue.

This approach requires owners and managers to provide these outcomes for patrons:

◆ comfort;
◆ a feeling of being wanted and special;
◆ good food and drink;
◆ a sense of belonging;
◆ something to do and see; and
◆ something to look forward to.

The total experience must provide reasons for staying and reasons for returning. The objective of modern hotel marketing is to provide a refuge for the customers—a sort of 'headquarters' for many of the things they want to do away from home. This list of outcomes contains no real surprises—after all, they are basic to hospitality. However, the way in which these outcomes is provided gives an establishment a special place in the hearts and minds of the customers.

We now consider each of the outcomes listed above.

Comfort

Under this heading, establishments should consider:

◆ seating;
◆ air-conditioning;
◆ décor and surroundings;
◆ music, radio, satellite television;
◆ spaces and places; and
◆ toilets.

Seating

Tables and chairs are the first things to consider when providing comfort. Some chairs need to be a resting place for a prolonged time, whereas others are nothing more than a handy place to sit for a short time. The utilitarian examples found in most establishments—chosen because they are cheap—offer customers no reason for wanting to sit in them again. They can be hard, wrongly shaped, awkward to move, and even difficult to get on and get off. A table and chair setting should constitute an inviting and accommodating place of comfort. The selection and cost of this simple item of furniture is worth a lot of time and trouble.

Bar stools are also worthy of careful selection. Most seem to be made for tall basketball players and offer no invitation to be sat on by people of average dimensions! They result from the practice of building bars to suit the bar server, rather than the customer. The 'dangling-legs' posture produced by most bar stools is a perfect example of poor design and negligible thought for customer comfort.

Air-conditioning

Most hotels these days have air-conditioning. However, air-conditioning can trap smells and recycle fetid air. Although the use of air-conditioning is unavoidable in climatic extremes, every opportunity should be made to utilise a flow of fresh air when the weather suits. The restrictions on smoking that now apply in most establishments means that areas where smoking is allowed must have their own air-conditioning or air circulation.

Décor and surroundings

Appearances count. Getting the right balance that produces the right mood and attracts clientele is a skill—especially as a local hotel usually has a mix of people types to consider. Making a statement with violent colours and strong patterns has its purposes if the hotel is catering for a young late-night night-clubbing crowd. Many (perhaps most) patrons would prefer that the background be more neutral, and acceptable to a wider range of tastes.

Music, radio, satellite television

Nothing sets a mood more quickly than music. Different music is required for the separate spaces provided for the customers. The front bar requires music that is different from the dining-room. The provision of a radio and a television in certain locations, so that customers can be in touch with news and programs, is vital. Pub-TAB, poker machines, gaming machines, pool tables, and so on might be required. All of these facilities must be located so that they do not intrude on the comfort of others who want quiet.

Spaces and places

Providing separate places and spaces for the different socialising needs of customers is very important. Some people want privacy, whereas others prefer to be with everyone else. The arrangement of the rooms and the spaces within the rooms needs to be planned. A bar, lounge, or dining-room should be broken into separate conversation areas. Each customer will gravitate towards a section of the room that suits his or her concept of a 'comfort zone', and will then return to that same area on later visits.

In contrast, some areas need to be larger. There are many people who enjoy activity and noise. They like to see and feel the things happening around them.

Toilets

Cleanliness of toilets is vital. They must be checked constantly to clean up accidental messes, and to ensure that the toilet is always fresh, tidy, and clean. Soft toilet paper and soap (and perhaps even talcum powder) are little considerations that are appealing to people. Having a room where parents (fathers as well as mothers!) can change a baby is another example of catering for customer's needs. The cost will be outweighed by the appreciation and additional business that will be returned.

Feeling of being wanted

Under this heading, establishments should consider:

◆ a friendly attitude;
◆ welcome for strangers;
◆ prompt attention;

- interest and care;
- customised services; and
- care for those with special needs.

A friendly attitude

The attitude of the staff and owners quickly conveys to the customers whether they are wanted and whether their custom is appreciated. Warmth and friendliness is the basis of hospitality, and this ingredient always makes the difference between one place and another, and whether people will return or not. Being greeted by name in a small community or in a close-knit suburb is very important to people. It should not take long for management and staff to learn the names of their regular customers. Nothing says 'we appreciate you' better than a friendly greeting by name.

Hiring the people who can share the gift of friendship with their customers is the first priority. This first priority will be readily recognised by owners and managers who have the right personality, patience, and interest in people to be successful in the hospitality business.

Welcome for strangers

A person who enters an establishment for the first time might only be passing through. But more frequently, such a person will be a new customer who has come to look the place over.

Many local hotels that are used to a regular clientele treat a stranger with suspicion and reserve. This attitude might also be found in the regular clientele. Management might not be able to change the attitudes of customers who give the newcomer an uncertain 'once-over', but staff and management should always counter this by an effusive welcome, followed by introductions to the more loquacious regulars.

Prompt attention

Receiving fast attention is part of feeling wanted. Even if the place is busy, there is still time for a greeting and an acknowledgment to new arrivals that they will be looked after as quickly as possible. Putting a beer down without waiting for payment is one way to handle a difficult busy time. The beer will almost certainly be paid for later by a grateful customer.

Interest and care

Many establishments go through the motions of hospitality without a sincere interest in their guests. This lack of real interest manifests itself in a lack of real concern and care. See the case study on 'Mrs Hitchens really cares' (page 241) for an example of how genuine interest and care can make an enormous difference to the experience of guests.

CASE STUDY

Mrs Hitchens really cares

The Criterion Hotel at Moree won an award for being the most hospitable hotel in New South Wales—even though there were hotels far better equipped than the Criterion.[2] The town of Moree, about 700 kilometres north-west of Sydney, is on a hot bare plain devoid of hills and features of consequence. The Criterion was not exactly a 'showpiece'. However, Mrs Hitchens, the wife of the proprietor, knew what hospitality was all about, and she made sure that something more was provided to her guests than simply keeping them alive until they paid the bill.

From the beginning of their visits, Mrs Hitchens was positively pleased to see her guests. She talked about the guests' trips, and asked questions in an interested, quiet, and unhurried way. From then on, a series of little, thoughtful services gave the place its reputation, and ultimately resulted in its receiving the award. These little services included mosquito repellent, extra coat-hangers in the wardrobe, iced water on the dining-table, breakfast brought to a guest's room (without asking) if that guest missed the meal time, suggestions on what was best to eat, and so on.

None of these is significant in itself. However, taken together, they add up to a thoroughly pleasant, caring relationship with the guests—a relationship established by management and staff from the time that the guests arrive until their departure.

Customised services

The showing of interest and care for customers can be extended to the provision of personalised services. See the case study on 'How do you like your fish?' (page 242) for an example of how an establishment took a little extra trouble, and gained the loyal custom of influential guests by treating each of them as a respected individual.

Care for those with special needs

There are dozens of ways of telling customers that they and their friends and family members, whatever their needs, are wanted and appreciated. These might include having high chairs for young children, child-minding facilities, toys, and special meals for children, heating facilities for baby bottles, and changing tables. It might also include cushions for seniors, appropriate provisions for people with disabilities (more than the strict requirements of access regulations), and meals for diabetics, vegetarians, and some religious faiths.

CASE STUDY

'How do you like your fish?'

A group of businessmen had just sat down for lunch when one of the chefs appeared beside the table.

'Do you like fresh fish?' he asked. 'I have some bream in the kitchen. It came straight off a boat this morning. Would you like me to cook some for you?'

'Certainly!' replied the delighted diners.

But the chef's concern for his guests did not end with this offer.

'How would you like it cooked?' he then asked.

'How do you do it?' asked one of the diners.

'However you like it sir,' smiled the chef.

He and the waiter then proceeded to take down individual orders for cooking preferences.

'No problem,' the chef told them. 'Just give me fifteen minutes and it will be on your table.'

True to his word, the fish arrived on time, and every diner had it cooked just as he wanted.

Good food and drink

Most customers have an expectation that local hotel food should be popular and not too different. It should follow the prevailing trends. However, this does not mean that the food has to be bland and tasteless, and nor does it preclude innovation. Hotels should certainly satisfy the patrons who are not adventurous, but they should also offer temptations for the bolder patrons who might prefer to try something different. Always present menus and dishes that are better than expected.

It is important to have food available anywhere and at any time—rather than restricting availability to set times and set places. Allowance should be made for snack meals to be quickly heated when the cook is off duty so that no one ever goes without. Appetites do not work to the cook's hours, and hospitality means being hospitable to the needs of guests. Meals should be available in the bars, courtyards, and out in the street if that is what people want. The patrons should be invited to eat. Not only is there profit in food, but also there is goodwill. Being hospitable means making kind offers and helpful suggestions all the time.

Beer is the staple drink in a local hotel, and customers can be very fussy about their beer. Keeping the lines to the keg clean and open is essential to good delivery to the glass. Maintain the levels and avoid too much of a collar. Provide mats or coasters. Think at all times of the patron's comfort. Always serve the next beer in a fresh glass.

A sense of belonging

To be successful, a small hotel must not only cater for the needs of the community but also demonstrate that the hotel is part of the community and belongs to it. This requires involvement. If this is done well. the community will believe that it really needs the hotel (and its owners and staff). The objective is to make the hotel the centre of the community's activities as much as possible. Under this heading, establishments should consider:

◆ sponsorships;
◆ giveaways and prizes;
◆ clubs;
◆ recognition of notable people and their achievements;
◆ notice boards—advertising space; and
◆ a local history museum or gallery.

Sponsorships

Sponsorship of local teams and clubs should be offered and provided. This sponsorships could include football, tennis, netball, cricket, bowls, and car clubs—indeed, any club that requires support. Sponsorships indicate involvement and interest to the local people, In addition, from a commercially pragmatic perspective, sponsorship brings the followers and players to the hotel to socialise. Hotels, wherever practicable, should have rooms or areas allocated for clubs to hold meetings, or simply to have an area where they can feel at home. Even better, some hotels offer a room that is adorned with a club's trophies, banners, photographs and memorabilia.

Sponsorships can also include local charities or fund-raising drives. Hotels can be the venues for a whole range of activities including games nights, raffles, quiz evenings, and so on.

Giveaways and prizes

Along similar lines to sponsorships, an hotel should always be willing to provide prizes for any worthwhile event such as free dinners, bottles of champagne, crates of beer, trophies, certificates, and so on. Different situations merit different offers.

Clubs

Service clubs such as Rotary, Lions, Apex, and so on hold regular meetings. These can be 'bread-and-butter' functions for most hotels. Service clubs are cost-conscious organisations, and these meetings and associated meals usually have to be priced such that hotels break even (at best). However, the hotel must demonstrate its role as an important contributor to the community. This is the paramount issue.

In addition to service clubs, every community has groups of farmers, tradespeople, and businesspeople. These include chambers of commerce, agricultural associations, unions, and so on. They meet to discuss problems and opportunities that affect them and the area. The hotel should be right behind all of these, contributing and offering facilities for meetings and social events.

Apart from these established clubs and organisations, smart hotel owners can use their imagination to originate social clubs, food and wine clubs, sports clubs, hunting clubs, fishing clubs, public-speaking clubs, or music clubs. Indeed, they can create a club from any type of activity that brings people together on a regular basis. The objective is a place of involvement for local groups with common interests.

Recognition of notable people and their achievements

A camera should be standard equipment for any hotel to 'snap' functions, interesting people, and events that occur at the hotel. These pictures should be displayed on the walls.

Similarly, every club or sponsorship with which the hotel is involved should be captured on film. Even opposition teams can be displayed and their members invited to come and see themselves portrayed. Local individual champions in darts, pool, snooker, bowls, basketball, and netball can be given recognition, as can their teams.

Better still, the acquisition of a video camera provides an extra dimension to the capturing of special occasions. A video recording can be replayed for anniversaries of weddings, birthdays, and sporting events at which participants can bring friends and relatives to relive the experiences.

A 'hall of fame' is a good idea—featuring photographs of people from the district who have won or achieved some form of distinction, no matter how minor. An 'honour board' is another way of giving customers a sense of belonging. This can feature lists of people involved in a function, a rescue operation, or a fund-raising effort—indeed any noteworthy deed that deserves a mention and that gives everyone a sense of pride and belonging.

Notice boards—advertising space

A notice board is always a focus of attention for locals and visitors. Provision of this low-cost facility for the people is appreciated. It can be used for advertising local businesses, things for sale, hire or rent, work wanted, or employment available.

Local history museum or gallery

Most districts have an interesting history. An hotel can display old photographs of the area and any memorabilia that can be collected. The locals will bring visitors to view the displays and recount the past, and a free collection of historic memorabilia will attract tourists. If an hotel is on a tourist route, a gallery or museum can provide a reason for coaches to stop and have lunch, morning or afternoon tea, or a refreshment stop.

Something to do or see

There are many ways in which an hotel can provide ongoing activities that entertain and interest the local population. Most ideas are simple and cost little to do, and they are proven winners.

Marketing is essentially about satisfying people's needs and wants, and this does not require special skills, imagination, or money. Common sense and a bit of consistent hard work are all that are required. Good hospitality marketing requires an interest in people and a real desire to give them a good time.

The dart board is possibly the oldest pub game in existence, and is a staple form of entertainment. Pool tables, pin-ball machines and, in some areas, poker machines, are similar forms of simple entertainment.

But there are other novel ideas that can also be considered. Marbles is a simple game that even the oldest drinker can try. See the case study on the 'Royal Australian Court House Marble Club' (page 246).

Other games to think about are indoor bowls (all that is needed is an open strip of carpet), quoits, and board games (such as chess, draughts, cards, mah-jong, and so on). The key is to encourage people to play by offering small prizes for the winners and consolation prizes for losers—so that everyone gets something. The objective of these strategies is to get the customers involved so that they find there is always something to do and see at the hotel.

Some outdoor games can also be considered. These include a basketball ring, a mini-cricket pitch, rounders, or a mini-golf putting green.

The less-frequented nights of the week for the hotel are best for the introduction of occasions that will bring people out of their homes and into the

---

CASE STUDY

'Royal Australian Court House Marble Club'

The Court House Hotel at Lithgow, New South Wales, reintroduced its customers to the ancient game of marbles by forming the 'Royal Australian Court House Marble Club'.

Sunday was designated as being the day of 'serious' competition at the hotel. It was made into a family occasion, and the children had their competition, in addition to the parents' competition. No one was excluded. Pool and quoits competitions were also features of the day.

Apart from having a lot of fun, the provision of prizes gave the competitors an extra incentive.

---

hotel for some fun. The idea can be as simple as the old favourite of a dance night, but other ideas worth considering are karaoke, charades, and the many parlour games that have entertained millions over the years.

There are other ways of providing an evening that creates a special occasion. Visiting celebrities provide an opportunity for an evening to 'meet the interesting and famous'. Bar and lounge promotions such as 'happy hours' have been popular for years. A 'wheel of fortune' period is another idea—in which the wheel is marked off into discounted drink prices and turned every fifteen minutes. Whatever price that comes up is the price that everyone pays for the next fifteen minutes. The owner and staff enter into the spirit of the occasion and moan loudly when the price is at rock bottom! Raffles, free food snacks, auctions for parcels of meat, mystery passwords, trivial pursuit games—anything at all that can provide interest for the patrons should be used.

Dining-room promotions are important. Food has become the main attraction for extending the customer base beyond that which sees the hotel as nothing more than a place for a drink. The dining-area can the focus for bringing in the whole family to be entertained as well as fed. There are several promotions that can be run on a regular basis. An amateur talent event on a Saturday night, or as part of a Sunday afternoon barbecue, is an idea that usually appeals. It is amazing how much talent can be unearthed in a small district, and a talent quest is an ideal opportunity to bring them forth. It is a good idea to have a professional band or singer to assist in the occasion, and a good compere is important. The customers can be the judges, and an enormous amount of fun can be had with the performances of both the bad acts and the good acts.

The mandatory occasions—such as Christmas, Easter, New Year's Eve, Mothers' Day, and Fathers' Day—should never be missed. But there are many other religious and ethnic feast days—such as Chinese Spring Festival—that can be turned into occasions for a special night out. They work best when everyone enters into the occasion with enthusiasm so that room decorations (and perhaps costumes) are tied to the event.

People's birthdays should never be forgotten. Neither should wedding anniversaries, announcements of forthcoming marriages, and other special milestones in people's lives. Special mention should be made of people who have achieved something of interest. The simplest and most effective strategy for winning the hearts of patrons is to record people's birthdays and anniversaries in a diary. Then, a week beforehand, they can be rung and told that the hotel has baked a cake for the occasion and has put aside a cold bottle of something special for them. The person can be asked when he or she would they like to come and celebrate the occasion, and how many people would they like to bring along? This is a friendly, thoughtful thing to do. It is obviously good for business too, but the hotel is unlikely to receive any complaints about that from the patrons.

Something to look forward to

Giving the customers something to do and see is a major strategy for a local hotel, and this leads to another good strategy—to have something for people to look forward to. Patrons will eagerly look forward to what the hotel is going to do next for them.

Planning is necessary. Events such as the ones mentioned above do not happen without careful thought, planning, and promotion—preferably well in advance. Successful promotion can be ensured by passing out leaflets, and by ringing or otherwise contacting those most likely to appreciate the event.

Running a local hotel should be fun for everyone. It is an opportunity to get to know people, and to become close and friendly. When that happens, the place makes money and no one will mind because they will be getting value. Remember, business is people.

Questions for discussion or revision

1 Involvement is a critical issue for the customers when building the business of a local hotel. This chapter noted six outcomes for customers that should be provided so that customers are given reasons for staying and returning. The first one was comfort. How would you go about making a place 'comfortable' for its patrons?

2 Another vital outcome is to convey to customers the feeling of being wanted and special. How would you achieve that if you were running a country hotel?

3 Everyone has an individual idea about what constitutes 'good' food and drink. How would you go about making sure that the food and drink you serve in your local hotel is considered 'good' by the majority of your customers?

Chapter 19

Strategic Solutions

Aims of this chapter

The aims of this chapter are:
- to explain how to deal with marketing problems and opportunities;
- to explain how to choose a balance of strategies; and
- to discuss how to achieve an organisation's goals without forgetting the customer.

Theory

Problems and opportunities arise in business all the time. A market analysis or a marketing audit, or any other form of assessment of the market conducted on behalf of a property, usually reveals problems or opportunities.

They might be *problems*. These can include a sales decline, reduced market share, loss of certain types of customers, reduced revenue, reduced profit margins, increased competition, product failures, need for refurbishing, and so on.

Conversely, *opportunities* might present themselves. These can include new markets, excess accommodation capacity, achievement of initial goals (and thus opportunities for new goals and further expansion), changes in the market opening up opportunities for new markets and new products, and so on.

So what should management do about these problems and opportunities? Obviously, this depends on what is revealed by the analysis. Strategic solutions are the means by which an organisation deals with the ever-changing circumstances of marketing an establishment. When confronted with the need for change, management cannot just sit and hope that the situation goes away. The corporate goals of sales and profit have to be satisfied.

Goals give an organisation strategic direction and are therefore the rudder of strategic planning. For goals to have meaning they must be timed and quantified. If not, the strategies become well-meaning intentions—as opposed to their real purpose, which is to achieve results.

Most corporate goals can be classified into four broad categories:

◆ expansion;
◆ survival;
◆ consolidation; and
◆ diversification.

There is always a risk that corporate goals can make owners and managers pursue profit alone, and lose sight of their strategic marketing goals. It is not hard to find examples of owners who are so busy being in business that they forget that the customers are the reason that they are in business.

Choosing a strategic solution

Once a problem or an opportunity is identified and properly analysed, the question arises: 'What are we going to do about it?'. To answer this question, management must make a decision about the elements of the marketing mix that need to be changed. This decision will involve one or more of the following:

◆ people strategies;
◆ product strategies;
◆ pricing strategies;
◆ positioning strategies;
◆ place strategies; and/or
◆ promotion strategies.

The decisions about the marketing mix strategies then become a strategic marketing plan. Each of these elements of the strategic marketing plan is considered below.

People strategies

People strategies to be considered include:

◆ changing or modifying the customer mix;
◆ targeting different demographic or psychographic groups;
◆ targeting heavy, light, or non-users; and/or

◆ targeting those markets that have certain purchase reasons or behaviour patterns (for example, corporate meetings, conventions, tour groups, visitors, holidaymakers, sporting groups, and so on).

Product strategies

Product strategies to be considered include:

◆ changing, modifying, or improving products;
◆ changing the product mix;
◆ introducing new lines or deleting some;
◆ changing the service procedures;
◆ changing the manner or style of service; and/or
◆ changing or retraining the staff.

Place strategies

Place strategies to be considered include:

◆ relocating the establishment;
◆ rebuilding, refurbishing, or redecorating;
◆ changing geographic sales outlets; and/or
◆ changing agents.

Price strategies

Price strategies to be considered include:

◆ changing the prices;
◆ becoming price competitive;
◆ creating value-added offers;
◆ introducing price discrimination or flexible pricing; and/or
◆ using price ranging.

Positioning strategies

Positioning strategies to be considered include:

◆ creating a market demand for the service or product; (this involves a wide-ranging approach bringing in other strategies such as promotion and pricing);
◆ improving or changing the corporate look; and/or
◆ changing internal attitudes.

Promotion strategies

Promotion strategies to be considered include:

◆ improving the 'in-reach' sales techniques (that is, the handling of customer enquiries);

- improving 'out-reach' selling techniques (that is sales representation);
- rearranging the tactical mix;
- introducing new promotions;
- changing the advertising approach;
- organising better brochures and collateral material;
- increasing or decreasing the promotion budget;
- using direct email or mail;
- organising publicity; and/or
- changing the signage on the property.

Which strategy to choose?

The choice of strategy depends on the circumstances. If the decision were easy we would all be richer! Choosing a marketing strategy is about knowing the options that are available and, based on the information available, selecting the option that best suits the situation. This takes experience and knowledge.

As a guide to the best strategic solution to choose, management should always begin with a market, select a product, and improve it to satisfy the requirements of the chosen market. Management must ensure that the establishment is right for the product, that the price offers value for money, that the establishment is positioned to appeal to the perceptions of the market, and that the promotion strategy is appropriate.

The procedure sounds simple—and the basics *are* simple and logical. Agonising over the consequences causes most of the pain in marketing.

Effects of change

A major change to any of the marketing strategies will affect the other elements of the marketing mix. For new strategies to work effectively, there must be benefit to customers as well as to the organisation. Therefore new strategies must be scrutinised for their effect on other strategies and a forecast made of their impact on the whole property.

For example, by adopting a strategy that pursues a new market consisting of sporting group tours, some of whom might be rowdy carousing men and women, it is worth considering that this might drive away many quieter customers (for example, businesspersons) who constitute a large proportion of the existing customer base.

As another example, a restaurant with a corporate goal of increasing sales might decide on a strategy to allocate a large section of the building to wedding receptions and convention groups. The problem with this strategy might be that such groups are generally very price-sensitive. As this move will limit the restaurant's capacity to cater for full-charge diners, the strategy might cause a consequent drop in profits.

The above examples illustrate that, with every change, a marketer has to forecast its impact on:

◆ markets (people strategies);
◆ selling (promotion strategies);
◆ market perceptions (positioning); and
◆ pricing strategies.

In addition, the effect on profit has to be considered. What will the new strategies do to sales or market share? How will the new strategies affect the perceptions of existing customers and new customers? If travel agents or distributors are involved, how will they react to the change? How difficult will it be to re-educate them? A large change will be noticed by the general public who are influencers of customer perceptions. How will they perceive the change? The interests of the staff also need to be considered. How will staff members react? Can they cope with the change? Will they have to be retrained or even replaced? Suppliers, unions, and government agencies all need to be involved.

All of these matters can present difficulties. This does not mean that a new strategic approach should be regarded with anxiety. It simply means that change can have wide implications, and that these implications should not be overlooked in the planning process.

Concepts, ideas, and copying

The functions of the human brain can be divided into activities in the two halves of the brain—called the left and right hemispheres. The left hemisphere is usually considered to be responsible for convergent thinking; it is the analytical and logical part of the brain. The right side is usually considered to be responsible for emotions, feelings, and concepts; it is the source of creativity. To illustrate this division, we might say that the left side is responsible for playing the piano, whereas the right side experiences the music. Some people are more developed in the functions of one or other of the hemispheres. 'Creative people' have a greater ability to use the right side to consider concepts and use their imagination. However, such people are not always able to evaluate their creations effectively.

It is not necessary for marketers to think of new ideas. There are many ideas that have proven to be effective, and which are therefore worth copying, or adapting. To be weigh up the strategic options effectively, and to decide on the best solution, are matters of experience and education. In assisting this process of education, much marketing theory involves lists of steps to take in undertaking various procedures. This provides the practitioner with a checklist of matters to consider, and helps to avoid overlooking vital factors. In the case of responsible strategic planning, the following sequence of steps needs to be followed:

◆ market analysis;
◆ identification of problems and opportunities;
◆ deciding which strategies will achieve the corporate goals;
◆ analysis of the effects of a proposed change on all elements of the marketing mix;
◆ forecasting the effect of change across all the categories of people who comprise the target markets;
◆ analysis of the resources required to cope with the changes;
◆ setting of the marketing goals; finalising the strategies, and setting strategic objectives; and
◆ implementing and analysing the consequences of the change.

Change usually causes disruption—varying from minor irritations to major upheavals. For this reason, it is worthwhile experimenting with change before implementing it. Alternatively, consider researching its consequences.

Dialectical method

One way of reviewing a proposed new strategy before advancing to a decision to proceed is to undertake a process known as the 'dialectical method'. The dialectical method is sometimes referred to as the 'devil's advocate method'.[1] A marketer considers possible strategies, and then deliberately looks for problems and difficulties. For example, if assumptions are made on continuing economic growth, the dialectical method suggests that the opposite assumptions should be made. That is, the marketer should imagine conditions of declining economic growth, and then consider the implications for the project.

This method looks for problems. Much time is spent on problem-*solving* in modern organisations, but very little time is spent on problem-*finding*. More emphasis on problem-finding would enable organisations to prepare solutions in advance, and be more flexible and fast-moving in revising its strategies in the marketplace.

Make sure the base strategies are in place

The basics of marketing success lie in having sound *people* strategies, carefully planned *product* and service strategies that enhance the customers' experiences, and good *place* strategies that create comfortable environments for the customers. Then come *price*, *positioning*, and *promotion* strategies.

A *people* strategy that targets the most viable customer groups is always the first essential. Then, provided that the *product* strategies meet with the approval of the targeted customers, a satisfactory flow of sales should follow. Large hotels and motels depend on location and the appeal of their premises (*place* strategies) as an essential part of their marketing planning. Restaurants are not so dependent upon place strategies. Indeed, some establishments are in basements of back streets with no frontage at all, and have only stone floors and walls as a backdrop to the eating experience. They can do extremely well purely on the basis of their food, ambience, and service (*product* strategies). *Pricing* strategies always have an effect on the outcome of marketing, although not to the extent that many believe. Cutting prices does not necessarily bring in more sales. The product has to be in demand for a discounted price to have meaning. An upmarket restaurant or hotel with a high-profile reputation can often get away with quite outrageously high prices.

Most strategic solutions depend on the people who have been targeted and the fulfilment of their expectations at the time. Night clubs for example, are particularly vulnerable to change because of the quixotic nature of their markets—always subject to the music trends and the fashions of the entertainment industry. Theirs is a continuing quest for solutions that match their customers' needs, and choosing the right products becomes an essential ingredient of their strategic planning.

At the luxury end of the hotel and tourist resort market, strategic solutions are mostly sought in changes to product lines within the complex. The overall strategies of the properties have already been decided by long-term commitments to business travel and vacation markets, which are more consistent users of hospitality.

Large properties that rely on accommodation for the bulk of their revenue contributions refer to these contributions as 'yield'—the number of rooms occupied on average over a month, a season or a year, and the sales value received from them. The yield figures are compared with previous periods for other years, or against sales and budget forecasts. A low yield is the stimulus for corrective action.

Most properties give priority to the most profitable market segments to maintain their yield, and increase remaining room nights with sales from less profitable segments. Some do not seek to maximise profit from ancillary outlets such as bars and restaurants. They use these facilities as a means of enticement or as 'add-ons' for their main business of room hire. A casino, for example, which has a large accommodation and entertainment complex, makes its money from gambling, and management is sanguine about losing money from other areas.

Questions for discussion or revision

1 In which circumstances would a property consider 'consolidation' as a corporate objective?
2 If a private (unlicensed) hotel decided to apply for a liquor licence, which elements of the marketing mix would the owners have to consider changing? What would be the reasons for their choice?
3 It is said that every change to the marketing mix has an effect on other areas of importance to the owners of a property. Explain why this statement is true.

Chapter 20

Growth Strategies

Aims of this chapter

The aims of this chapter are:
- to explain the concept of market growth;
- to explain various growth strategies; and
- to discuss how to implement growth strategies.

Theory

It is an accepted fact of business that growth is important to survival. A property cannot expect to depend on existing business indefinitely. There is always change—a turnover of customers, different trends, variable market conditions, the natural attrition of customers—so management always has to consider attracting new business. For example, a restaurant should consider setting itself an annual growth target of twelve and a half per cent. This growth rate builds on the existing customer base by constantly improving products and making the place a better experience for the customers. Word-of-mouth recommendation does the rest.

Organisations can grow through an increase in sales, profit, size, products (diversification), number of customers, or number of employees. One could say that only profit matters, but there are other benefits to be gained from growth. Growth provides pride and satisfaction for the staff, as well as for the owners. Size also gives a place a better chance of survival in the marketplace. For example, the sheer size and brand-name power of leading hotel chains often assures them of a sound market in any location they choose to enter. Size through growth can also achieve economies of scale and have profit benefits for investors. In the case of large hotel, motel, or tourist resort properties, increased size also implies a diversity of products. This has the advantage of providing many profit-earning centres. When one is down others can compensate for lost revenue.

However, there is also a 'downside' to size and growth. Unless management and staff are competent, size and diversity can stretch an organisation's resources to breaking point. In fact, rapid growth places such strains on the human, physical, and financial resources of an organisation that it is a major cause of business failure. Many owners, somewhat unwisely, perceive growth at any cost is the cure for every marketing ill. The examples of numerous failed takeovers demonstrate how disastrous this headlong pursuit of size and growth can be. Nevertheless, growth is the constant corporate goal for most organisations.

Growth: opportunities and constraints

Growth strategies should always be contemplated in terms of market demand opportunities. Such strategies should also consider the effects on the base business because the customer mix not only should dictate the product mix, but also should dictate the corporate attitude towards growth. It is not sound business practice for a property to embrace a new product opportunity unless the product has a market that:

- ◆ is proven; and
- ◆ is not in conflict with existing customers.

Hotels usually offer a variety of products and therefore have many profit-earning products. Growth can occur by adding to, or improving, products including:

- ◆ accommodation and room service;
- ◆ dining-rooms, restaurants, cafés, coffee shops, and eating areas;
- ◆ bars;
- ◆ function & banquet rooms, and catering services;
- ◆ laundry, valet, mending, and hire facilities;
- ◆ business facilities including fax, computer, Internet, and secretarial services;
- ◆ indoor recreational facilities including gymnasium, spa, sauna, massage, and swimming pool;

◆ sports facilities including tennis courts, squash courts, badminton courts, billiard tables, and (in the case of resort properties) golf courses; and
◆ more specialist facilities such as casinos and boat marinas.

When an organisation the size of a large hotel, motel, or tourist complex contemplates product or market growth, it should ensure that there is synergy between all of these profit-earning products. Promotion of the whole complex enables all products to benefit from the main positioning thrust of the property, and each product can feed off the customers attracted by another.

The products of a property are not all purchased by the same people—some use the accommodation and room service but do not dine in the restaurants; others use the pool and the gymnasium, and nothing else, and so on. Nevertheless, there will be clusters of similarities among those who comprise the customer mix because the positioning of the property has attracted a particular type of person. This is the synergistic effect.

A property has to take into consideration the type of operation it is, and its physical location. Sustainable growth is difficult to achieve in a finite market such as a country town with a static population. Growth in this instance has to come from 'market penetration' (that is, selling more to the existing customers) or from diversification (that is, getting into areas of activity separate from the main business).

Some properties are also constrained in their growth ambitions by the needs of the customers and the expectations that customers have of establishments that fall into specific hospitality categories. For example, a bed & breakfast place would become something else if it obtained a liquor licence, or a tavern would become an hotel if it accommodated guests. In these cases, it is best for an establishment to do what it does best, and grow by doing it better and more often.

Growth through positioning and service

The customer mix has to have synergy, and this synergistic relationship should dictate the product mix. Therefore customer groups define the growth strategies of a business.

For hotels, motels, and tourist resort complexes, the perceptions of customers (which management has created through positioning) therefore become as important as the products themselves. Consequently, in the hospitality industry, in which service is the main product, growth can be achieved through service without a cent being spent on tangible facilities or on promotion.

However, even today, when the importance of service is well recognised, only a small percentage of management respondents to surveys really believe that service can be quantified and measured. Nor do they think that service is anything more than an 'add-on' to ambience and facilities. A prevailing belief among many operators is expressed in this quotation from an article by Professor Robert C. Lewis:[1]

> A hotel's offerings comprise a bundle of goods and services ranging from tangible to intangible. Because the lion's share of the hotel's products—services—is at the intangible end of the continuum, it is often difficult [especially for those properties that do not have a commitment to service] to determine which attributes are most important in the consumer's purchase decision . . . Moreover, because every hotel property offers a heterogeneous range of services, the consumer's risk in the purchase decision is high. Finally, because service offerings are easily duplicated, the consumer cannot always draw clear distinctions among competitive offerings.

However, good service *is* a marketable difference which provides enormous potential for growth. Service is the memory taken away by satisfied customers, and good memories frequently result in the invaluable 'pass-on' recommendation of satisfied customers to other consumers. So the soundest basis for growth is to consider service strategies that capitalise on a good image and a reputation for outstanding customer satisfaction.

Intensive growth strategies

Intensive growth strategies endeavour to obtain increased sales and market share by:

◆ market penetration—selling more products to existing customers; or
◆ market development—seeking new customers for existing products; or
◆ product development—improving the existing products or developing new products to build on the customer base.

Market penetration

Market penetration is best achieved by finding new uses for existing products or by creating reasons for existing customers to use other products. A ballroom, for example, can be used for many occasions—such as banquets, conventions, training seminars, large meetings, trade shows, weddings, and so on. Some of these potential uses might not occur to existing customers until it is drawn to their attention.

Market development

Market development can be achieved by finding new reasons to attract customers who seldom use the property's facilities—by encouraging customers away from competing properties, or to attract new users from other locations.

In the case of encouraging customers away from competing properties, this can be done by better prices, by better value or, most effectively of all, by an improved customer service experience.

In the case of attracting customers from different localities, promotions, extensive advertising, or sales representation are required.

Product development strategies

The third intensive growth strategy—*product development strategies*—is considered in the next section.

Product development strategies

Through the growth of profit-earning products, large hospitality establishments can make significant gains, provided that there is an unsatisfied demand. If there is an undersupply of accommodation, an establishment can add more rooms. If a restaurant is filling regularly, it can expand into an adjacent area. If a bar consistently overflows, it can be extended. This is called 'horizontal stretch'.

If a place has earnt a reputation for a product, another growth strategy is to capitalise on this reputation and attract a new group of customers by introducing a similar (but differently rated) product. If the base product is accommodation, other forms of accommodation can be added—such as higher-priced luxury suites, budget-rated family rooms, or low-priced single rooms. If the base product is a continental restaurant, other styles can be offered—such as an Asian restaurant, or a smorgasbord. This is called 'vertical stretch'.

The assessment of the opportunities for growth should be based on a careful analysis of:

- the establishment's customer base;
- the things that an establishment does best, and the things that it does better than its competitors;
- how an establishment can build on its strengths, or overcome its weaknesses; and
- the primary assets of an establishment—such as staff, management, location, and image.

To summarise, product growth can occur through two sources:

◆ current customers—by selling them more of the same products, by offering improved products, or by offering new products; or

◆ new customers—by increasing awareness of existing products, by offering improved products, or by attracting customers with new products.

Growth through diversification

Corporate growth, as opposed to product growth, can occur by a corporate organisation entering fields that are allied or connected with the hospitality business. These growth strategies are:

◆ horizontal diversification;

◆ diversification through vertical integration; and

◆ horizontal integration.

Horizontal diversification

Horizontal diversification occurs when an organisation invests in new products that are allied to hospitality, but that are dissimilar to their existing style of operation. Such products will attract entirely new markets. They include such products as a new large entertainment centre, a casino, a sports centre, and so on.

Diversification through vertical integration

Diversification through vertical integration occurs when an organisation controls or owns its suppliers—such as laundry, linen supplies, a winery, a butchery, flower supply, vegetable supply, and so on. This can make sense if a place has a special skill or reputation in an area and wants to maintain it. It might also be justified if an organisation has such a high turnover in its operation that it can make additional profit).

Diversification through vertical integration is also said to exist if an establishment 'owns' its source of customers. This might occur if an organisation owns its own travel agent, airline, bus company, and so on.

Horizontal integration

Horizontal integration occurs when an organisation buys out or buys an interest in its competitors. This can also entail building or acquiring another establishment and gaining a different market unavailable to the present style of operation. This move usually entails operating under a different company or brand name to avoid confusing customers, and possibly losing an existing customer mix.

Market expansion

Market expansion occurs when property owners decide to expand into different geographic locations and, by utilising the same expertise, set up a chain of operations. This can be achieved:

◆ by buying properties;
◆ by selling its management expertise and name; or
◆ by franchising.

The Six Continents Hotels group, for example, is a professional management company that owns a few properties of its own, and also manages a chain of properties under various brand names. In 2001, the group had 53 hotels and resorts in Australia, New Zealand, and the South Pacific—including the Holiday Inn brand (positioned in the mid-range of the market), Inter-Continental, Crowne Plaza, and Parkroyal (upmarket), and Centra (business class).[2]

Hilton, Sheraton, Hyatt, and Continental are among the best known hotel chains in the Asian, Pacific, and American regions. They run high-profile, luxury properties that provide consumers with an assurance of standards of service well above average.

Most hotels are owned by investment groups which contract with chains for the reputation of a high-profile brand name and management expertise.

New market assessment procedures

To enter new markets by acquisition, diversification, or integration requires an assessment of the following factors:

◆ good market size—an adequate number of customers, or the potential to develop an adequate number before making the move;
◆ good market growth—ascertained through research and growth projections of a likely growing market;
◆ good profitability—a logical test to apply before proceeding with a new venture, but one that can be overlooked by management if it becomes carried away with 'growth for growth's sake', and fails to assess the return on investment properly;
◆ low competitive intensity—a move into a new market is a risk at the best of times, and even more hazardous if the competition is strong and firmly entrenched;
◆ manageable volatility—hospitality is subjected to seasonal conditions in travel and tourist activity, and these factors have to be investigated and understood;

◆ economy of scale—a new product, or the acquisition of another property, can often provide savings by avoiding duplications, and can also add to the purchasing power of the group and allow for better trading arrangements;

◆ good customer fit—a new product should be assessed in the light of its acceptance by the existing customer mix because old customers can be lost if the new product conflicts with their perceptions of the property;

◆ good fit with the existing product mix—a new product can disrupt the positioning of other products; a new product might also be such a specialised operation that specialised staff are required, causing difficulties in transferring staff when needed;

◆ the human and physical resources to handle it—for example, changing the style of a restaurant from Western food to Japanese food might be a good idea if the market demands it, but such a change will require specialised staff and equipment; and

◆ market knowledge and business management experience—as a rule, it is always best to do what one is best at doing; diversification usually requires new management skills and this has to be acquired or specialists have to be appointed to handle the new situation.

Questions for discussion or revision

1 Suggest some circumstances in which different profit centres (outlets) of a big city property (such as an upmarket restaurant, gymnasium, hairdressing salon, or self-service cafeteria) can prosper even though there is no synergy between them.

2 What is most likely to happen if a property decides to break with its existing customer mix and seek growth in an unrelated activity?

3 Explain the probable outcome if an hotel with a strong market base of family holidaymakers and retired bus tourists decides to run a disco in its function room on two nights a week.

4 'Too much growth too soon' has been identified in government statistics as being a cause of many business failures. Why do you think this is so?

Chapter 21

Pricing Strategies

Aims of this chapter

The aims of this chapter are:
- to explain how to select an appropriate pricing strategy;
- to describe hotel pricing strategies; and
- to describe restaurant pricing strategies.

Theory

Price is usually set by examining what the market will bear. As there are many markets, there are many opportunities for pricing strategies, and therefore many opportunities for various contenders in a market to position themselves according to price.

The balance between price and value largely determines the success of an establishment. With an hotel, the room rate sets the pricing levels for the rest of the hotel's products. Therefore price is part of positioning. For example, a customer expects to pay more for a high-class, five-star hotel than for a middle-range three-star hotel. Price helps to determine the customer mix; conversely, the customer mix targeted by an establishment determines the price.

The hospitality industry is fiercely competitive and sensitive to economic conditions. The relationship between rates and occupancy therefore has to be finely tuned.

Hotel, motel, and resort pricing strategies

Prices and strategies

There are various prices and pricing strategies utilised in the accommodation industry.

Rack rate

The *rack rate* is the regular published room rate. In a perfect market, the rack rate is set as a result of 'cost-plus' pricing, which is based on a simple sum:[1]

$$\text{price} = (\text{operating costs} + \text{capital recovery} + \text{profit}) \div \text{forecast number of customers}$$

Rarely is there such a thing as a perfect market. Therefore, the rack rate in many instances becomes a starting price for negotiation—the price that management would like to achieve throughout the year and at all times during the week. However, fluctuations in demand dictate that different rates apply at different times of the year, week, or even day. This leads to the following variations from the rack rate.

Target pricing

Target pricing occurs when the hotel endeavours to determine a price (based on average occupancy) that will provide an adequate return.

Perceived-value pricing

Perceived-value pricing occurs when an establishment sets a price based on the value or benefits being offered. This pricing strategy is generally aimed at a specific customer mix.

Going-rate pricing

Going-rate pricing is based on averaging—that is, keeping pace with the competition.

Price-ranging

Price ranging is employed by nearly all hotels. It is the setting of a high price for its best suites or rooms, ranging down to its cheapest rooms—with each drop in price representing a consequent drop in size, views, facilities, and extras.

Value-added pricing

Value-added pricing occurs when extras are discounted and coupled with a going rate to provide an attractive package offer—often referred to as a 'product'.

Therefore, when a customer asks the price for a room, the room rate can cover:

- room only;
- room and breakfast;
- room and all meals;
- room plus all recreational facilities; or
- room plus free enticements (such as champagne, opera tickets, shopping vouchers, and so on).

The purpose of a value-added pricing strategy is to make direct comparisons with competing properties difficult while making the offer appear to be worth more than is being charged.

Price skimming

Price skimming is a strategy adopted by new properties with a well-known brand name, a grand façade, and high-profile positioning. From the outset, such an establishment charges a high price for their rooms and other products because it has a new, exciting, prestigious image that usually attracts a 'high-flying' customer who wants nothing but the best. The customer who takes to a new establishment immediately is known in marketing an 'early adopter'.

This strategy is maintained for as long as the property holds its position. The strategy is called 'skimming' because it takes the 'cream' of the market at the time. However, when other (newer) properties are built, and as the facilities become a little tired, prices are gradually reduced.

Changes in policy

Management usually has a policy on pricing that varies from being rigid to being flexible. The objectives are survival, profit maximisation, market share, quality leadership, and capital recovery.

However, price changes can be forced upon a property by competition—a close competitor can 'steal' guests by offering better deals, or by market conditions. Or a general economic downturn can force every property into a price-cutting war.

The market and demand for accommodation set the price *ceiling* and the costs of an establishment set the price *floor*. The price ceiling is the maximum price people are prepared to pay in a given market environment. The price floor is the lowest price a property can charge without losing money. Competing properties struggle for market share between the price ceiling and the price floor. Price is an equation between value and money over which potential guests have to deliberate before making a decision. In some markets setting a rate is almost a daily decision as rivals have the option of raising or lowering rates with every enquiry.

Demand differential pricing strategies

In most capital city markets, there is an oversupply of rooms for the majority of the year. Special events and seasonal demands are the only occasions when all rooms are filled. The marketing challenge therefore is to fill as many rooms as possible in the seasonal gaps of market demand. Price and perceived value become significant in this situation.

On different days and times of the year, a room might be hired out to guests at rates that vary considerably. Similarly, the rate varies to attract specific customer groups—such as tour wholesalers, large companies, convention holders, and frequent travellers. This is *demand differential pricing*. This produces the following rates and packages:

◆ holiday packages;
◆ cooperative rates for wholesalers of tours, travel packages, and airline seats;
◆ weekend rates;
◆ business rates;
◆ frequent user rates;
◆ corporate rates;
◆ family rates;
◆ share room rates;
◆ convention rates.
◆ upgrading; and
◆ 'no-frills' rates.

Each of these is considered below.

Holiday packages

Holiday packages are products that the property markets as its own. For example, an establishment might offer a three-day stay at the property combined with sightseeing tours or with a special-interest package that takes in sporting or cultural events. These are products that can be advertised, promoted to corporate clients, or marketed through other tourism-related companies.

Cooperative rates for wholesalers of tours, travel packages, and airline seats

These are special discounted room rates that are struck for tour wholesalers so that they can market their own holiday packages. Such rates enable an airline, for example, to offer a stay of one or more nights at the property as part of an attractive package holiday of benefits and events. Most large travel agents and transport companies package holidays in this way. From the hospitality establishment's perspective, the discount is offset by the volume of business it receives.

Weekend rates

Businesspeople and organisers of conferences and conventions tend to use the facilities of hospitality properties on working days. As a result, most properties find that they have excess capacity over weekends. Weekend rates are therefore offered as discounts designed to attract businesspeople to stay on after their business, or to attract locals to indulge themselves. Weekend rates can also be marketed in conjunction with transport operators to entice country and inter-state people to have a 'short-break package', and enjoy the luxury of staying at the property.

Business rates

Business travellers are the most frequent users of hospitality, and are therefore the target of nearly all properties. To attract their business, special incentive rates are offered. As additional attractions, the use of special business services is offered. These include secretarial assistance, Internet access, fax facilities, computers, photocopying, meeting rooms, video-conferencing, and perhaps language translators.

Frequent-user rates

This is a strategy designed to encourage frequent users of hospitality products to stay with the property regularly, and to build credit points that reduce the rate over time (and perhaps provide the recipient with a free stay after a certain number of bookings). Such an arrangement is sometimes called a 'frequent stayer club' (or similar). The rate is usually created to attract businesspersons to become loyal clients. Another form of the same strategy is an offer to stay another day for free.

Corporate rates

Corporate rates are aimed at large companies, or companies with a high usage rate of hospitality facilities. These are offered at a low rate for continued custom, and special deals are often included for the use of other hotel services. A variation of this strategy is to enrol such clients into a special 'club' that provides discounts for every facility of the property, and discounts at participating stores, airlines, hire-car firms, theatres, and other attractions likely to appeal to corporate customers.

Family rates

To attract family customers, many properties offer to accommodate children for free, or offer free child-minding services. A variation of the strategy is to offer family suites or adjoining rooms to allow families to be together. These types of products are frequently sold to use the excess capacity over weekends or at times of seasonal downturn.

Share room rates

For budget-conscious customers, a shared room is a 'bargain-basement' offer that can be useful. It is a particularly useful strategy when a special event has filled a town's properties. Many potential customers are prepared to accept such a deal in these circumstances. The strategy enables establishments to 'squeeze' more customers in, and provides more revenue from one room.

Convention rates

Professional, trade, business, or social groups hold conventions, conferences, training seminars, celebrations, and special sporting or cultural events. They always hunt for the best value they can get. Most properties 'bid' for this type of business and have a negotiable rate with a 'floor value' to the property— which means that they recover costs and retain a bare minimum of profit. Most properties offer an all-inclusive price including meals and use of other facilities. Often, the objective is to confuse the issue with 'add-ons'—such that price comparison with other properties becomes more difficult. Some places negotiate with suppliers to help them with special prices to win the deal. A transport element in the offer is not uncommon.

Upgrading

Some high-profile hotels do not like discounting because it can harm their 'prestige' image. Instead, when they are in a competitive situation, they upgrade favoured clients from a normal room to the executive floor so that they can provide added benefits at no extra charge. As an alternative, the establishment might include business facilities for no additional charge. Such establishments are, in effect, giving away some of their profit—but they are not seen to be discounting and they thus preserve a claim that they do not have to reduce their prices to win business.

'No-frills' rates

Another form of discounting is a published 'no-frills' rate that offers basic accommodation. This is a last-resort pricing strategy for large properties, but is a common strategy for properties struggling to be competitive in other ways.

There are variations on all of the above strategies. All of them have the same intention—to win business at all costs, especially during difficult times or flat spots in the year.

Yield management

Yield management is a method of pricing that attempts to match the demand for rooms with purchase patterns to maximise revenue from the sale of accommodation. This is a delicate balance, for if the price is set too high for customers who are price-conscious, they will not make the purchase. And the room–night, once past, can never be reclaimed.

Airlines have refined yield management practices so that they maximise the seats they sell on each flight, but they have an immense potential database of all past seat sales to use to assess demand at various price levels. Hotels do not usually have as much information as airlines, but managers and marketers can use historical information to assess how many rooms they can sell at various times at various rates. In Coltman's words: 'The objective of yield management is to maximise hotel room revenue by using basic economic principles to allocate the right type of room to the right type of guest at a price the guest is prepared to pay'.[2]

Yield management works by determining the high-demand periods and the low-demand periods, and then determining which categories of customers are likely to be attracted by which rates. Reservation records and forecasts are used in this context. Some periods can be identified as heavily booked, and other periods can be noted to have had light bookings, or perhaps high levels of cancellations. The marketing personnel can respond appropriately. For example, when marketing to a business or convention group, an hotel's sales director might be prepared to offer lower rates if the bookings are made in a period of low demand. In peak holiday periods, the hotel would not offer discounts at all.

Yield management can operate on a daily and weekly basis. For example, a transient guest who arrives at 9 pm could be offered a discounted rate (provided that other hotels in town are not booked out). In contrast, a guest who makes a reservation the day before could be quoted the rack rate. Over weekends, hotel demand generally declines because business travellers want to go home. At these times, special discount 'deals' can be offered.

It is important to note that these discounts must not cause problems with other guests who have booked at higher rates. Weekend specials usually have some conditions attached, so that other guests who have paid a higher rate do not resent the price differential. For example, to receive a discount deal, a prospective guest might have to pay in advance, and might have to agree to stay a minimum number of days. There might still be a need for some customer education, but hotel customers are usually aware that there are categories of guests who pay lower rates for different deals.

Marketing people need to have flexibility in setting rates in a yield management context. They also have to have good knowledge of their market segments, and must conduct an analysis of their guests' wants and preferences. Yield management must be a joint effort with the manager of the rooms division so that blocks of rooms can be allocated at various rates.

E-commerce has made effective yield management simpler—because computers can easily handle analyses of booking patterns and cancellation patterns at times of high demand, and can match customers' room rates with their length of stay.

Selling up and selling down

Customer mixes differ in their perceptions of value. Many establishments have price levels for each segment (for example, top rates for businesspeople and low rates for families). This can result in a disparate customer blend that harms the image of the place. A policy of 'get what you can' in setting different price levels for different people can lead to a loss of regular patronage. However, even the best hotels sometimes resort to a 'sell-up, sell-down' pricing approach—sometimes called an 'open-door' strategy, as opposed to a 'closed-door' strategy in which there is price rigidity.

A 'foot-in-the-door' strategy applies when an enquiring customer asks about rates. The potential guest is given a number of alternatives—ranging from a very low price to the highest price. The client will often choose the middle price—not wanting to appear to be too cheap or too extravagant (and, of course, seeking the best value). With a 'foot-in-the-door' strategy, the establishment then suggests to the client that, for only a small amount of extra money, he or she can get some added benefit—such as a king-sized bed, or a room with a view. This is called 'selling up'.

A 'face-in-the-door' strategy is the opposite of the above. The price quoted is the highest. Often this will be accepted. If it is not, other alternatives are offered until an acceptable price is reached. This is called 'selling down'.

A market-penetration pricing strategy is used when an hotel sets a price lower than usual because it wants to capture market share. This is a pricing strategy that will, at times, achieve much-needed cash flow. It also makes sense if the establishment wants to introduce a new product and needs to gain quick recognition and win some early sales.

Pricing impacts on other products

A price strategy will impact on other elements of the marketing mix, depending on the corporate goals and the marketing objectives. For example, long-term discounting will affect decisions regarding product quality. Management must have cost and profit predictions that reflect the consequences of price strategy decisions.

Although the room rates set the overall position of an establishment, a different pricing strategy for ancillary products is desirable. This is called 'product-line pricing'. This approach can be used to put value back into a room rate that is perceived by the customers to be very high.

Product-line pricing is used to offer customers a choice of values. Thus, an establishment with an expensive, quality restaurant might also offer a low-priced café-style dining-room. Similarly, an establishment might offer a cocktail lounge, a medium-priced saloon, or a club bar. In this way, different customers can find their own price level.

Another strategy is to maintain a high room rate and recover profits from other products and services. For example, incentives such as off-season rates, early booking discounts, preferred customer discounts, or special promotional offers can be offered.

Restaurant pricing strategies

In making offers, a hospitality establishment operates like any other retailer. Everyone likes a bargain, which is why sales promotions and premium offers usually attract additional customers, or bring regular customers into the establishment more often.

The strategies used by larger properties can be adapted by other hospitality businesses. The principles do not vary, but some businesses are perceived in a certain way by their consumers and therefore sensitivity to market demand has to be recognised. For example, a restaurant that has the same prices for dinner and lunch, on weekdays and at weekends, is certainly inflexible (and also rather hopeful!). At different times of the day, and perhaps on different days of the week, customers want a different type of eating experience. The luncheon period is usually patronised by businesspeople who want a quick, light meal with minimal liquor. A restaurateur could decide that he or she does not wish to cater for that market segment, but the restaurant could be passing over valuable business. More importantly, the restaurateur might be forgetting that the same luncheon customer is also a potential customer for dinner, supper, and even breakfast.

Menu and price structures can be changed according to the demands of various customer needs. For example, a restaurant might offer a lower-priced luncheon menu. For dinner, it might offer an 'early birds' menu (at half the normal dinner price) to cater for those who have to eat before going on to a function or the theatre. Such a menu might also appeal to people looking for a cheap meal. During the normal dinner time, full prices can still apply because this is the time of greatest demand. The restaurant could then offer a supper menu for late eaters, or for those who have come from their evening's entertainment.

A varying level of prices and menus makes sense because it maximises the use of staff and facilities. Such a variable pricing strategy can help a property to use the tables several times in the course of a day.

Questions for discussion or revision

1 What is the likely long-term outcome for a property that consistently reduces its rack rate to fill unused room capacity?
2 There are many different pricing strategies. List the five main types and explain what they mean.
3 Would you advise a new tourist resort on a tropical beach island to offer special discounts to fill the place and make a good opening impression? Or would you price it at the normal rate and hope that extensive promotion and advertising will achieve a full house by the time that it opens?

Chapter 22

Promotion Strategies

Aims of this chapter

The aims of this chapter are:
- to explain how to use the tactical mix;
- to discuss target markets and the selling messages of a property; and
- to describe promotion objectives.

Theory

There is a firmly held belief in the hospitality industry that selling is the most important function in the marketing mix. Some might disagree. The general attitude of experts such as Professor Peter Drucker is that good marketing makes selling unnecessary.[1]

It can be argued that getting the product and service quality right comes before anything else, and there have been many success stories in the hospitality industry without a cent being spent on advertising. The referrals of satisfied customers by word of mouth provide a large proportion of the custom of most businesses. The place, and what happens to customers in the place, has to be right—otherwise no amount of selling will bring customers in the long term.

Despite these valid points, promotion is still important. Potential customers need to know how good a place is. There are many markets that have to be reached and told the good news about a place. They have to get the message and get it often.

Promotion is the communication process that uses information persuasively to achieve a positive customer response. Promotion is divided into a number of functions (called 'tactics') embracing advertising, selling, publicity, brochures, sales aids, direct email, and mail promotions. How much is spent on each tactic, and the degree of emphasis on each one to achieve strategic marketing objectives, is called the 'tactical mix'. Despite the variety of tactics available, the best promotion tactic is personal, one-to-one contact.

Outreach and inreach selling

The two main sales functions can be termed 'outreach' selling and 'inreach' selling. *Outreach selling* refers to the communications going out to existing and potential customers. *Inreach selling* refers to inward enquiries from interested customers. Although different, both have the same intention—to secure business. For some reason, many establishments have experienced and accomplished salespeople handling outreach selling, but entrust inreach selling to inexperienced (and sometimes disagreeable) clerks. The handling of clients in both functions is equally important.

Outreach selling encompasses promotion as well as selling. It utilises both direct and indirect contact. Indirect contact includes advertising, publicity, displays, signs, and brochures. In most cases, the people being addressed are unknown. Direct contact includes personal contact, direct email, and telephone contact. In most instances the people are known.

Inreach selling is the handling of people who have made enquiries via telephone or correspondence, or who have personally attended the property.

Both of the communication processes are *message-delivery* systems because promotion strategies are messages about places and products that need to be communicated to the target markets. The information to be communicated concerns differences, advantages, and benefits of the property in question.

The intention of a promotion strategy is to use tactics to achieve a desired consumer result—in other words, a sale.

Tactical mix as a sequence

Types of message delivery

The tactical mix is a combination of message-delivery systems. They can be categorised as being in direct contact with the customer, or indirect contact with the customer.

Direct

Direct contact message-delivery systems include:

◆ personal outreach and inreach selling;
◆ direct email;
◆ direct mail;
◆ sales promotion;
◆ product presentation; and
◆ point-of-sale activity.

The advantages of personal contact are:

◆ physical presence—the dynamics of face-to-face confrontation and adaptability to individual behaviour can be useful;
◆ sales can be clinched on the spot;
◆ it is cost-efficient when targeting is used.

Some of the limitations are:

◆ the high cost of employing people to make personal contact;
◆ buyer resistance as a result of a feeling of pressure; and
◆ the impracticality of reaching large numbers quickly.

Indirect

Indirect contact message-delivery systems include:

◆ advertising;
◆ brochures;
◆ publicity; and
◆ signs and displays.

The advantages of indirect contact, using various media, are:

◆ the message can be communicated to a broad audience;
◆ an image can be conveyed;
◆ costs per contact can be small; and
◆ a high rate of return can be received.

Some of the limitations are:

◆ it is impersonal;
◆ there is no need to react to message; and
◆ advertising, in particular, is very expensive

Choosing a mix and communicating the message

The task for management is to decide which mix of these tactics will be employed to make its promotion strategies work and achieve message comprehension. Message comprehension can be slow or fast, depending on which message-delivery systems are utilised, for how long they are used, and to what extent they are used. With a large budget, a combination of advertising, publicity, direct email, and selling can get a message to a large number of people. And if the message is clear and contains an obvious benefit for customers, large-scale comprehension can be achieved quickly.

The comprehension of the consumer is measured on a graduated scale:

◆ no awareness;
◆ some awareness;
◆ interest;
◆ desire;
◆ conviction; and
◆ action.

Several things happen in communicating a message to the consumer. These are:

◆ the sender (the management of the property) originates the message;
◆ the message contains favourable information about the property and its products;
◆ the message is in various forms—the spoken word; the written word (in electronic or hardcopy form); pictures (in a brochure or an advertisement); images and sounds (in television or radio commercial);
◆ a message vehicle takes the message to the receiver; the message vehicle might be another person, a letter, an email, a fax, a telephone message, or an advertising medium;
◆ the message reaches the receiver;
◆ the receiver places an interpretation on the message;
◆ the receiver responds to the message, or ignores it;
◆ feedback occurs—perhaps in the form of a sale.

From this communication process, it can be seen that much depends on the clarity of the message and the effectiveness of the message-delivery system. This requires good salespeople, effective advertising and brochures, and proper identification of the best people to receive the message.

Target markets

There are many segments in the market to target, and each one requires a different promotion strategy. These include:

◆ corporate and professional clients;
◆ social clubs, business and professional associations, and sporting clubs;
◆ government departments and educational institutions;
◆ fraternal, ethnic, and religious organisations;
◆ travel agents;
◆ tour operators and wholesalers; and bus, train, and airline companies;
◆ suppliers of goods and services to the property;
◆ media; and
◆ individual business and holiday travellers.

Each of these is considered below.

Corporate and professional clients

For corporate and professional clients, personal contact is the most effective promotion strategy, supported by direct email, mail, and brochures. Corporate clients do not necessarily react to image advertising. However, for the launch of a property or a significant refurbishing that repositions the property, advertising can set the scene and establish a climate of interest for sales representatives to open dialogue with prospective clients.

Social clubs, business and professional associations, and sporting clubs

The clubs and associations most likely to use a property's services should be contacted personally, with regular mail follow-ups. Most corporate an professional clients of a property belong to an association, and these contacts offer an ideal opportunity for an introduction to their association. This is called a 'networking' strategy.

Government departments and educational institutions

The strategy for this segment is to identify and make personal contact with the decision-makers and those who organise conferences, travel arrangements, and training seminars on behalf of these organisations. The senior departmental heads are not always the people who do the organising and the selection of the venues. Sorting through the labyrinth of the bureaucratic process is not always easy.

Fraternal, ethnic, and religious organisations

For fraternal, ethnic, and religious organisations, the same approach can be used as for government departments.

Travel agents

Travel agents pose a geographic problem because they are scattered all over the world. For the local ones, particularly those who package their own travel products, it is obviously best to maintain frequent personal contact, supported by mailing and brochures. For those interstate, it is essential to select the main ones and have personal area representation if possible. Otherwise, contact should be maintained by fax and email. Overseas agents have to be selected for their viability as an influencer of travel to your region, and it might be possible only to update their files regularly.

Tour operators and wholesalers; and bus, train and airline companies

These segments are significant creators of business for a property, especially if the property is targeting holiday makers. The development of offers and attractive packages for them to use, and the negotiation of mutually suitable arrangements, can be a time-consuming (but profitable) exercise for the sales department.

Suppliers of goods and services to the property

For this segment, personal contact is best.

Media

This segment is usually the province of the public relations department, depending on how the property has structured its marketing division. Personal contact and mailing is used to establish good rapport with each medium.

Individual business and holiday travellers

Because they are usually unknown to the property until they become customers, advertising is the only way to reach these segments. Then direct email and mail, with special offers, are used to stimulate return business.

Products to be sold

Communication and promotion is a multidirectional effort requiring constant contact with existing and potential customers to convey the benefits of a property's products. These include its function and convention facilities, accommodation, business facilities, meeting and conference rooms, dining and restaurant facilities, sporting amenities, holiday packages, and special deals.

A large property usually divides the selling function into market segments rather than into products. This means that department personnel who concentrate on, say, corporate accounts, can communicate all the products and services applicable to corporate clients and be in a position to respond to any type of enquiry from those clients. Corporate customers who use accommodation one day might hire a conference room on another day, be diners the next, organise a convention on another day, and be holidaymakers in a few months' time.

Such a division of tasks (by market segmentation) is more successful than a division of tasks by products (with each person making his or her own contacts). The latter arrangement is unsatisfactory because it involves duplication and inefficiency, and can cause confusion for both the establishment and the client. However, dividing the tasks by market segmentation does require coordination of the dissemination of brochure material and electronic messages with product line managers, and small properties often do not have the luxury of a sales team to whom they can allocate market segments and coordination tasks. In these smaller establishments, product line managers might have to take sales responsibility for their product lines.

Measuring feedback

Tactics are a major expense item, and therefore must be result-orientated and measurable. The money allocated to each message-delivery system, and to the overall information mix, has to be budgeted to meet forecasts of sales. For example, the tactical mix for telling existing customers about a special one-off rate offer might involve only some calls on large corporate customers, and letters to all other regular clients. In contrast, a major initiative affecting all levels in the customer mix would involve most of the tactics and be expensive.

After a tactical campaign has been running for a while, the communication effects must be analysed to measure their impact on the target markets. The objective is to find out the level of message awareness and message comprehension, how many reacted favourably and unfavourably to the message, how many intend to purchase, and how many did purchase.

Some of the areas to be analysed could include:

◆ the promotion objective;
◆ the targeted customer mix;
◆ buying behaviour and patterns of purchase;
◆ the product mix; and
◆ budgets based on forecasts of sales and profit.

Each of these is considered below.

The promotion objective

What does the promotion have to achieve? In the case study of 'Randall's city cocktail bar' (page 283), the aim was to create awareness of the bar, and selected people (target markets) were targeted as potential patrons. In this case, a minimal budget was needed and not all tactics were employed. If the whole property had to be promoted to form an umbrella positioning for the sale of all of its products, the budget would have to be large, and most tactics utilised.

The targeted customer mix

The target markets and the sales objectives for the property or for individual products determine budgets and message-delivery systems. Was the targeted mix successful?

Buying behaviour and patterns of purchase

Each market has its own ideas about the type and style of establishment it prefers. Understanding the differences in market behaviour and choosing the right benefits to present to each market is critical in the formation of promotion messages. It is important to use a message-delivery system that suits the pattern of purchase of each market. Evaluation of the budget and the message-delivery systems to use becomes a question of numbers. How many people were attracted by a specific occasion or situation, what was the likely sales return, and how much was spent to promote it?

The product mix

Which products need to be promoted more? A restaurant might have only two products—its main dining area and a function room. A large hotel or resort has many products. Advertising a smorgasbord of products usually fails to impress anyone in particular because it is general information and many customers do not think the promotion is meant for them. A property can group some of its products and promote them efficiently to selected target markets. Feedback should be sought to assess the success of the product mix.

Budgets based on forecasts of sales and profit

All promotions should be considered for their ability to produce sales and profit from an investment. A restaurant advertising campaign which costs $10 000 and which produces only ten more customers is obviously a failure in cost/benefit terms. An establishment therefore needs to assess sales increases recorded after the marketing campaign.

CASE STUDY

Randall's city cocktail bar

Randall's had a sustainable competitive advantage, and the promotion strategy was a tactical mix aimed at delivering the message to specific target markets. These included:

- a range of senior executives, corporate clients, and important people who were, or had been, their clients;
- a number of 'society people' and 'social climbers', many of whom had never been their clients; and
- interstate and overseas visitors.

Randall's was not for everyone. Cocktail bars never are. The customer mix had to be selective.

The tactical mix was:

- publicity in the fashion pages of the daily press;
- telephone calls with invitations to existing and past clients;
- telephone calls with invitations to potential clients known to the sales staff;
- a general information colour leaflet to travel agents, airlines, and their sister hotels in the chain; and
- a special mailing with a personalised invitation to a list of well-known society people.

There was no general media advertising

The invitations asked people to attend the opening of the bar over several nights. Randall's management hoped that those who responded to the invitations would pass the word on to others. The publicity and the brochures were more long term. Their job was to create awareness and arouse interest.

The response to the invitations was good, and the bar was packed on the opening nights. After the opening, there were two slower weeks. However, the word had gone out that Randall's was fun, and business settled to a steady and satisfactory level. The promotional mix had proved to be a success.

Distribution: selling by intermediaries

Both inreach and outreach functions can be handled by intermediaries (such as travel agents and tour wholesalers) and through cooperative deals with associated businesses in the industry. However, the changing marketplace brought about by the spread of Internet and Intranet selling means that small-to-medium

Figure 22.1 A large amount of information can be quickly and effectively conveyed through a website with attractive graphics and links.

Thanks to INDULA Safaris and Tours

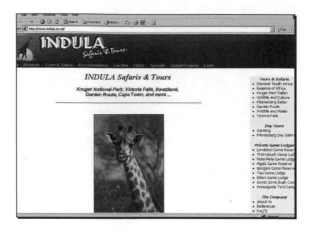

properties can now also take reservations and queries directly from customers. Web marketing is now part of the marketing strategy, but it does not exclude other sources of business, such as intermediaries.

Travel agents can be businesses in their own right, or can be departments of other operations. Banks, building societies, airlines, train and bus companies, department stores, and so on all have travel departments that capitalise on the lucrative business of securing travel and accommodation bookings for a commission. Non-competitive hotel chains in many instances will also take bookings for a commission.

Tour wholesalers who put together holiday and travel packages (and include accommodation as part of the package) are an important source of business for an hotel. Cooperative deals involve organisations which, in the process of selling entertainment, conventions, sporting events, and various festivals, will do a deal with an hotel to have a travel and accommodation component included in their arrangements.

All large establishments depend on intermediaries. The disadvantages are:

◆ margins have to be allowed and, in some 'deals', the profit is minimal;
◆ sometimes there are advertising subsidies involved;
◆ a huge amount of expensive literature is required;
◆ often the representation by intermediaries is poor and can even be misleading;
◆ intermediaries have to be constantly 'sold' on the product and serviced with information and inspiration; and
◆ the control of the selling process is passed over to the intermediary.

Questions for discussion or revision

1 Which tactical mix would you recommend for communicating with customers in the event of a complete reorganisation of the décor and menu for the dining-room of an hotel?

2 Which tactical mix would you recommend for communicating with customers in the event of the provision of four more 'presidential' suites in an hotel?

3 The hotel you work for has built a casino attached to the main building. How would you handle the selling of this new facility?

4 Sales from travel agents have been falling slowly over a period of six months. Some agents claim that many customers regard the service as 'not being as good as it used to be'. What steps would you take to change this attitude?

Chapter 23

Inreach and Outreach Sales Tactics

========= Aims of this chapter =========

The aims of this chapter are:
- to outline the procedures to use when guests make their first contact;
- to discuss how to handle enquiries; and
- to describe how to turn contacts into clients.

Theory

An enquiry at the front desk or by telephone is 'the moment of truth' for the customer and the property. Here is a person seeking assistance from the establishment—whether it be seeking a place to sleep, a place to eat, entertainment, or a site for a banquet, conference, or seminar. Whatever the request, what happens next is critical. There are three keys to successful telephone selling, and one author calls them the 'three jewels'—energy, enthusiasm, and passion.[1]

Customers come in all shapes and sizes, are derived from many countries, have different nationalities, speak different languages, have contrasting backgrounds, and come with little or plenty of money. And they all have varying needs. Will these people be 'processed' as one of many to be 'dealt with', or will they be welcomed as individuals? Will they be judged by their appearance, pejoratively labelled in a particular way, and relegated to anonymity, or will they be treated with respect, concern, and genuine interest? Will they telephone and wait while they listen to the telephone ringing interminably and remaining unanswered, or will their call be answered promptly? When the phone is answered, will they be told to 'hold' for another five or ten minutes, or will they be treated promptly with respect and courtesy? If they come to the reception point, will they wait and watch with growing irritation as other people query, complain, enquire, and chatter until it becomes their turn, or will they be dealt with quickly and efficiently?

How they are treated is a measure of the property's 'inreach' selling techniques. How they are treated will have a significant effect in determining the future of the property and its ultimate success.

There are two critical factors in the management of inreach selling:

◆ having people in sales reception who have the ability and product knowledge to handle enquiries, to assist people, and to make sales; and
◆ having a service strategy and operating procedures to ensure that salespeople have the support of all departments in serving customers effectively.

Every prospect who makes an enquiry—by phone, by mail, or in person—has opened the dialogue. This might be a result of outreach selling or influence from a third party. Invariably, the person making the enquiry is 'half sold', and this person is really seeking reassurance (or a little more information) before making a final decision to purchase.

For some reason, many properties regard telephone reception as a separate procedure from other aspects of marketing—a department tucked away in another room and operating in isolation with a different set of standards. The receptionists are told that their job is to sell, but they are not integrated into the overall marketing strategy of the establishment.

Five principles of front-of-house management

Anyone on the reception desk who calls out 'Next please!' to waiting guests should be frog-marched out of the foyer! Does the host of a party greet the guests with 'Next please!' at the door?

The principles of inreach selling are as follows:

◆ appoint the right staff;
◆ have a measurable set of procedures;
◆ have effective operational procedures in place;
◆ establish effective follow-through procedures; and
◆ maintain contact with the customer.

Each of these is considered below.

Appoint the right staff

Staff members appointed to guest reception positions should be people who like and respond well to people. They should be the epitome of charm, grace, and good manners—efficient, intelligent, patient, knowledgeable, multilingual (if possible), well groomed, and well presented. For the prospective patrons, these people *are* the property and everything it stands for.

Have a measurable set of procedures

Have a measurable set of procedures for the sales staff to follow. Their performance must be monitored and measurable.

Have effective operational procedures in place

Make sure there is immediate implementation of any action affecting the likelihood of a customer or prospect concluding a sale. Operational procedures need to be in place to support the salesperson with a minimum of delay.

Establish effective follow-through procedures

Establish follow-through procedures that constitute, in effect, a traffic-flow system which monitors every action by the property to ensure that it provides the best outcome for the customers. This means logging the enquiry into the system for other salespeople to take the enquiry through the various stages.

Maintain contact with the customer after the sale is made

Maintain contact with the customer after the sale is made. Once a service is provided, a customer exists, and that customer can be nurtured into a long-term friendship with the establishment. Otherwise, the customer will become just another entry in the filing cabinet under 'past sales'.

Management styles

Various hospitality establishments have different approaches to front-of-house procedures. In its management style, each establishment places a different emphasis on various aspects of management, and this emphasis dictates its attitude to customers and, in turn, the perceptions of the establishment by the customers.

Management styles can be considered as follows.

Sectionalised

This style involves sectionalised front desk, sales, marketing, advertising, publicity, and promotions functions, and these perform separately. However, customers can come from a variety of sources and no one, except perhaps the general manager, is actually in charge of the smooth transfer of information about a customer from one section to another to ensure that what happens to the customer is coordinated.

Product-orientated

This style involves each product being a profit centre. All enquiries are sought by, and steered towards, the separate managers in charge of each product. If the enquiry is about a banquet it goes to the banqueting manager. If the enquiry is about a restaurant booking, it is transferred there.

Market-orientated

This style involves different markets—businesspeople, group bookings, conventions, functions, and so on—being handled separately by different departments.

All of the above management styles have inbuilt problems that need to be recognised, but the market-orientated style has certain advantages. See the case study 'Who looks after Jane?' (page 290).

It must be remembered that an hotel client can be a businessperson one day, a family on holiday another time, a convention organiser on another occasion and, eventually, a wealthy, retired visitor. The value of loyal, regular clients and their pass-on recommendations cannot be overestimated.

The 'departmentalising' of many establishments makes continuing contact and after-sales service difficult. At best, customers go into a databank and receive emails or letters or phone calls once in a while. The salesperson is in the best position to maintain the client relationship and to recommend other products to the client. If someone else does this, the client perceives the exercise as pressure selling; but if the person who helped them in the first place does it, the client perceives it as ongoing good advice.

'Whatever it takes'

A standard operating procedure is important. The steps that make up this procedure are not just 'nice things' that should happen if everything goes right, or when the place is not too busy. They should constitute a standard operating procedure for handling customers at any reception point.

However, although there should be a standard operating procedure, there are always exceptions from the rule. Management should allow staff members to exercise discretion, and have sufficient confidence in their ability to depart from procedures and do 'whatever it takes' to satisfy the customer. See the case study on 'Whatever it takes' (page 291).

CASE STUDY

Who looks after Jane?

Jane Baker is the head of the (fictitious) Harbours Board, and she wants to have a conference at your hotel as a result of an advertisement. After her initial enquiry she is put through to the property's conference organiser. She has several conversations and an inspection of the property, and decides to proceed. A sale now exists.

Who tells the front desk, sales, marketing, advertising, and publicity departments? In some properties, these various departments will not know that Jane Baker exists. Eventually the word gets around the establishment that the Harbours Board is holding a function in Conference Room B4. But who, in the other departments, actually knows Jane Baker? After the conference, who talks to Jane Baker about the possibility of trying some of the other products that the property can offer? The probable answer is that no one does.

For efficiency, a 'traffic department' is required. Someone has to recognise Jane Baker as a customer who can be developed into a friendly client whose business could be worth tens of thousands of dollars to the property. This takes into account the business that she can generate herself, as well as the business that she could generate by word-of-mouth recommendation.

The best (but seldom used) style is marketing orientated. Under this arrangement, outreach and inreach marketing are coordinated under the marketing manager, and salespeople handle all clients as account customers and maintain contact from beginning to end.

Jane Baker is a person, not merely 'the lady from the Harbours Board'. Through the salesperson, a personal bond with Jane Baker is established.

Inreach sales procedures

Staff members should be provided with clear guidelines for successful inreach sales procedures. Here are some suggestions.

- If the initial contact is in person at a reception point, greet the customer immediately, and make eye contact. If busy, acknowledge the customer, indicate interest, and say: 'Be with you as soon as I can, sir'.
- If the initial contact is by telephone, answer within three rings, and do not use 'hold'. Answer and ask the person to wait, or offer to ring back.

CASE STUDY

'Whatever it takes'

A porter of a New York hotel noticed that a customer, Mr Schuster, had left his briefcase behind at the desk. He had just put Mr Schuster into a taxi for the La Guardia Airport so it was apparently too late to catch him. But the porter had been given freedom to depart from procedures if necessary to keep a satisfied customer.

The porter grabbed the briefcase, hailed a taxi, and followed Mr Schuster to the airport. He arrived just as the Chicago plane left. The porter considered the situation for a moment, shrugged his shoulders, checked with his hotel to find out which hotel Mr Schuster would be staying at in Chicago—and then followed on the next flight! Two hours later, as the amazed Mr Schuster was booking into his Chicago hotel, the New York porter arrived and handed him his briefcase.

'You left this behind, sir,' said the porter.

He then turned and left, leaving Mr Schuster with the impression that it was the type of service the New York hotel always provided!

When the porter returned to New York he wondered if he would still have a job. The story goes that he kept his job—and was thanked, congratulated, and promoted to duty manager. Today, so the story goes, that same porter is manager of a six-star hotel!

(Holding with recorded music and taped sales messages is considered a 'put off' by most people.)

◆ During frantic moments of business remain calm. There should always be a back-up for unexpectedly busy periods.

◆ Make the first contact count. Give the customer undivided attention. Never act uninterested or bored. Show that you consider the person to be special.

◆ Get the person's name, and get it right. Put it down on paper. Get a contact address or phone number. Pass the customer's name on to colleagues who become involved. (From now on, the customer should be addressed only by name.)

◆ Listen carefully to the person. Do not try to handle two customers at once. Treat every person as an individual. Treat every person with respect and friendliness. Do not have standard answers. Treat each person as a unique individual and each situation as a new event. Concentrate on key points. Demonstrate efficiency. Make sure you understand exactly what the person wants.

◆ Have pride in your role. To the person standing in front of you, you are the hotel's representative. Accept the responsibility with pride, interest, and enthusiasm. Your role is essentially that of a salesperson, but you also act as an adviser and problem-solver.

◆ You are the liaison with other sections. Smooth the transitions. Hand over your valued customer to the next person with care to ensure a seamless transition. Always leave an opening to make contact again. Never 'close the door'. Assume that you will be seeing the person many times in the future. Ensure that you leave the person on good terms. Make your last contact count. The last impression is just as important as the first.

◆ Do not criticise other people—including your colleagues, the competition, other guests, or other people seeking your attention. Never blame others for any mistakes you or they make. Indeed, do the opposite and take responsibility for the errors of others. Remember, you 'are' the hotel. Never ridicule the opposition; rather, convey the impression that they are professional colleagues, not enemies. Do not argue with difficult customers. When you have a rude customer, seek the help of someone in higher authority and let the disagreement happen away from other customers.

◆ Remember that the job is to sell by solving problems and answering enquiries. Understand the customer's needs. Provide factual information. Never lie. Present benefits, and support the benefits with facts. Create awareness, create interest, create desire, provide conviction, cause action. Always seek a decision. Try to close the sale. Always try to 'upsell', but remember that the customer's interests and the hotel's objectives must coincide. The best deal is the one that makes both parties happy.

◆ Use common sense. If you find yourself in a situation that is not in the manual, take the initiative or check with your superior. Try to avoid acting out a service ritual and doing everything 'by the book'. Rules do exist (to make procedures work efficiently), but if the rules get in the way of solving a customer's problem, bend the rules if necessary.

◆ Assess the result of the enquiry as the conversation comes to a conclusion. Let the customer know that the establishment appreciates the enquiry even if the person did not make a purchase. If an order is placed, thank the person for his or her business. Be genuine in these responses. Always remember that if the person was not there, you would not have a job. Check to make sure that all the things that were supposed to happen for the customer did happen.

Seven deadly sins of sales and service

As well as providing guidelines for successful inreach sales procedures, advise staff of 'the seven deadly sins of sales and service'. These are:

◆ apathy—insensibility, indifference, laziness, indolence;
◆ condescension—racism, sexism, being patronising to small or poorer clients;
◆ the 'brush-off'—not having time; not being bothered; not considering someone to be important enough;
◆ coldness—being aloof, superior, unfriendly;
◆ being robotic—going through the motions; it is only a job;
◆ giving the person the 'run around'—someone else can do it; it is someone else's problem; it is not my department; you will have to speak to someone else; and so on;
◆ being bound by the rule book—we cannot do that; it is not our policy; we are not allowed to do that; we do not accept that; and so on.

The seven deadly sins infect many places and their evil can spread. The hospitality business is service. The people who understand service succeed in the hospitality business, and enjoy what they do. The seven deadly sins are the real 'competition' for every hospitality property. They represent a very nasty enemy. The hotel or restaurant down the street is a much less significant threat.

A good manager of a property needs people who believe in what they do— people who are always thinking about how they can give the customer a good time. 'Selling' is a bad term. Guests resist people who sell. But guests enjoy friendly interest, enthusiasm, and genuine service.

Theory of outreach sales tactics

Outreach selling has one initial purpose—to open the door for a prospective customer to step through so that he or she can experience the property and become a client.

Once the client has tried one of the property's facilities—provided that the experience is enjoyable and represents value for money—the selling approach enters another dimension. From then on, it is no longer a 'cold' call. Rather, it is a follow-up to the beginning of an established relationship whereby the client is entreated to repeat the experience or to try other products offered by the property.

Outreach selling faces a daunting task if the property fails to live up to expectations. Selling cannot replace the interest and excitement of a well-organised property that treats its customers as welcome guests.

The tourist industry sells dreams and images—of journeys to faraway places and enticing scenery, of service, fun, relaxation, sport, sex, excitement, and escape. But hard-nosed executives want speed, efficiency, and convenience first. Nevertheless, the 'extras' usually make the difference when they choose an establishment.

All prospects are interested in only one thing. What is in it for them? To open the door therefore requires an enticing offer—an irresistible appeal that will cause the prospects to take the first step over the property's threshold. A general presentation that merely outlines a string of the property's attributes is as boring as it sounds. Finding the benefit that will appeal most to a prospect is the skill required for successful selling.

Some properties try to get prospective clients to join a 'club' that has benefits for members—such as free introductory meals, a night's accommodation, or an interesting speaker. There are many ways of creating an offer that will break the ice with the prospective customer.

Most big hospitality establishments employ sales representatives to handle large account customers—such as companies, professional groups, government departments, sporting bodies, institutions, and so on. In addition, salespeople are required to liaise with travel agents, airlines, buslines, tourist bureaux, convention bureaux, tour wholesalers, and organisations connected with the tourism and hospitality industry likely to produce business. In all cases, 'the deal' is usually the justification for the guest to purchase. In such a 'deal', the add-on benefits count most. Usually the salesperson has to 'give to get'.

Role of sales representatives

Salespeople involved in outreach selling can be called 'marketing executives', 'account executives', and even 'public relations executives'. The job of these outreach sellers is to persuade prospects or existing clients to use the establishment's services, rather than those of rival establishments. The way in which sales staff go about this task varies, depending on the buying readiness of the contact. The most common tasks of sales representatives are:

◆ 'cold call'—to initiate new business;
◆ follow-up to a lead;
◆ regular customer contact;
◆ to tender for a conference or seminar; and
◆ trouble-shooting.

To be effective in their work, sales representatives need:

- company knowledge—they must have a full understanding of the establishment's objectives, strategies, and policies;
- product knowledge—they cannot sell if they do not know what they are talking about;
- market and industry knowledge—they must understand the tourism and hospitality business; and
- knowledge of the competition and its activities—so that they can respond to property and product comparisons.

An ideal salesperson needs to be able to plan, to 'prospect', to manage time, to speak fluently, and to keep basic books. Such a person must be attentive to detail, likeable, confident, persistent, and have people skills.

Selling process

A sales plan follows the same principles as a marketing plan. It requires:

- an analysis of the market;
- an identification of opportunities;
- the setting of sales objectives;
- a series of strategies for winning the maximum number of clients; and
- detailed tactics that will achieve the strategies.

There are various ways of getting to a prospective client. The salesperson might write, fax, or email, inviting the prospect to call for more information. Alternatively, the salesperson might speak directly to the prospect, giving a reason for calling him or her. However it is achieved, this is called a 'cold call', and is usually the most difficult part of selling. The planning procedures for making a 'cold call' are:

- target marketing—start with 'prospecting' and choose those organisations suspected of having a need;
- research—make initial enquiries and narrow suspects into prospects; find out who has the authority to decide and who influences these decision-makers;
- market analysis—find out as much as you can about the organisation and the contact; establish which opposition establishments the prospects have used in the past, and in what circumstances;
- strategies—develop your offer;
- contact—write, fax, or email beforehand, or make a telephone call (as described above).

The target markets for hospitality are reasonably obvious—business and professional people, and government departments of all descriptions. The larger companies are easy to identify and they make the best targets. The problem is that everyone else thinks so too, and competition is therefore tough.

If your property has been established for a while it probably has a sales history consisting of several successes and a litany of dashed opportunities. Many of the target companies will have tried your place, but will have remained loyal to other properties. Some might have had bad experiences and be currently hostile. Some will have had good experiences and be regular users of your property.

The task for the sales department is a continuing one. It involves:

◆ developing the present users and selling them more products;
◆ converting users of another property to become users of your own;
◆ attempting to turn uncommitted occasional prospects into regular clients; and
◆ trying to bring back the hostile ones.

It is vital to have an attractive offer that will get the attention of the prospect. But good sales strategies involve more than this. Good sales strategies consider the best outcomes for the clients. Good sales strategies aim to solve problems for the clients. Sales is sometimes a maligned occupation. Many people fear that salespeople will make them do what they we do not want to do. They feel threatened by salespeople. The way for the seller to overcome this natural worry is by the seller being a problem-solver, rather than a product-seller. An effective salesperson must be consumer-orientated, rather than product-orientated. The best selling strategies are those that provide the best outcomes for the clients.

To achieve this consumer-orientated idea of selling, the following are required:

◆ matching products and services with the client's expectations;
◆ calling frequently to demonstrate the property's advantages to clients;
◆ possessing strong personal credibility; and
◆ inducing the clients to experience the property by making value-for-money offers.

There are several problem areas that affect a new client's choice of establishment. Feeling strange in a new environment is the most common. Most people like to be in familiar surroundings, and this is why they go back to the same place repeatedly—even though they might complain about things from time to time.

A property is selling an experience—a bundle of benefits that add up to customer satisfaction. How can you sell satisfaction in advance of the customer getting it? Referrals from other satisfied customers are merely *persuasive*, but giving away some services is *convincing*. It overcomes fears of making a bad decision.

Conferences, seminars, and meetings are wonderful opportunities for collecting a large number of people together at one time and making a big impression of the property's benefits. But many properties miss this opportunity. Having secured the conference for a special 'no-frills' price, they treat the attenders like 'no-frills' citizens. This is not very clever, and is definitely not the way to make friends and influence prospective customers.

A conference is a nightmare for the organisers. Their great fear is that something will go wrong. Here is an ideal opportunity to win a customer for repeat business, and simultaneously make a big impression on the delegates—who might well be planning a conference of their own in the future. A smart operator therefore goes 'all out' to make sure that nothing goes wrong from beginning to end—irrespective of the price that was paid for the occasion. This means covering every detail and contingency, including little things such as having spare globes available for the overhead projector, ensuring that coffee arrives just when it is needed, deferring to every guest's requests, triple-checking the sound system, and keeping outside noise to a minimum. In other words, management must think ahead all the time on behalf of the organisers and the attenders.

A miserly approach to hospitality makes everyone miserable. It is the antithesis of the generous style of operation that attracts and keeps customers. The bottom line is not the final balance in a ledger. The bottom line is the size of the customer base, and the potential customer base. Of course, management must be aware of costs. Staff salaries cost approximately 40–50% of outgoings for some large properties, and food & beverage costs amount to approximately 12–15% of outgoings. However, financial controls on such matters should be kept in the office, out of sight and well away from the customers' eyes. If the budget has to be trimmed, it has to be anywhere except in areas that directly affect the customers' experiences. Otherwise the sales staff will have to sell in a climate of 'making a dollar at every opportunity'—in which case sales staff will be fighting a losing battle as they lose unhappy and disillusioned customers.

Sales presentation

There are various ways of setting up an initial appointment. Breaking the ice is the first part of the sales approach, and there are several ways of doing this. For example:

◆ an introduction approach—'You don't know me, but . . . ';
◆ a letter in advance approach—'The letter that I sent contained a . . . ';
◆ a referral approach—'Jack Smith suggested that I call you . . . ';
◆ a question approach—'Are you planning to go to . . . ?';

- a benefit approach—'We've cut the cost of . . . ';
- a new product approach—'We have just added on a . . . '; or
- a free gift or sample approach—'We thought you might like to be our guest for dinner . . . '.

The best approach is the referral approach—if it can be arranged. This is the basis of 'networking'—that is, moving from one contact to the next by using the previous contact as a 'lead-in'.

Having made the appointment, the sales presentation is a series of steps. These are not in any special order—everyone has his or her own style. But the essentials of the sales presentation are:

- involve the client—talk in terms of his or her interests; keep the initial statements short and simple; do not use superior jargon;
- explain the features and sell the benefits—but listen to the customer and find out what he or she really wants; ask questions; probe; suggest; advise; listen;
- keep emphasising the benefits, and support what is said by demonstration—show pictures, slides, films, videotapes; talk about satisfied customers;
- watch for verbal clues and body language for signs of conviction—go back and explain if there is any misunderstanding;
- summarise the main points;
- give the prospect a chance to buy; ask for the order.

There might be objections from the client. But objections should not be seen as being entirely negative—they often demonstrate interest, and they present an opportunity for the salesperson to establish conviction in the mind of the prospect. The techniques for handling objections are as follows.

- Listen to the objection. Sometimes it is a real difficulty that the prospect has identified with some aspect of the property or product, and the salesperson might recognise the identification of a genuine problem. If so, take the objection seriously, and attempt to reply with a fact or feature that really overcomes the difficulty. Sometimes the real difficulty might not be apparent to the salesperson. If so, the salesperson should ask: 'What makes you say that?'. This might reveal the real reason for the objection.
- Avoid arguing. Even if you win the argument, you will lose the sale. No one likes to be proven wrong, and the prospect has the last say! Instead of counter-attacking, say: 'I can understand your concern, but I think you will find that . . . '.
- Defer an objection. A good formula of words is: 'Can I come back to that?'. Often, the objection will be forgotten. If it is not forgotten, at least you have time to consider your reply.

- Sweep aside the objection. This is a more dangerous strategy, but it sometimes works by distracting the prospective customer. 'Oh that's not a big problem between us. Let me show you this . . . ', and present more features and benefits.
- Present additional information to counter the objection. 'Of course, I haven't told you about this yet, but . . . '.

Good salespeople plan for objections and anticipate them. An objection should seldom come as a surprise. Indeed, some salespeople deliberately raise objection themselves, and use them as a way of getting across a benefit: 'I guess you are concerned about such-and-such? Well, that's not a problem, because . . . '.

Closing the sale is the objective of the sales presentation. And yet there are salespeople who are frightened to ask for the order in case the prospect refuses. But if a prospect does refuse to place an order, this simply means that he or she has not yet been convinced. The salesperson can treat this as an objection (see above on 'objections') and endeavour to find out why the client remains unconvinced. The word 'no' does not necessarily mean that the prospect has a taken a final position of disapproval of the salesperson or the property.

Some proven closing techniques are:

- a simple, direct closure—'Can we have your OK?';
- a recapitulation of the main benefits followed by a simple direct closure;
- an assumptive closure—'If you wouldn't mind just signing here . . . ';
- a 'benefit-in-reserve' closure—'What I haven't mentioned is this . . . Can I have your OK now?';
- a 'dual-choice' closure—'There is this one or that one. Which one would you like?';
- a 'last-chance' closure—'I don't know if one is left, but if there is, would you like it?';
- a 'balance-sheet' closure—'If we add up the positives and the negatives, it is clear that . . . ';
- a 'trial-order closure—'Take one to begin with, and if you like it order the rest';
- an 'impending-event' closure—'The price goes up next month. If you say "yes" now . . . '.

The presentation should not be without selling aids and sales support. Outreach requires selling support, especially if the prospect has never seen the facilities. Videotapes, colour pictures, brochures, and advertising are mandatory.

The outreach functions of selling, advertising, publicity, sales promotions, brochures, travel agents, and other staff members are not separate functions. They must be coordinated activities. In selling, no one should ever feel alone.

For a very large sale, other people might need to be personally involved. For example, it might be necessary to bring the food & beverage manager into discussions with a prospective client before the sale is made.

The closing of the sale is not the end of the affair. A sale should not be perceived as having a beginning and an end. It is the foundation for a continuing relationship with mutual advantages. It is therefore important to follow-through and provide constant contact—reinforcement of the relationship is vital. Building a customer base is the 'name of the game'.

Because selling is a coordinated activity, and because the client will come in contact with a variety of facilities and staff, *everyone* should be encouraged to contribute to the selling effort. When every person—from the potato-peeler to the chief executive—realises that he or she is contributing to the selling effort, the property becomes a customer-driven organisation and success is likely.

One last word of advice—do not 'oversell'. There is a tendency for many salespeople to be carried away with their own enthusiasm and make promises that are difficult to fulfil. This might even extend to 'protecting' the prospective customer from the truth—that is, in effect, to tell lies to the client. This is a highly dangerous and short-term approach and must never be contemplated.

Overstating the case with adjectives is understandable. 'We'll give you the time of your life' might be something of an exaggeration, but it is not reprehensible in the course of a sales presentation. However, when the offer is being made and the deal is being formalised, the delivery of products and services must be absolutely precise and leave no room for argument or error. In selling, the absolute truth is the only sensible course of action to pursue.

Questions for discussion or revision

1 Imagine that you have made a successful contact with a corporate prospect who has exhibited a strong interest in opening an account for the company's business users. However, the person is hesitating. How would you go about securing the business and close the sale?

2 Let us assume that you have been told by a friend that a wealthy football team is unhappy about its accommodation arrangements for an end-of-season holiday. The team has used the same place each year for a long time. What are some of the means you would use to make contact, and how would you plan your presentation?

3 While talking to a good prospect for a corporate account, you are informed that the person takes exception to the hotel's rack rates. How would you handle the situation and secure the business without giving too much away?

Chapter 24

Advertising Strategies

The aims of this chapter are:
- to explain how advertising strategies are used;
- to explain how to create awareness of a property and its products; and
- to explain how to convey messages that create a competitive position.

Theory

Advertising is one of the main message-delivery systems used in promotion. Advertising is not merely paid space or time in the mass media. Advertising includes signs, brochures, leaflets, and cards. Advertising also includes 'signature' items that feature the name of the property—such as an array of sold merchandise or giveaways, and towels, linen, crockery, and glassware. In short, advertising is any opportunity to communicate the name of the property, or a message about it.

Advertising can be general or specific. It can send a message about the whole complex or concentrate on individual products. There are four broad classifications of advertising:

- reach advertising;
- teach advertising;
- preach advertising; and
- reminder advertising.

Each of these is considered below.

Reach advertising

Reach advertising involves selling a promotion or product when the objective is immediate results, and advertising is the main tactic to achieve that objective. Examples include an announcement about a special restaurant price offer or an announcement about a cut-price weekend accommodation rate. In these cases, the advertising is expected to generate enquiries from interested customers. Reach advertising is 'retail' in its approach, and a price offer is usually an essential component of the message. It can achieve its aim through paid media, through brochures mailed or delivered in person to prospects, or through a simple 'tent card' or leaflet on a dining-room table. Reach advertising of this sort can also be a sandwich board at the front of the property, a sign in a window, a voice over a public address system, or a recorded phone message for callers who are waiting on hold.

Teach advertising

Teach advertising involves telling a specific segment of the market about the benefits of the place or one of its products, with medium-term results being the objective. Advertising in this instance might be a support role in a phone canvass for various establishment initiatives—for example, special 'club' memberships, a new holiday package, or the opening of a new facility. Price is seldom mentioned because teach advertising is not meant to make offers. Rather, it assists in securing the final sale.

Preach advertising

Preach advertising is meant to achieve a position in the market for the property. It therefore makes general statements about the attractions of a place. Such advertising creates an image (or ambience) about a property such that awareness is heightened—especially in the case of a new property. Preach advertising can also be used to reposition a property that has undergone considerable refurbishing. Alternatively, it can remind would-be customers by restating the key benefits of a property (which many might have overlooked). The intention of preach advertising (sometimes dubbed 'corporate' advertising by the advertising industry) is to present the establishment in an appealing way by positioning it as offering better value than the opposition. For existing customers it reaffirms their opinion that they are making the right choice in continuing to use the establishment. For new customers, it sets the scene for the general position of the property.

Reminder advertising

Reminder advertising is simply keeping the name of the property foremost in people's minds so that it will be remembered when an occasion arises for the use of one of its facilities. Reminder advertising is similar to preach advertising except that reminder advertising is passive—mostly achieving the objective of maintaining awareness by the use of corporate advertising, signs, giveaways, and signature items.

Shortcomings of advertising

Services are easily duplicated. Customers cannot always draw clear conclusions about competing offerings so advertising fills the breach by conveying the messages about differences, advantages, and benefits. However, it is not a panacea for poor marketing in other areas of the marketing mix, especially product strategies. Wild claims are not convincing. Tangible evidence, cleverly communicated, is more likely to attract attention.

Too much is usually expected of advertising. It is simply public communication. It cannot make a sale on its own. It can only generate an enquiry. Someone still has to close the sale physically. Advertising will not work if the message is wrong, if the product is wrong, or if there are no people in the market who want what the advertising is offering.

A major shortcoming of advertising is its limited ability to communicate with the main business markets—the largest users of hospitality. By the nature of their occupations, business and professional people are light watchers of television, indifferent radio listeners, scanners of newspapers, and readers of only certain magazines (those of particular interest to them). To make matters worse for those attempting to communicate a message, there is a plethora of communications aimed at businesspeople through every medium, especially direct mail. Businesspeople are already 'submerged' in information. Consequently, they have to be very selective in choosing which messages they wish to note. Unless the communication has immediate relevance and an immediate benefit, it is likely to be ignored.

The other major difficulty for advertisers is the high cost of advertising—not only the cost of buying the space or the time, but also the cost of preparing the communication. Colour photography, type, copywriting, finished art, and colour separation work (used in print magazines and brochures) is a very expensive process. Even more expensive is the filming or videotaping of television commercials—with the cost of actors, sound effects, music, graphics, and editing running to very high amounts indeed.

With so much advertising bombarding the population, the majority of people switch off mentally and do not notice the advertising unless it obviously applies to them. 'Cut-through' is a term used to describe getting through the clutter of messages, and being noticed and understood. Most marketers attempt to achieve 'cut-through' by clever advertising or by volume advertising. The problem with creativity is that it can be so obsessed with achieving 'cut-through' that it can lead to a very expensive production that, in effect, sells the advertisement but not the message. Segmentation, careful strategic positioning of the advertising message, and a cleanly executed creative approach are most likely to achieve 'cut-through'.

Too many hospitality advertisements are 'me-toos'. They look the same as everyone else's advertisements. They end up selling travel, holidays, and luxury accommodation *in general*, but fail to sell one place *in particular*.

Who does the advertising?

Most large properties use the services of an advertising agency, some leave it to the medium to prepare the advertisement (based on a brief and a rough outline of what is required by the property), and others do it themselves.

Clearly the best way is to employ an advertising agency—because an agency has the expertise and the experience. A good agency also has the discipline to coordinate several advertising thrusts and to maintain consistency of the look and presentation of the client's messages. However, few smaller properties can afford to have their own advertising specialists for the creation of advertising. Those that allow the media to do the work usually get the worst advertisements because the various advertising media seldom employ people with specialist expertise in the field. For most media, designing advertisements is an add-on facility provided at the cheapest price, or even for free.

For a large property with many products to promote, advertising has to be coordinated by one person whose function is to assess the various requests and needs for advertising so that the promotions of the property are efficient and cost-effective. This can be a specialist position or be part of a sales executive's job specification.

There are three essential elements of advertising:

◆ aiming at the target markets;
◆ competitive positioning; and
◆ establishing the brand personality.

Each of these is considered below.

Aiming at the target markets

As in every aspect of marketing, the people who form the most viable customer-mix groups must be targeted. Aiming the advertising at target markets and selecting media to reach these markets avoids wastage in 'impacts' (the number of people reached by the advertisement). Given the high cost of advertising, this obviously makes sense.

Having specific target groups also gives the advertising direction. It is like writing a letter. If you know to whom you are addressing your message the composition is easier and more telling because you know the person and have a good idea of how he or she will react. If you do not know the person, even beginning the letter presents a problem—'Dear Sir, Ms, Miss, or Madam' you might say—and you are in trouble already!

This is the problem with much advertising—it talks to people who are stereo-types that exist in some creative person's mind, but who are hard to find in the real world. Consequently, the message misses the mark and the tens of thousands of dollars—spent in production costs and buying space or time—are wasted.

Competitive positioning

Chapter 17 (page 223) explains the importance of positioning a property to gain a competitive edge. Much of what was said in that chapter also applies to advertising. With so much hospitality advertising already looking the same, having a clearcut difference in positioning is an added reason for advertising that expresses a difference. This does not mean going mad with a bizarre-looking advertisement, but it does mean using advertising to express a property's personality—referred to by advertising people as the 'brand personality'.

Establishing the brand personality

The advertised positioning of a property has to be consistent and persistent. Therefore, individual promotions that concentrate on products and special package offers must support the basic positioning of the property, even though each of the promotional messages will have separate marketing intentions. For example, advertising for a chain of five-star hotels always maintains a consistent profile and presents the various properties as members of an exclusive group at the top end of the market. This positioning strategy is maintained by every piece of literature and communication item used by their properties.

All advertising communicates best if the message it delivers has an offer and strategically positions the property with a sustainable competitive advantage. This advantage might be a price, a product or service difference that few others have, or an apparent benefit from a special feature of the property. This is why 'the message comes before design'—meaning that the message is more important than how the advertisement looks.

In summary, if the market aimed at by the advertising does not receive the message (that is, if the wrong media are used) or does not understand the message (that is, if the copy is poor), the message itself fails. Therefore, the success of advertising depends on:

◆ knowing who to talk to (the target markets);
◆ knowing what to say (the message);
◆ knowing where to say it (the medium); and
◆ knowing how to say it (the creative approach).

Communication objectives

Communication objectives have to be set for advertising and used as a means of measuring its effectiveness.

Communication objectives might read like the following examples.

◆ 'To increase the awareness of our property among lawyers, accountants, architects, medical practitioners, dentists, and other professional people, and to communicate that our property has a closed-circuit video-conferencing facility which is ideal for training seminars.'
◆ 'To communicate to married couples with children in the middle-to-upper income groups that our property has full-time child-minding facilities to enable them to have a care-free weekend at a very attractive weekend package rate.'

Objectives such as these clearly state what is required from the advertising. By stating objectives in this way, it is possible to measure the cost-efficiency of the advertising, although some forms of advertising can be more accurately assessed than others. Reach advertising (page 302), for example, has a specific aim, and specific sales can be measured and set against advertising costs. Teach advertising (page 302), in contrast, can be assessed only in a general way because it communicates the overall benefits of an establishment. Over a period of time, teach advertising has a cumulative effect and builds an impression of the establishment which at some time leads to an enquiry and then to a sale. It is thus difficult to establish whether the advertising worked or if the enquiry came from a referral. Few people will ever admit that they were 'sold' by advertising.

Segmentation of markets for advertising

Segmentation avoids talking to people as though they all think in the same way, and sends a message to a specific group of people who have been defined as having a need or preference for a product or service.

Some of the primary segments at which advertising is aimed include:

◆ existing patrons of the establishment or its profit-earning products;
◆ travel agents, tourist bureaux, convention and visitor bureaux, and tour wholesalers;
◆ allied business operators—airlines, railways, bus lines, tourist resorts and facilities, and so on;
◆ professional and trade organisations;
◆ suppliers and service providers;
◆ customers of other hotels, motels, clubs, and so on;
◆ business, leisure, entertaining, sporting, and holiday populations; and
◆ prospective customers in specific geographic locations that offer potential for market penetration.

Positioning advertising steps

When preparing an advertising campaign, it is best to assume that the reader or viewer knows nothing. No one can talk back to an advertisement and ask it questions. Therefore the advertisement has to say enough to interest the audience and provide enough information to answer the most pertinent questions without spoiling the communication with an overload of detail.

The factors to consider include the following.

◆ Does the property occupy a geographical and physical place in the minds of people making up the target market? Communicate where it is—on an island, or in the middle of the city, or by the sea, or wherever.
◆ Does the advertising communicate a clearly defined benefit or reason for the establishment's existence? Communicate the existence of the golf course, or ten gourmet restaurants, or four thousand rooms, or fax machines in every room, and so on.
◆ Does the advertising indicate who mainly goes to the place? Communicate that they are business and professional people, or film stars, or sporting identities, or young families, or whatever. Not everyone, please!
◆ What else is special about the place? Communicate what is different in the way of facilities, surroundings, ambience, and features that no one else has.

Value of persistence

Advertising works by attrition and constant repetition. Marketers have to sustain awareness of the message. If they do not, the advertising will soon be forgotten.

Communications should also be consistent. Frequent changes of image present a confusing picture to the market. Some of the best advertising for the hospitality and tourism industries utilises simple imagery to capture people's emotions, but repeated again and again. Some properties present a different aspect of the same message, but always the same message comes through. They achieve positioning through an image that tells the market 'Hey! This is what we are on about. Come and experience it!'. Then they ensure that future advertising is in keeping with the image.

Sales promotion campaigns

Short-term tactical objectives give direction to much of the advertising required for a property. These short-term tactical objectives might be to take advantage of a change in the market, or to offset a competitor's move. Tactics to achieve this might include such matters as a special event, a sales promotion, or a product promotion.

Sales promotions have become a way of life for many establishments. They provide immediate reasons for customers to come and use the facilities. Giving a reason to 'act now' is the best use of the advertising dollar because it is immediately productive. Sales promotions, special offers, rewards for sending a coupon, discounts, early booking reductions, off-peak specials, weekend rates, and so on work best with a jaded public that has become used to the glossy hype associated with the industry. 'What's new?' is the question that has to be answered if advertising is to achieve 'cut-through'.

The large, successful establishments use advertising in a support role for a concentrated sales promotion, and they have the money to involve all the promotion tactics in the mix.

As opposed to image advertising (from which results are almost impossible to assess with certainty), sales promotion advertising is more of a direct investment in future sales, and the results are measurable. This is why sales promotion advertising overcomes many owners' fears of spending a dollar and not seeing a return for it.

Supplementary advertising

The aim is always to make the advertising dollar go further. This can be accomplished in several ways. Some of the options are:

◆ contra-advertising—when a medium commits to use the facilities of an establishment and repays it with an equivalent dollar value of advertising;

◆ cooperative advertising—when the establishment and another company combine their advertising as part of a joint marketing arrangement; the partnership could include a casino, a bank, an airline, a tour wholesaler, a tourism operator, a festival organiser, and so on; and

◆ region or industry advertising—when all the establishments in a geographic area combine to conduct a large campaign to attract a market to the area that will benefit all the participants; tourism authorities can also be involved in these exercises.

Collateral

Collateral (or below-line) advertising consists of brochures, fact sheets, tent cards, signs, posters, and folders. Even a menu can be classified as a collateral advertising item. Collateral advertising is the foundation of most of the advertising effort, and arguably the most effective for the majority of properties.

Small properties can use collateral without resorting to main media advertising and its associated expenses. Some can do this just as well as the larger properties. However, much depends on the quality of the collateral material— not its gloss or cost, but on the distinctive messages, the use of pictures, the clever imagery, and the offers that are relevant to the markets being aimed at.

Some of the simplest and least expensive advertising media are giveaways— such as pens, pads, notebooks, mouse pads, paper hats, diaries, and so on—all of which carry the name and perhaps a simple message about the property's difference, advantage, and benefit (DAB).

There are also 'reminders' featuring the hotel's logo and messages—in the form of take-away menus, brochures, calendars of events, recipes, and signature items (such as ash trays, coasters, spoons, glasses, towels, soaps, and toiletries).

Some places sell novelties that pay for themselves—such as postcards, maps, gifts, toys, and tour guides. These usually feature the hotel's logo, and are often sold through the property's shops and other outlets. These are sometimes called 'self-liquidating' advertising media.

Questions for discussion or revision

1 Name four of the essential factors that have to be considered in the preparation of an advertising campaign.
2 Explain what 'cut-through' means in advertising parlance. Give an example.
3 What is 'contra-advertising'. In what circumstances is it best used?

Chapter 25

Advertising: Creative Strategies

================ Aims of this chapter ================

The aims of this chapter are:
- to explain what creative strategies are all about;
- to discuss creativity in advertising; and
- to discuss creativity in promotional literature.

Theory

The intention of commercial advertising activity for hospitality is to communicate benefits and values, and to invoke a favourable response from people in the market. The response will vary from group to group—depending on the message, and on the needs and wants of the individuals in each market group that have been targeted. Just as it has to be certain about its target markets, a hospitality property has to be clear about the type of response it wants. The creators of an advertisement have to anticipate the silent questions from the audience.

- What sort of place is yours?
- What are you offering me?
- What will I get for my time and money?

In anticipating these questions, and preparing answers for them, many larger hotels and resort properties present an array of breast-beating self-indulgence. Their advertisements boast of their gloss, glitz, marble, slate, brass, and crystal.

How do people react to these breast-beating propositions? Some might say: 'If I stayed at that hotel I think I would be treated very well'. Others might think: 'Looks good, but I know it will cost a lot of money and I doubt that I need to spend that much'. Others will say: 'It's very impressive and I believe it would be excellent, but I can never afford to stay there; it is out of my league'. Others will simply be unimpressed. For them, it is just another hotel advertisement.

The basis of effective advertising is to know in advance what the target markets are likely to think, feel, believe, or know as a result of being exposed to the messages in the advertising. Thinking ahead and putting oneself in the position of those in the target market is part of the preparation of good advertising. This is sometimes called 'formatting the consumer action proposition'. It means predetermining the reaction to the presentation of the message. Its essential purpose is to answer the question: 'Will the advertisement deliver the message to the people we want, and will they react in the way that we expect?'.

Messages, objectives, and media

Creating an advertisement for mass media or other message-delivery systems has to be driven by the communication objectives. The creative process, which determines the way in which the message is presented, has to encode the message into words and pictures such that the target markets get the message quickly and easily. The creative process must therefore ensure that it suits the chosen message-delivery system. Consider the case study on 'Communication objectives for Smith's Family Bistro', page 313.

Creative solution—the KISS principle

The purpose of a creative approach is to use a message-delivery system, such as a newspaper, to its best advantage by drawing attention to the message and making it easy to read and understand. Effective creativity should considerably enhance the possibilities of the advertisement being noticed and read. However, creativity on its own will seldom save a poorly conceived or uninteresting message.

Any advertisement that obscures the message is a foolish waste of money. In print media, it is the headline that has the main job of conveying the words that spell out the key points of the proposition. It must be assumed that the readers are largely uninterested in reading advertisements, so the headline is no place for subtlety. See the case study on 'Effective communication for for Smith's Family Bistro', page 314.

CASE STUDY

Communication objectives for Smith's Family Bistro

'Smith's Family Bistro' is a fictitious family-style restaurant. The message to be delivered is: 'Smith's Family Bistro has half-price meals for children under 12, and a special TV viewing room for them to use while their parents finish a leisurely meal'.

This attractive offer has a good difference, advantage, and benefit (DAB) in comparison with other places in the vicinity.

The communication objective for this advertising project might read as follows: 'To make people with children aware of the offer, and to achieve a 40% penetration level of the message within a month'. Note that this objective has: (i) a target market, (ii) a measurable level of awareness, and (iii) a time criterion.

To achieve the objective, the media chosen to deliver the message might be a letter-box drop to all the homes in the area, supported by a weekly press advertisement in the local newspaper. In an area that has approximately five thousand homes with children, 40% awareness means that two thousand homes should get the message and understand the offer. The other three thousand do not get the message for various reasons—because they do not read brochures, because they missed the advertisement in the newspaper, or because the offer simply did not 'register' in their minds.

The response to the advertising will depend on:

- how enticing the offer is perceived to be;
- how many people were actually interested in eating out with their children; and
- the success of the creative approach.

Experience suggests that a 5% response is good—that is, approximately 100 couples and their children respond to the message during the course of the campaign, and take the action of actually coming to the bistro. At least 40 of those, it is to be hoped, might become regulars. Thereafter, with the help of word-of-mouth recommendation, and perhaps with the help of some reminder advertising, Smith's should experience continuing growth—thus justifying the advertising expenditure.

CASE STUDY

Effective communication for for Smith's Family Bistro

Here are three creative alternatives for the headline of the 'Smith's Family Bistro' (page 313) brochure and press advertisement:

■ 'We'll mind the kids while you eat'
■ 'Kids are half the trouble and half the price at Smiths Family Bistro'
■ 'Half price for children under 12! TV room available!'

Which one do you prefer? Which one do you think would work best?

The first headline is misleading even though the copy below it might go on to explain the offer in full. It takes a single benefit approach and latches onto the belief that most parents want the kids taken off their hands while they eat. This is a dubious assumption because many parents do not trust others to look after their children.

The second headline is a clever play on words but it still relies on the copy to explain the offer.

The third headline is dull from a creative perspective, but it gets the message across without the reader having to get the details from the copy.

According to an old adage, 'a picture is worth a thousand words'. Advertisements work better by using an illustration. The 'Smith's Family Bistro' advertisement could show two children in the foreground watching television and, through a picture window in the background, illustrate a typical restaurant scene with their parents being waited on at a table. The advertisement now has the readers' attention and communicates a situation that is appealing and hard to misunderstand.

One of the most common mistakes in advertising creativity is being too clever. The use of puns (the humorous use of a word with two or more meanings) can be clever. But it can also be obscure, and many people can miss the meaning. Advertising is too expensive to waste on cleverness at the expense of clarity. Every so often, a headline with a pun is stunning in its creativity. Even though such gems are rare, the world's advertising copywriters spend their working lives dreaming of emulating those great statements! Unfortunately, few succeed. See the case study 'Too clever by half!', page 315.

Too clever by half!

A Sydney hotel once tried a pun by advertising with the following headline: '72% of Business People Visiting Sydney ask for Something on the Rocks'.

As most people know, a drink 'on the rocks' means a drink poured onto ice cubes in the glass. The intended double meaning was a reference to the hotel's location in the area of Sydney known as 'The Rocks'. But the reader has to read the copy to establish this second meaning, and how many 'visiting business-people' know 'The Rocks' area? And how many really care? The reader has to guess at the hidden meaning, and then wonder whether 72% of visitors really do ask for a place situated 'on the Rocks'.

The message is obscure, and unlikely to appeal.

To ensure that the message is communicated, one of the first rules of creativity is the 'KISS' principle—'Keep It Simple Stupid!'.

A general checklist

Here is a simple checklist for advertising copy. The following apply to most advertising and brochures.

◆ Know the target markets the advertisement is aimed at. Try to understand the people and how they are likely to respond to the message itself and to the presentation of the message as contrived by the creative approach.

◆ Get attention—usually with an interesting picture. If the picture can deliver the message on its own, the words only have to confirm (and perhaps add to) what the reader sees. Use colour if you can. Colour provides warmth and feeling for the message.

◆ Hold attention. Make the advertisement easy to read and follow. An uncluttered simple presentation that allows the eye to follow the story naturally adds considerably to the effectiveness of the message.

◆ Build interest. Have a headline that ties in with the picture and delivers the main benefit of the message. The copy provides the details. It should never have to solve a riddle presented by the illustration and the headline—as happens in so many advertisements.

◆ Create desire. Write copy that points out the benefits and confirms the facts for readers. Spell out the reasons in favour of a purchase.

◆ Be credible. Prove the point with testimonials. Endeavour to reassure the readers that they will get what is promised.

◆ Make it easy for the prospective client to obtain the product. Provide the reader with enough information to find the place and make the purchase. For some reason, in many advertisements, the purchase details are contained in type so tiny that it is hard to read.

Some basic creative rules

To make the communication more effective, there are several basic 'rules' to follow. These can be considered under general rules for all media, and specific rules for different types of media.

General rules

◆ Keep the communication simple. Do not try to communicate too much. Advertising should be single-minded.

◆ Although there might be several salient features to present, highlight the main ones. Memories are short. No one gets all the information. Make sure that one or two benefits stand out.

◆ Use pictures to tell the story. 'A picture is worth a thousand words.'

◆ Present the message in a friendly, pleasant way. Shock has a place, but that place is not usually in advertising. (Keep shock for horror films!)

◆ Utilise emotion wherever you can. Human beings are emotional creatures. Human beings respond to emotional appeals.

◆ Do not introduce sex, nudity, religion, racism, sexism, or violence into the advertising unless it is directly related to the advertising objective. It might achieve 'cut-through', but it might equally 'cut out' a large percentage of your audience.

◆ Do not be a 'copycat'. A copycat runs the risk of being confused with another advertisement.

◆ Criticising the opposition is dangerous. To do so is to draw attention to the opposition for free. The best examples of this are political campaigns. 'Slanging matches' can help to elect the opposing candidate.

◆ Reinforce the message at every opportunity. Coordinate the creative approach throughout the tactical mix if more than one message-delivery system is used. One helps the other by reminding the audience of what they have seen or heard before. This also helps to build trust and conviction.

◆ Use advertising to position the property or product. The tone and manner of the advertising should reflect the personality of the property. Run 'theme' advertising. Although several campaigns (perhaps aimed at different markets) might be running concurrently, one can support the other as a member of a 'family' of advertisements.

◆ Avoid making 'introverted' statements that refer to the establishment ('We have . . . '). Rather, make 'extroverted' statements that involve the customer ('You can have . . . ').

◆ 'Humanise' the advertising by portraying people. Advertising and media research has proven conclusively that a voice or picture of a person draws the attention of the audience more effectively than objects or words.

Rules for specific media

Television

Due to high costs, it is unlikely that many hospitality establishments will use television. When it is used, make sure it works by following these principles.

◆ Keep it brief. Too many commercials attempt to be 'mini' feature films. Have one central core of action.

◆ Avoid telling stories to make a point. Such advertisements do entertain, but the audience frequently forgets the message. Often, people remember the commercial but cannot say whose commercial it was.

◆ What is seen and heard must work together. No one can read one thing while watching something else.

◆ Utilise music that sets a mood. Music is important for communication and quickly sets the scene.

◆ Be original.

◆ Be believable.

◆ Be informative and interesting.

◆ Take care with casting. Casting is critical in a television·commercial. The target market must be able to identify with the people portrayed. But remember that people will see themselves as they would like to be, not how they are.

◆ Remember that the pictures are the key element in the advertisement. Moving, colour pictures are the principal means of communication, and are proven strong communicators. Use them to send the message. Words are used to reinforce what people see.

◆ Maintain the action but avoid visual clutter. Do not cram the time available with too many scenes.

Radio

- Do not raise the volume to attract attention. This annoys listeners. Radio is an intimate medium.
- Use the theatre of the mind. Listeners imagine what they cannot see, and what they imagine is often more impressive than reality.
- Do not cram the available time with words. An advertisement is not a 'word race', and advertisers who try to cram as many words as possible into an advertisement get less value for money, not more. Allow no more than fifty words for every thirty seconds.
- Construct the commercial like a melody. That is, it must have an arresting beginning, a developing middle, and a recapitulated close. Make a statement about the benefits, explain the facts, and then repeat the statement.
- Ensure that one point stands out in every commercial.
- Set the mood with music. A few bars of evocative music carefully chosen can transport the listener to anywhere in the world (or even into deep space!). Similar comments apply to other sound effects.
- Humour works well on radio. But do not allow the joke to overwhelm the message.

Web advertising and print media

- Always use an illustration.
- Have one or more people in the picture.
- Use the headline to present your basic message. The headline must support the picture. They work together.
- Do not puzzle the reader with the picture or the headline. Clever advertisements often fail.
- Keep the headline short enough to catch the attention—that is, fewer than, say, seventeen words.
- Use a typeface that is big enough to read easily. Never use smaller than 10-point type for copy. People older than 40 have trouble reading small print.
- Serif letters have been used in printing for centuries, and this might be because the serifs make the letters more distinct and hence easier to read.
- Do not put type on an angle to make people turn their heads to read it. They will not do this.
- Avoid 'widows' (that is, a word that is 'turned over' to the next line or page and sits there on its own. It is best to keep one thought to one line. Readability is essential.
- Do not use white type on a black background, except for special-effect headings. This is difficult for some people to read.
- Keep the advertisement 'clean and open'. Retain plenty of white space.

◆ Do not try to attract the readers' attention to everything. There is an old saying in layout: 'All display is no display'.

◆ Lead the reader through the advertisement from top to bottom—just like reading a book.

◆ Maintain one type style throughout. Adopt a typeface that becomes part of the corporate advertising 'look'.

◆ Use enough copy to make the point. When readers are interested they want information. There is a mistaken belief that people do not read long copy. Uninterested people do not; but interested people do.

◆ Do not stint on the size of the advertisement. Smaller advertisements are less likely to be read.

Advertising agencies

Most large establishments employ advertising agencies. The tasks of these agencies are:

◆ to plan the media;
◆ to create the advertising;
◆ to produce the advertising; and
◆ to place the advertising in the media.

Some agencies offer additional services—such as marketing planning, public relations, brochure preparation, and print and sign work.

Agencies usually retain a commission from the media (perhaps 10%) in which the advertising is placed. Many add a service fee (perhaps 7.5%). Others work on a flat fee for services.

The main benefits derived from having an agency are: (i) expertise in interpreting the advertising brief creatively; and (ii) expertise in choosing the best media to present the message effectively. However, the hospitality establishment must not let the agency 'run away' with creative flamboyance. The agency should be pulled back to the brief. If necessary, quote the 'rules' noted above (see 'Some basic creative rules', this chapter, page 316). Marketing is the client's responsibility. The client should set the communication goals and give the agency the task of achieving those goals. The communication goals should have measurable criteria so that the work of the agency can be measured.

When checking on an agency's work, the establishment should ensure that:

◆ the agency has the necessary expertise and experience; in this e-commerce age, this expertise should extend to Web-based advertising;
◆ the advertisement is in accordance with the brief;
◆ the advertisement is aimed at the right target markets;

- the media reach the target market;
- the advertising 'talks' to the target market;
- the message is clear and simply stated;
- the message is not offensive in any way;
- it achieves 'cut-through';
- it achieves attention, interest, desire, and conviction;
- it calls for some action by the respondent and that this action is obvious;
- the establishment is positioned correctly by the advertising;
- the advertising will achieve the communication objectives;
- the costs are not excessive; as a 'rule of thumb', production costs should not be more than approximately 10–15% of the amount spent on media exposure;

When choosing an agency, the hospitality establishment should note the following.

- Do not call for creative submissions. Look at the work that agencies have done for other clients. Ask other clients for references. Check with the media.
- Choose people with whom the establishment can relate.
- Do not be bemused by hyperbole; the biggest is not necessarily the best.

Questions for discussion or revision

1 List seven basic creative rules for advertising.
2 You have employed an advertising agency to build awareness of your motel. The agency puts forward some press advertisements for you to consider. What criteria would you use to evaluate their creativity and potential effectiveness?
3 Explain how an advertising agency is remunerated.

Advertising: Media and Budgets

Theory

There is no doubt that promotion, using a mix of message-delivery systems, is essential to the development of a customer base and to the retention of existing patrons. But promoting an establishment can be one of the most expensive parts of running a business. Before money is spent, each campaign has to be carefully assessed for its ability to contribute to sales and profit. Promotion is goal-driven. Therefore the sales objectives and the time frame have to be compared against the costs of communication.

The markets also have to be carefully considered. For example, large hotels, even though they are mainly targeting travellers for accommodation, still must consider promotions for the local market. The local market is the major user of food & beverage products. In addition, local people are an important source of recommendations for visitors.

Because of its high cost and low efficiency, there is some doubt about the value obtained from large-scale mass-media advertising as a primary means of securing new business. Mass-media advertising is more often used in a supporting role for sales promotions.

The questions that have to be answered before proceeding with an advertising campaign concern the selling load that has to be carried by advertising.

◆ Is it meant to have a support role for a sales promotion?; or
◆ Is it the sole communication vehicle to promote a product?; or
◆ Is it meant to position the hotel by creating an image that sets the stage for other selling activities in the tactical mix?

In the case of the third alternative, it might be difficult to calculate how much should be spent compared with the anticipated sales return—because there is no way of knowing how much advertising contributed to the securing of a particular customer. A person or a corporation might have been influenced to come to the property by information obtained from several sources—from a sales presentation, from a price promotion, or as a result of a referral (from a satisfied friend, a business acquaintance, or a travel agent). Or perhaps, the new customer was simply passing by the property.

And the question cannot simply be resolved by asking respondents questions such as: 'Did you decide to come to us after seeing our advertisement?'. Most people do not like to admit that they have been influenced by advertising. Indeed, people might be unaware that they *were* influenced by advertising. Much advertising to which people are exposed merely establishes a favourable impression of the property, or provides 'name memorability'.

The effectiveness of the contribution made by image or positioning advertising can be measured only by research. This research reveals:

◆ how many people are aware of the establishment (as a result of the advertising);
◆ how many people know where it is (as a result of the advertising);
◆ how many people recall its chief attributes (as a result of the advertising); and
◆ how many more people hold favourable attitudes towards it (as a result of the advertising).

To confirm that the effects are due to the advertising, research should be conducted at regular intervals (perhaps every six months) to identify these changes in awareness and attitude, and to establish that advertising contributed towards the changes identified.

Budgeting

There are three basic budgeting approaches that can be used to estimate the amount to be spent on advertising when preparing a realistic budget. These are:

◆ the retail approach (how much money the property *can justify in spending*);

◆ the market approach (how much money the property *needs to spend*); and
◆ the corporate approach (how much money the property *can afford to spend*).

Each of these is considered below.

The retail approach

The retail approach is decided on the basis of how much money the property *can justify in spending* on the campaign. The budget can be decided by:

◆ allocating an amount of money for each anticipated sale; then
◆ estimating the number of sales; and then
◆ multiplying the estimated number of sales by the amount allocated to each sale.

The final answer is the budget under the retail method.

The market approach

The market approach is decided on the basis of how much money the property *needs to spend*. The budget can be decided by:

◆ fixing on a market and estimating the number of prospects it contains; then
◆ forecasting the likely return (in dollars) from the advertising; then
◆ deciding which media will reach the market; then
◆ estimating the number of times the message will have to be exposed; and then
◆ costing the schedule according to the amount of money required to meet the communication objectives.

The final answer is the budget under the market method.

The corporate approach

The market approach is decided on the basis of how much money the property *can afford to spend*. The budget can be decided by:

◆ calculating the establishment's anticipated gross income for the year; and then
◆ allocating a percentage for advertising.

The percentage to use in this approach can be decided by checking the industry average. Although this is a broad yardstick approach, it is not uncommon among all industries to do it this way—with some exceeding the industry average, and others spending less.

This figure is then divided into two parts: (i) image or positioning advertising; and (ii) promotional support and direct response advertising campaigns.

The large hotel chains allocate a higher percentage of their gross income to advertising because the cost burden can be shared by many properties. Individual properties find it difficult to justify large advertising budgets—even though it can be argued that they are more in need of the exposure. To overcome this problem, many individual properties belong to a marketing group that pools the advertising and provides an international booking service.

General advertising principles

Here are some general advertising principles to remember before embarking on a mass-media advertising campaign.

An offer

Always try to have an offer in your advertisement. Even if the advertisement is carrying a positioning message, it will work better if the recipient of the message is given something to do, or is given information that enables him or her to make a decision.

A clear message

The message of the advertisement must be clear. People must be given an interesting and compelling purchase reason to consider. Good advertising is noticed but good messages are remembered! The content, the offer, the reason for being considered will usually override a poor layout or small size.

A distinctive style

Irrespective of the content or intent of each individual advertisement, ensure that each one fits in with the distinctive style of a 'family' of advertisements.

Time to work

Give advertising time to work. It takes time for a message to get through—especially in the case of image advertising. A property should not go in for large-scale advertising unless it can be sustained over a period. 'Surge and saturatc' advertising is the name given to intensive advertising for a period, followed by a break—for example, two weeks on and two weeks off. This has been proven to extend the life of a campaign, and to improve its performance (in terms of awareness and retention).

Timing

It is always best to cue advertising bursts to the seasons or times when travel is being considered. It makes sense to tie in with special events which bring large volumes of traffic to the area.

Realism

Be realistic about what advertising can achieve. Advertising does not have the power to put several thousand dollars into someone's pocket so that he or she can go on a holiday. Advertising cannot influence a businessperson to take a trip and do a deal simply because you want him or her to stay at your hotel.

Advertising cannot achieve miracles. Restaurants in the doldrums are the chief culprits in trying to reverse poor sales by advertising—and invariably they throw good money after bad. Advertising can only support sound product strategies. Advertising cannot change poor perceptions unless the reality is changed.

Follow through

Follow through your advertising at the point of sale. It reminds people that they have seen the message elsewhere. Marketers of packaged goods use the technique of having a 'memory trigger' at the point of sale—perhaps through the label or a display card. Such companies recognise that they are still competing with other brands being displayed. In the hospitality industry, the competitors are down the road, but a memory trigger is reassuring for new patrons. If a well-known personality is part of the advertising creative approach, cards at the desk can show this person. (Better still, have the person there if you can!)

Supporting media

Use supporting media. Two forms of media are more effective than one because they reinforce each other. This might be two radio stations, a radio station and a newspaper, or a radio station and a letterbox drop. The principle is the same as receiving more than one recommendation. If one person tells you that a place is 'great', you might be interested; but when two or three say the same thing you are convinced.

Social norms

Remember that advertising serves only to reinforce existing knowledge, social values, and habits. Advertising is unlikely to change established social habits.

Below-the-line advertising material

All establishments require below-the-line advertising material. Below-the-line advertising is any promotional expenditure that is not main media. This includes brochures, leaflets, folders, catalogues, and so on. In the USA, this is referred to as 'collateral'. In every case, media advertising and collateral must be coordinated to achieve a corporate 'look' that presents the same image or personality of the property. To be effective, collateral has to be informative and persuasive—but the emphasis is on information. Information 'sells as it tells'.

Flowery phrases and exaggerated claims are puffery that, ultimately, do not fool anyone. Some places do not spend money on main street advertising. They produce only collateral material. Indeed, the trend in the industry world-wide is for less money to be spent on media advertising, and more on direct response marketing.

Choosing media

Advertising in mass media is more obvious to the general public than other forms of advertising, and it can work very well if it is selectively chosen. The choice of the most appropriate and efficient medium to use is influenced by:

◆ the intention of the message;
◆ the type of message to be delivered; and
◆ the market to which it is to be delivered.

Based on these factors, an assessment has to be made of the following forms of media:

◆ Web advertising;
◆ print media; and
◆ broadcast media.

An assessment of each of these main mass-media vehicles follows.

Web advertising

Users surf the Web either from curiosity, or to satisfy a need for certain types of information—such as a guide to financial markets, share trading, weather, shopping, sporting events, and so on. Web advertising has to be carefully directed to get the message across. Many users browse websites without reading more than the headlines, and most 'hits' are of only a few seconds in duration. For this reason, advertisers must take as much care with the design of their advertising as they do with their website, and the rules discussed earlier on website management (page 144) apply just as much here. For Web advertising to be effective, it must 'hit' the right market and gain attention in a crowded electronic information marketplace.

Directory advertising on the Web can be good value because such directories contain information sought by the readers (such as where to stay or dine). Some directories have a long life and 'hang around' for years. Therefore, make sure the message will last for years.

Print media

Newspapers

Newspaper advertising might be in daily, weekly, national, suburban, or regional newspapers. With most of the population preferring to get their news in short bites from broadcast media, newspaper circulations around the world generally are not keeping pace with population increases. In many cases they are static, or even decreasing. With this in mind, hospitality advertising objectives are better served by using newspapers for retail-type announcements and customer information—rather than for the longer-term intentions of image-building. If the advertisement does not contain news and an offer, it will probably not be suitable for placement in a newspaper.

Magazines

Magazine advertising includes glossy publications such as women's and men's magazines, business magazines, holiday and travel magazines, and special interest magazines on subjects such as beating, fishing, rock-climbing, and so on. Magazines usually represent good value for the hospitality advertiser because they are bought by people with specific interests, thus enabling the advertiser to reach particular markets that have high sales potential for their products. Quality magazines also provide a prestige environment for hospitality establishments. Colour is virtually essential. Cheap publications suggest cheap products and should be avoided. Products are judged by the company they keep.

A drawback with magazines is the long 'lead time' required to meet the publishing deadlines of most magazines. Special price offers or deals therefore have to be planned well in advance, and require a long life. Magazines are expensive—but ideal for long-term positioning.

Trade publications

A special subcategory of print media is that of trade publications. Trade publications are those magazines and journals that are distributed primarily to the hospitality and tourism industries, and to associated industries (such as wine, beer, provisioning, food, and so on). These publications can be used to good effect to reach the important group of 'influencers'—those whose opinions are sought and respected by some markets, especially the corporate sectors. Marketing messages need to be carefully handled when placed in trade publications. Advertising in such publications has the advantage of being relatively inexpensive. The circulations of the publications are seldom large, but respected industry publications are well read.

Placement of advertising in print media

With all print media, page positioning is relevant. There is no conclusive evidence that a right page is any more effective than a left—although many people believe that the right side is better. Some pages—such as front, back, and the early pages—are far more read than others. It is worth paying the extra asked for these.

Do not allow your advertisement to be lost among a lot of other advertisements. For this reason, as a general rule, avoid industry features in newspapers or magazines.

Broadcast media

Television

The term 'broadcast media' (or 'electronic media') refers to television and radio. For consumer products, television is the most popular of these media because it has all the communication advantages of sight, movement, sound, and colour, and because so many people watch it. It is an excellent means of building a position through imagery.

But television has some disadvantages. It can be very expensive. For this reason alone, television is not favoured by the hospitality industry—an industry that is often nervous about getting a return on its advertising investment. In addition, in many Western countries, 'free-to-air' television is losing its audiences to home video and pay television, as well as facing competition from an assortment of new forms of entertainment. Moreover, the all-important corporate and professional customers and the wealthier holidaymakers do not usually watch very much television.

Selected programs with proven ratings among the markets being targeted is the only way to buy television advertising. Packages of spots that are exposed to a general market might appear to be cheaper. However, most of the viewers are never likely to be prime candidates to become customers at a restaurant, or at an expensive hotel, motel, or resort.

Radio

Radio can be used for image positioning, but it probably works best as a retail medium—communicating new developments, special offers, and price deals.

Targeting of the market is again important. As with television, 'run-of-station' spot packages (which can be aired by the station over 24 hours of transmission) are not recommended unless the station chosen has a consistent audience type throughout all sessions. The commercials are better placed in sessions in which the major proportion of the audience represents the property's target markets. Announcers and music styles, for example, build loyal listeners of particular audience types. Radio stations, both AM and FM, are proliferating. The stations to choose are those that have captured a market that suits the communication objectives of the hospitality establishment.

Most people listen to radio as a background to what they are doing. They do not listen intently unless something of interest to them is being discussed. 'Cut-through' is therefore important for radio advertisers. However, all too often, cut-through is attempted by silly gimmicks that lose the message. The announcer who has already captured the audience is the best presenter of a message, provided that he or she does not suddenly put on a false 'selling voice'—and thus turn off the audience.

Buying media space

To evaluate one medium's costs against another, compare the unit cost-per-impact for a given sized advertisement (or length of commercial) and find out how many impacts can be obtained in each medium for the same cost.

Here is a simple example comparing a '9 cm × 7 cm' press advertisement appearing in three different newspapers circulating in the same market:

Newspaper	Cost	Readership	Unit cost-per-impact
Newspaper A	$4000	150 000 daily	$0.026
Newspaper B	$5000	170 000 daily	$0.028
Newspaper C	$3000	120 000 daily	$0.024

On a cost-per-impact basis, Newspaper C appears to represent the best value provided that it reaches the target markets the property wants. It is false economy to buy on price alone. Media know this so they conduct research and maintain a vast mount of statistical data to help advertisers make their choice of medium. However, care must be taken when analysing statistics, because they can be used by a medium to prove almost anything.

Television and radio stations use a ratings formula to assist buyers in their choice. Television sets switched on at any given hour of the day are called 'sets-in-use' and are expressed as a percentage of all homes with television sets. Thus, in a city with 500 000 homes with television sets, 50% sets-in-use means that 250 000 homes are watching television at a particular time.

A rating is a percentage of television sets switched on to a particular station and program. Thus, a program that has attracted 22% of all homes with television sets has a rating of 22. When television commercials are purchased in several programs, the percentage ratings obtained each time are added together into gross rating points (GRPs) as a means of determining the total 'reach' of the commercials.

Ratings can also be measured by target audience segments—such as 'men aged 18 to 39'. These are called target audience rating points (TARPs). Costs per impact for each station can be compared by using either GRPs or TARPs. TARPs are the better means of comparison because the advertiser usually has an interest in reaching a defined audience.

Radio stations use a similar ratings formula but also employ the term 'cumes'—meaning the number of listeners who have been 'accumulated' every quarter of an hour in a given session.

Miscellaneous media

Outdoor advertising is the oldest of all media, and remains one of the most effective. Outdoor advertising is excellent for creating awareness and acting as a brand name reminder.

The keys to outdoor advertising are visibility, simplicity, and impact. The message has to be shortened to few enough words to be read and absorbed in two or three seconds. This effectively amounts to no more than ten words at the most. Pictures therefore have to carry the main impact load.

The first sites to consider for outdoor advertising should be the property's building itself and its vehicles. These are obviously cheap sites to use, and costs are limited to the cost of creating and producing the signs or displays used. For aesthetic reasons, the temptation to put signs and posters all over a building has to be resisted. In any case, most councils restrict the use of signs to prevent visual pollution.

All forms of public transport should be considered for advertising for their relatively low cost and high visibility. They are noticed more if the creative approach makes good use of the area hired.

For properties wanting to reach inward-bound customers, consider the purchase of carefully located sites on major roads near airports, large sporting venues, and convention and business centres. Many people who have not made bookings will be influenced by these signs, and those who have already made their decision will have their decision reaffirmed.

The clue to the use of outdoor advertising is to change the posters and displays frequently. Outdoor advertising works best on initial impact, and on subsequent sightings for about a month. By that time most people who have passed by have seen them several times. After about a month, people lose interest, and the advertising becomes part of the scenery.

'Point-of-interest' advertising

It is becoming apparent to many advertisers that 'point-of-interest' advertising is the most effective form of advertising in achieving high awareness and interest in the message. When people are at a place or doing something connected with the advertiser's interests they are more susceptible to receiving allied messages.

Points of interest for an accommodation property include airlines, airports, restaurants, buses, trains, bars, travel agents, high-fashion dress shops, and so on. A place that has a golf course would be advised to expose its messages wherever golfers are likely to be—pro shops, other golf courses, golfing publications, golfing programs, and so. In general, wherever people are in a spending or recreational mood, it is easier to divert them into considering similar interests—places to go and stay. This point-of-interest approach is particularly true of theme resorts and hotels.

Similarly, there are many opportunities within the property itself for conveying important items of promotional information to existing and potential customers at the points and moments of greatest interest. Good examples are tent cards or brochures on counters, on restaurant tables, in the guests' rooms, and in the bars. Also consider signs, information boards, and displays in foyers.

Window displays at chosen places, especially if you can tie in with a retail promotion, represent good value at relatively low cost.

Questions for discussion or revision

1 Before you spend money on advertising you need a budget. What are two of the procedures that can be used in the preparation of a budget?
2 Explain what 'surge and saturate' means when buying media space.
3 What do the terms 'GRPs' and 'TARPs' mean?

Chapter 27

Sales Promotion and Publicity Strategies

Aims of this chapter

The aims of this chapter are:
- to explain the purpose of sales promotions;
- to describe the staging of promotional events; and
- to discuss the effectiveness of promotions in generating sales.

Theory

Sales promotions are special selling efforts for boosting sales or introducing new products. They are usually short-term projects. Although they can be repeated at a later date, they can seldom be extended for long. Promotions should be thought of as a means of providing immediate reasons for customers to use the establishment's services. In this chapter, we are talking about promotion events rather than sales drives—such as discounted packages, clubs, and special deals.

Surveys of customers reveal that one of the main reasons that people use an establishment's facilities is for 'special occasions'. Special occasions also mean special reasons. Instead of waiting for the customers to find a reason for coming to the place, promotions offer the reason.

The challenge is to come up with interesting things that make a place distinctive, unusual, and exciting. The object is not to sell, but to fill the place with people, and generate word-of-mouth advertising. In supporting a promotion, people are looking for a social experience. They are not going to a bar because they are thirsty. They are going because other people of interest are in the bar. Promotions are for people not profit.

For well-marketed hotels, promotions have become a way of life.

Benefits

The benefits of sales promotions include the following.

- They address specific needs and opportunities.
- They establish relationships with customers and the public.
- They appeal to basic human motivations.
- They involve people who might not otherwise be customers.
- They generate word-of-mouth advertising.
- They can show the place in a different light.
- They can solve weekly and seasonal down periods.
- Prices can be submerged into add-on value products.
- They raise staff morale.

Each of these is considered below.

Specific needs and opportunities

Sales promotions address specific needs and opportunities. Promotions can fill low-occupancy periods by attracting guests who might have had no intention of staying or dining at the property. If a property is having an awareness problem, a sales promotion can draw attention to it and renew interest in the property. Staging an international cooking competition that attracts media attention and public interest is one type of promotion that can be considered.

There are thousands of ideas for promotions—both original ideas and ideas that can be copied or adapted. A property does not have to wait for an event to happen. Most promotion concepts are generated by the property. The intention is to solve a business problem by bringing together a number of unrelated elements by the use of a central theme. The more outside businesspeople who can be involved the better—because it spreads the interest and often spreads the costs.

Establishing relationships with customers and the public

Promotions establish relationships with customers and the public. Strong promotions can indicate to the public that the property is a 'good citizen' by organising events that involve the physical and cultural environment of the city. They also enable the management to come into contact with executives and public figures at a personal level. Most of all, promotions stimulate existing customers and bring them closer to the property and its staff.

Appealing to basic human motivations

Sales promotions appeal to basic human motivations. Promotions often have a cost advantage for customers, and this is appealing in itself. More importantly, many members of the public love being involved in a special occasion that offers excitement, interest, and a chance to be part of a 'happening'.

Involving people who might not otherwise be customers

Promotions involve people who might not otherwise be customers. Regular customers can be targeted for promotions as a means of bringing others. Promotions do not always have to make money for the property immediately. Although the intention is not to make a loss, a promotion that brings in new customers who later become regular patrons has been successful.

Generating word-of-mouth advertising

Promotions generate word-of-mouth advertising. They can also create media interest and coverage. People talk about good promotions. The ability to keep expanding the customer base is essential to a property's future, and the best way to do this to have many people passing on news of the good times they have had at a place.

Showing the place in a different light

Promotions can show the place in a different light. Attention can be focused on products and facilities that people know little about. A promotion might be held around a new cocktail bar, or a ballroom that many customers did not know existed. The whole property can be given a 'lift' by a good promotion.

Solving weekly and seasonal down periods

Promotions can solve weekly and seasonal down periods. Nearly every property has trouble with numbers at weekends. The time-honoured solution is to run special weekend packages and 'theme' weekends that involve special events such as music, personalities, games, gambling, food and wine fairs, and national celebrations.

Submerging prices into add-on value products

Prices can be submerged into add-on value products during promotions. Most promotions involve a package of events or situations that are offered at an attractive all-inclusive price that represents good value for the participants. For those properties that are conscious of their image and do not want to appear to be discounting their room rates, promotions are ideal.

Raising staff morale

Promotions can raise staff morale. Properties that are seen as being promotion-minded find it easier to attract good, talented staff because it is more fun to work there.

Marketing promotions

Promotions can be associated with:

◆ visiting celebrities;
◆ seasons;
◆ festivals;
◆ exhibitions;
◆ trade showings and demonstrations;
◆ historic occasions;
◆ national events and calendar days;
◆ international events and celebrations;
◆ food and wine events;
◆ sporting carnivals;
◆ holidays and holiday packages;
◆ openings;
◆ parties;
◆ training programs; and
◆ value for money packages.

Promotions offer an ideal opportunity for joint promotions with other businesses. Used in this way, they can spread the promotional dollar further. For example, a special travel package might involve an airline, a casino, a bus company, a winery, and shops. Everyone contributes financially to the staging costs, including the advertising. Moreover, each plays a part in using its own customer base to make the promotion a success.

Merchandise can also be sold with promotions—thereby providing additional opportunities for profit.

Objectives for promotions must be set to ensure that there are clear aims for the promotion in terms of monetary expectations, number of customers, and the reactions of customers. Remember, promotions are for people, not for profit. Greed can ruin the event.

There are three basic types of promotions, although a good promotion can combine all three. These are:

◆ price promotions that give people some extra value;
◆ party promotions that offer people an exciting different experience of the same property or one of its products; and
◆ new product promotions that introduce people to something completely new and different.

All promotions must contain an 'offer' of some type—a price advantage, a special value not normally available, or a sense of excitement.

Promotions need to be targeted at specific groups, and these are usually the people who best suit the customer mix of the place. For example, if an establishment finds that it is not gaining enough custom from a desired market, promotions can be devised that attract them. However, a place should not aim at customers who will come only for the promotion because of the value that is being offered. These people are unlikely to return. It is best to aim at those who are likely to be retained as clients and thus become part of the customer base.

When new people are pulled in by a promotion, the establishment should obtain their names and add them to the email and mail list. Because one of the aims of every promotion is to gather new customers, the establishment should give the customers a reason to provide their names and addresses—through a competition, a raffle, or a small give-away that has to be posted to them.

Care is necessary to ensure that the promotions are within the establishment's physical and human resources. Nothing will be gained by an event that overwhelms the place and leaves patrons disgruntled because they could not get in, or were not served properly, or missed out on some of the promised benefits.

The staff must enter into the spirit of the promotion. There is nothing worse than a badly run promotion that fails. This can ruin a hard-won reputation. Therefore, a property should never stint on the budget and the preparations.

Promoting sales promotions

Ascertaining the target market is just as important for promotions as it is for any other tactical effort by the property. The knowledge of the market helps to refine the message-delivery systems to be used.

Some of the message vehicles to be considered include:

◆ direct email to potential customers;
◆ leaflets to everyone who attends the place from six weeks to a month beforehand;
◆ informing regular customers in person;
◆ advertising in selected media that reach a large number of the target market; involving media and getting publicity;
◆ networking through organisations that are connected with the promotion; using their customer base; and
◆ using the property's outlets for cards, signs, posters, window displays, and notices to spread the word.

A promotion is a special event and it should offer value not usually available. To add to the attraction of a promotion, offers and enticements are nearly always necessary. Redeemable vouchers can be used as a method of getting a reasonably certain return. These might be handed out to customers and outsiders, posted to prospective customers, or included as coupons in advertisements.

Gifts and give-aways are hard to refuse. Merchandise at reduced prices is also very attractive. The world is full of bargain-hunters!

Raffles and prizes are probably overworked—everyone seems to run a raffle. However, they often appeal, as do quizzes and contests.

Value-added products and bonus packs (included with the price of the promotion) are excellent enticements. For example, a promotion combined with a casino might offer chips to a certain value, together with champagne and a free meal. This could be part of a 'wild gambling-spree weekend', offering the prospective customer a stake to get started.

Free samples are often neglected, but are one of the best means of enticing new customers or of selling something new to existing customers. A cultural event, such as a small orchestra or a dance night with a special band, can be enhanced as a proposition if the customers receive a sample CD or tape beforehand, or the offer of a free CD or tape at the promotion. The opening of a new accommodation wing might be promoted by giving away free bed–night samples to selected corporate customers. Alternatively, a function might be held with a lucky draw for the rooms, together with consolation prizes for the unlucky ones (so that no one goes away empty-handed).

Publicity and public relations

An organisation as publicly exposed as an hotel depends heavily upon its reputation. The goodwill of the public can significantly affect its viability.

Public relations (PR) is about the management of public attitudes, or the attitudes of those members of the public who are important to the organisation. This includes the customer base, the target market, and leaders in political, business, financial, union, and hospitality life who influence other people. PR can therefore embrace all marketing functions—because PR is concerned with image and positioning.

In a hospitality establishment, the PR person is very much concerned with using sales promotions to gain media exposure, and the PR person is thus often responsible for much of the organising of a promotion.

Every establishment likes to obtain free favourable exposure in the media. Promotions provide this opportunity—especially when the promotion is newsworthy. Gearing a promotion to obtain this sort of publicity achieves the objective of communicating the occasion to a broad audience and gives the promotion added impetus and stature. As well as gaining public mention through its own promotions, an hotel can also get its name mentioned by having someone else's event staged at the hotel. It can be worthwhile in these instances to offer a special deal and win the business—simply to achieve media mention.

Internationally acclaimed visitors and entertainers are chased by media, and an astute PR person can capitalise on this by arranging for television cameras to include the hotel's name in the background.

Summary

The sequence of steps in planning a promotion are:

◆ set the customer and product objectives;
◆ fix on a sales target and prepare a budget;
◆ get the right idea;
◆ sell it to the staff;
◆ organise it down to the last detail;
◆ promote it;
◆ turn it on and make it happen; and
◆ do it again next year if it works really well.

The risk with sales promotions is the tendency to extend them indefinitely—particularly if they are successful. This can be as counter-productive as repeating the same joke many times over. There is also a possibility that customers will think that a product is not good enough to be purchased on its own merits, and that some form of inducement has to be offered to compensate. This usually applies only to a property that continually has to resort to 'hype' to survive—like a run-down car yard that has a sale every week. This concern does not apply to a property with a strong position.

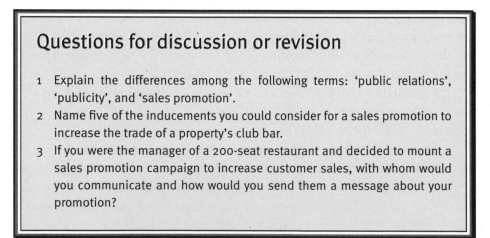

Questions for discussion or revision

1   Explain the differences among the following terms: 'public relations', 'publicity', and 'sales promotion'.
2   Name five of the inducements you could consider for a sales promotion to increase the trade of a property's club bar.
3   If you were the manager of a 200-seat restaurant and decided to mount a sales promotion campaign to increase customer sales, with whom would you communicate and how would you send them a message about your promotion?

Chapter 28

Direct Marketing Strategies

========= Aims of this chapter =========

The aims of this chapter are:
- to explain the reasons for direct email and mail strategies;
- to outline the techniques of direct messaging; and
- to describe how direct messaging can be used to build and maintain a customer database.

Theory

Direct marketing for hospitality establishments means direct approaches to existing and prospective customers—through email, mail, or by personal representation and customer contact. Such direct marketing has become an important source of business for hospitality establishments, especially as the cost of advertising has increased. Some places exist solely by this means of promotion.

This chapter concentrates on direct email and mail—selling a property's outlets, products, and facilities by sending electronic messages or postal letters with various enclosures (such as brochures, samples, incentives, reply-paid cards, invitations, and so on).

There are many advantages to direct marketing. The major advantage is that it can reduce the costs of advertising and distribution costs, and thus reduce many traditional marketing expenses.

email

The use of email is one of the cheapest means of marketing. However, the creation and maintenance of a database of customers is essential to its success, and this takes time and money to develop. The big advantage of email over postal mail is the cost differential. Similar comments apply to the cost advantage of email over the telephone—although the cost differential in this case is less marked.[1] However, mail and email, and to a lesser extent, the telephone, have less control over the communication relationship than does face-to-face contact.

The main advantage of email is its ability to deliver a personalised message to people known by their name and (email) address, with the effectiveness of the communication being considerably increased when details of the receiver's relevance to the sender are known. The more that is known about the customer the more personal the letter and its contents can become, and the more direct and effective can be the message.

Contact lists (from databases) usually originate from the establishment's own records, together with lists of people obtained from outside sources. There are brokers who sell lists of names, and some organisations sell or exchange their customer lists.

Database marketing is a 'buzz' term at the present time. It simply means maintaining a list of people on computer files. To have value, databases must be constantly updated with information about customers' purchases and any other facts relevant to their habits and preferences that can be used to influence a sale. The benefits of having customer information stored in a computer is that it can be easily cross-indexed to cluster and highlight various customer combinations by demographics, psychographics, buying behaviour, and purchase histories. By having accessible, historical information on file, an establishment can choose the most likely customers to mail with information about an offer or impending event. And, because email works best as a personalised message-delivery system, a good database provides customised information that enables the writer to refer to that person's interests.

There are several specialised email marketers who have expertise to offer larger organisations. For example, Starwood Hotels has selected specialists MessageMedia to deliver email messaging as part of a strategy involving a multi-media promotional campaign.[2] MessageMedia delivers monthly e-statements to Starwood Preferred Guest members, and informs customers of potential promotions and loyalty offers.

Mail by post

Direct mail by cost is a relatively expensive form of advertising. Taking into account the costs of labour, paper, envelope, and postage, the simplest letter is far more expensive per impact (people reached) than media advertising. Media advertising can work out to be less than a cent per impact (see page 329). In contrast, with direct mail—especially including enclosures such as multi-coloured brochures, reply-paid envelopes, cards, vouchers, menus, and even samples of products—the costs can soar to several dollars per impact. In these cases, each mailing impact must count. To be effective and cost-efficient it must be personal. Unlike media advertising (which, although it might have a defined target market, reaches unknown and unnamed people), direct mail has to be mailed to someone, identified by occupation at least, with an address that allows the postal authorities to deliver it.

When is used in an impersonal way—for example, by sending a large number of letters to companies or homes addressed to 'the Manager' or to 'the Householder'—direct mail ceases to have much advantage over general advertising. It is doubtful whether such mail (without a specific name) has any better chance of being read than does a media advertisement.

Some marketers consider a letter to have an advantage over print media because they can send 'kits' of collateral material. This is of doubtful benefit. Many print media allow enclosures in their newspapers or magazines, and often the costs of insertion or 'stuffing' in an envelope are such that any advantage is outweighed by the costs.

Reasons for using direct email and mail

Most establishments use direct email and mail to inform people about special offers, value-added packages, sales promotions, forthcoming events, and new developments. They choose the people they contact by their status. 'Status' refers to their being regular customers, infrequent customers, new customers, customers who have not used any of the facilities for a while, or potential customers.

The intention of the message is different in each case. The message might aim to attract new customers, or maintain contact with existing customers (and perhaps sell them more facilities or get them to use the facilities more often). It can be used to bring back customers who have drifted away. However, the most rewarding use of direct email and mail is to work through existing customers to keep them, or to encourage them to bring in new customers.

This form of contact is a more controlled diffusion of messages than advertising, and the messages do not conflict with whatever the competition is saying. The sender has the undivided attention of the recipients—provided that the message is matched with their interests.

It must be remembered that different categories of customers have different reasons for considering a property's facilities. The classic mistake is to send the same mailing piece to everyone—rather than distinguishing between types of customers. People do not think alike. They usually seek benefits associated with their occupations, their ages, and their desired lifestyles. Even if the offer is essentially the same, it should be customised to suit the situation of the recipient.

In terms of customising messages, email has several advantages. It is easy to adjust messages to suit particular recipients. Attachments, illustrations, and virtual tours of the property can be included as appropriate.

Privacy issue

Enterprises can compile mailing and email lists from their own records, or can purchase lists through list brokers. One such broker, British marketing group MM Group, claimed, in 2001, to have more than one billion names in its databank. Any business, especially one that is heavily dependent upon consumer goodwill (such as the hospitality business), should use address lists with care, conscious that there are privacy issues involved in the compilation of consumer information and details.

Address lists can be composed from publicly available information (such as electoral rolls) or from business records. An example of the latter are lists compiled as a result of computer card or electronic fund transfer point of sale (EFTPOS) usage. Loyalty schemes such as 'fly-buys' can also result in the compilation of direct address lists for marketing purposes.

A more intrusive way of compiling personal information is through a 'web cookie' or 'web bug'. This is a very small data file that can monitor webpage and website usage. Engage Technologies of the United States claims that it can monitor 72% of US Web traffic.[3]

Organisations that do not wish to receive unsolicited email (known as 'spam') or unsolicited mail can take certain actions to remove their names from lists when they realise that they are listed. Consumers can apply to the Australian Direct Marketing Association to have their names removed from mailing or email spam lists. The website of the association is <www.adma.com.au/consumer>.

Individuals and companies can also protect their electronic commerce with encryption software.

Main uses of direct email and mail

Direct email and direct mail can be used in the following ways:

◆ as an adjunct to an existing marketing plan;
◆ to sell new products;
◆ to sell promotions;
◆ to maintain confidentiality;
◆ to reduce old stocks;
◆ to generate new customers;
◆ to retain customers;
◆ to reactivate old or lost customers; and
◆ to upgrade some existing customers.

Each of these is considered below.

As an adjunct to an existing marketing plan

The combination of advertising, direct contact, and sales calls is a very effective strategy to employ when making a push for new customers. One of the truisms of marketing echoes a statement of the novelist Lewis Carroll: 'What I tell you three times is true'! [4]

To sell new products

Direct messaging works well when a new outlet has been created, when a new menu has been introduced, or when some important changes have been made. News is interesting. It is a good idea to make an offer around the new item to encourage the recipients to respond in some way.

To sell promotions

Direct messaging is also useful for inviting customers to become involved in a sales promotion. A message that details the features and the benefits often works better than advertising.

To maintain confidentiality

Some new products and sales promotions apply only to selected people. In addition, sometimes a property might not want to telegraph its intentions to competing establishments.

To reduce old stocks

Some establishments find themselves overstocked from time to time with various items—such as materials that were generated for previous promotions, but not used. Limited offers—perhaps on a 'privileged customer' basis—can not only shift these items but also develop a loyalty to the establishment.

To generate new customers

The generation of new customers is the most common use of direct messaging.

To retain customers

Keeping in touch with regular clients cheaply and efficiently is one of the best reasons for using email. Regular clients are the chief assets of the business and have to be treasured.

To reactivate old or lost customers

A friendly overture with an interesting offer from the property can work wonders with people who have drifted away over time.

To upgrade some existing customers

Upgrading some existing customers is a common technique of banks, credit providers, and retail stores. For a hospitality establishment, upgrading entails offering customers a series of special privileges not available to most people. These might include a club membership, extended credit, or access to certain 'private' facilities.

Building a database

Direct messaging is a dynamic marketing tool when used properly. If it is employed merely as a broadcast medium it becomes a communication with dubious sales value. Having a sound list of customers and prospects is the clue to effective direct emailing and mailing. In selecting an address list of potential customers, the rules of targeting apply—search for people who match the desired customer mix.

As the database grows, there is a need to update the list from guest records. The term 'merge and purge' refers to merging one list with another, and purging (or getting rid of) names that are no longer appropriate. These might be names of people whom your electronic mailer cannot find, are no longer responding, do not apply any more, or are duplicated.

A good database is programmed for correlations that are cross-indexed into categories that sort people by their demographic features, psychographic features, and buying habits—including recency, frequency, product type, and size of purchases. In addition, the database should note how the names came to be on the list (from where and when). This information is available from various records, including sales records.

New lists of prospects can be obtained by searching company shareholders records, club memberships, various government registrations, electoral rolls, and so on. But the best source is often existing customers, and some organisations offer them incentives for recommending names.

A low-cost source of email addresses can be achieved by exchanging lists with other businesses associated with hospitality.

When buying or exchanging lists, an organisation should evaluate their worth by using the test of 'recency/frequency/money spent'. This means a check on how recently the people purchased, how often they have purchased, and how much they spent each time. The organisation should ensure that the names on the list constitute an active list, and they should avoid old lists. After two years, most lists are worthless. The best ones are those compiled in-house from one's own customers.

Making an offer

Direct messaging works best if there is a specific offer. Although it is an excellent idea to keep in touch with existing and prospective customers, the point of the exercise is to obtain a response or a sale. This is better achieved if an offer or a benefit is the reason for the message.

It is impossible to measure the effect of a message that does no more than inform the recipient. Each message should therefore seek a response, and the type of response required has to be clearly identified. This provides measurement and accountability—feedback from the process that can be evaluated by numbers (sales and cost) so that responses can be tested and adjustments made to the approach.

A message about the right product effectively communicated to the right people should elicit a response. But even with the best offers there is always a problem with 'inertia'. Response rates vary, depending on the appeal of the offer, but anything over 3% can be considered good, and anything over 7% is outstanding. Different creative approaches and variations of the offer can be tried to test the best response rate.

Various offers that can be made

An offer of a free trial or demonstration is one of the best to make because it asks the recipient to do something without any conditions attached. The recipient simply has to try the meal, the drink, or the facility being offered. Such a trial offer suits the service products of hospitality, because hospitality products can seldom be seen, felt, handled, or experienced in advance.

A conditional offer of sale can be made. This means offering the use of a facility at a special rate—provided that, if satisfied, the recipient will continue to purchase.

Another offer used frequently by hospitality establishments is a 'positive option' offer. This means that, by paying a fee and joining a club, the customer can buy a range of goods or products at a very reduced price.

A 'your choice' offer can also be made. In this case, customers are offered a range of specially discounted products from which they can choose one or two. This is a good way of determining the popularity of various hospitality products by measuring the responses to each one.

Discount offers are straight 'money-off' propositions. There is no mystery about these. They can be offered to attract custom during a down period—such as at weekends at an hotel that relies mainly on business travellers.

A 'refund-if-not-satisfied' offer is a good way to introduce a new product—such as a special food item, business facility, or even a small item such as a new cocktail.

There are also 'you-can-win' offers. These are always popular with customers. They can be used as an inducement to try a facility, or simply to respond by sending back a coupon or token. The responses often reveal the degree of interest by customers in a product that can be used for a follow-up call by a salesperson.

'Limited time' offers are added motivations for customers to respond to any offer. They often overcome the natural inertia of people.

Direct email and mail strategic development

In the preparation of any promotion it is necessary to have defined and measurable strategic objectives. The choice of the right mix of message-delivery systems is determined by the markets to be targeted, and by their accessibility.

Direct mail is very popular in the hospitality industry—perhaps in the mistaken belief that it is relatively inexpensive. Direct mail is cost-effective only when it makes an offer and when the people to be targeted can be named so that the mailing can be personalised. Some messages are not suitable for direct mail. For example, building an image is more suitable for media advertising than for direct mail.

The use of email is more cost-effective than mail—although it might not have as wide a reach. But, like all correspondence, email is a more subtle medium than most users realise. It is useful to think of email in the same way as thinking of correspondence with a penfriend or acquaintance some distance away. One message does not bond the sender and the recipient, but consistent messages gradually develop a relationship and perhaps cement a friendship.

Customising should not be an act or gesture. An authentic offer presented genuinely is more likely to be effective. But the sender should not say: 'This is a genuine offer'. This implies that previous offers were not genuine. And few people are fooled by trite statements such as: 'Yes, that's right! For only $ . . . you will get . . . '. With direct messaging, the products being promoted, and the offer being made, have to suit the customer mix of the property and the individuals who comprise the mix. A proposition has to be developed that has a distinct price benefit or immediate advantage for the recipient. 'What's in it for me?' is the question that has to be answered by the proposition in the mailing piece.

Then comes the creative part—working the offer into a communication that tells the recipients what they will get in the clearest terms and that overcomes the natural worry of making a decision. In compiling your message, always get to the point in the first or second sentence. Make your offer early, and be quite clear about what you are saying.

It is essential in the composition of a direct message to provide easy response methods. Clearly, email is far superior in inviting a response, because a simple click can send a reply. Postal services need more care (and expense). The usual method is through despatching a reply-paid envelope. Other options for inducing a reply (with either email or post) are a toll-free phone number, or a voucher or coupon that can be redeemed only by personal attendance at the property.

Remember, your image and therefore the position of your property is on show when you write, so do not think of email or mail as being a separate part of your promotion strategies. However, do consider the advantages of these media. Their ability to be personal and their capacity to reach out to your receiver with an offer of friendship and interest should not be underestimated.

Questions for discussion or revision

1   A three-star hotel of 500 rooms is located in a city that is a major tourist destination for overseas visitors. The competition is intense and there are hundreds of hotels competing for the tourist dollar and thousands of travel agencies around the world that can recommend clients. With 500 rooms, the hotel is obviously large. It features two respectable dining-rooms—one catering for fine dining and the other a bistro for casual diners. Its recreational facilities include a swimming pool, a spa, a sauna, a well-equipped gymnasium, and four tennis courts on the roof. The sustainable competitive advantage of the hotel is its massive five-storey car park that can accommodate 400 cars. Your task is to plan a direct email and mail campaign that will economically produce awareness of the property and increase its share of the holiday market. You will need to decide to whom the message will be sent (target markets), what the main message will be, and which inducements you will use to interest the travel agents.

2   List the chief advantages of email.

3   Your licensed golf club is fifty years old but, due to increased competition from new clubs, membership has been steadily falling. You have upgraded the course and the clubhouse facilities. The next task is to increase membership. What direct email and mail strategies would you use to communicate the changes to members and potential members?

Chapter 29

Product Development Strategies

Aims of this chapter

The aims of this chapter are:
- to explain how new products are developed;
- to describe how existing products can be improved; and
- to discuss how product development can rejuvenate an establishment by giving the customers a better experience.

Theory

Every hospitality property in the world tries to sell accommodation, food, or drink. How a place does things makes the difference between an ordinary experience and a special experience and, in most cases, makes the difference between gaining customers and losing them. It is often thought that how a place does things is its 'style'. Actually, its style is how the place considers its customers.

The way a hospitality establishment does things is its product. If it wants more customers, it has to ensure that what it does is distinctively *its* product—an entity that provides a difference, and offers obvious benefits for its customers. When it does this, it has a sustainable competitive advantage.

Hospitality is a series of products that have to be customer-orientated to work. The emphasis, therefore, has to be on product strategies—the means by which a better experience is provided for the customers. The only way to succeed in business is to think about strategies all the time—to think about pleasing customers and appealing to customers.

A place should always aim to create for customers a sense of 'ownership' or 'belonging' to an establishment. Regulars at a local pub feel this and enjoy it. It is harder to achieve with transients. Even so, some sense of being wanted and being among friends is important to everyone. For the long-distance traveller, a place that offers these sorts of attributes is providing a haven of solace to which they will return when an opportunity is presented. And they will pass on memories of their pleasant experiences to others. This is how solid reputations are built—rather than with glass, brass, marble, and tons of slate.

The enemies of hospitality strategies are apathy, ignorance, and arrogance. In any failing establishment, one or more of these shortcomings is usually evident. They usually arise if the owners are in the business only for the money and not for the customers. Such owners 'push' for every dollar they can get. They weaken the drinks, cut back on the food portions, reduce the staff, minimise the hours they trade, and try to *sell* instead of *serve*. Such lack of empathy for the customers—an inability to understand their needs—is associated with owners who lack interest in alternative strategies and who are devoid of imagination.

Some people are so busy being in business that they forget that the customers are the reason for being in business. Of course, examples of apathy, ignorance, and arrogance are also common outside the hospitality industry. There are doctors and hospitals who treat people as commodities rather than patients in need of help, public servants who do not serve the public, builders who build to suit their own pockets instead of the owner's comfort, appliances that meet the manufacturer's cost economies instead of the users' needs, manuals that are difficult to understand, and public transport that suits the staff rosters instead of the needs of travellers. Many of life's frustrations are caused by people who do not consider other people. Such conduct is bad enough in ordinary business. In the hospitality sector, it is business suicide.

Business is people

Market surveys show that the benefits sought by customers from hotels are friendliness, compatibility with other guests, helpfulness, knowledge, location, comfort, reputation, cleanliness, value, facilities, minimal noise, personalised service, and consideration.

Few customers want size, impressiveness, luxurious surroundings, free facilities, discounts, gymnasium, pool, spa, restaurants, bars, shops, valet service, and free bottles of champagne. Further probing shows that customers do not assess an hotel by the amount of marble and brass, or the number of chandeliers. A free bottle of champagne is 'nice', but a cup of coffee is just as acceptable.

Of course, there are some customers who want the most luxurious place in town, and can afford to stay there—but they are human too, and their basic likes and dislikes are the same as those of other people. The hotels that concentrate on the basics of hospitality and develop product strategies that offer customers recognition, friendship, help, simple comforts, personalised services, and consideration will always be the winners.

Examples of product strategies

The fortunes of an establishment will not be changed by simply copying any one of the product strategies outlined in this chapter. Rather, the culmination of customer-orientated product strategies and the sum total of customer experiences make for success. When product strategies become perfunctory services performed by unenthusiastic waiters, the magic dies. Business is people, and these people include the people who serve the customers.

Here are some examples of product strategies that can provide a better experience for customers. The great thing about most of these strategies is that they do not cost a cent to implement.

Food strategies

Food starts 'dying' the moment it comes out of the oven or off the stove. To get the food to the customer quickly, use a runner. Michael Hurst explains:[1]

> We use waiters and waitresses. But food servers never leave their station. Runners bring the food from the kitchen and put it on the sidestands. This way, food comes hot from the kitchen and the server can befriend his other customers. By using runners I can serve 30% more people. Serve hot foods hot. Make an art of it, not an empty claim. Every restaurant operator claims he serves hot food, but how many do? Serve cold foods cold. Serve salads ice cold.'

Choice seems to be a problem for restaurants. Their ideal is to have a set menu because it avoids wastage. Are they so devoid of kitchen skills and imagination that they cannot develop ways of offering a selection of dishes that can still appeal to the customer without waste? The 'soup of the day' is a classic example of minimal thought by the chef. One soup? Why not offer thirty soups to the customer and make it a product strategy? If waste is a worry, soup can be frozen in portions and thawed in minutes by microwave. How about desserts (also called 'pudding' or 'sweets')? There are hordes of customers who regard the main course as something they have to eat before they get to the dessert—the best part of the meal in the estimation of these people.

Some places have the same menu for months and even years. Michael Hurst believes hospitality should be fun—for him and for the customers. He believes that creativity keeps customers coming back. 'I perceive us as not selling food and beverage, but as trying to provide a pleasant experience for our guests. That's the rule of hospitality.'

Hurst, who as well as running his restaurant, has taught restaurant management and merchandising at Florida International University, believes variety and improvement are the constant challenges of the business. He has devised a unique sampling and market research program that involves servers with customers. The programs are charged to the advertising budget.[2]

> When I develop a budget, I set aside a bundle for marketing. We have to do things for people who patronise the restaurant to help them enjoy themselves so that when they leave they talk about and recommend the restaurant.'

First, Hurst tests two or three new food items each week. Anyone in the restaurant can contribute ideas, but the final selection is his. When an item is good and has a chance to get on the menu, it is taste-tested by the employees. If 85 % of them think it is good, it goes into the first phase—which is to do nothing for 30–60 days except to have servers whet the customers' appetites by telling them something new and different and good is coming up. Then Hurst puts his market research program into effect. Each day a set amount of the new item is prepared. Hurst handpicks guests as they enter the restaurant, and tells them he would like them to try a new item. He does not tell them what it is, but he does ask them to let him know if they like it, and if it should go on the menu. After they have eaten it the server explains what the item is. Innovation—creating new product strategies all the time—makes people talk about a place, and talk brings more customers.

Hospitality is personal. One restaurateur relates how he creates special dishes on the spot for fussy clients.[3]

> I didn't run the place for the cook, I ran it for customers. If someone wanted a meal outside normal hours they were fed. Within five minutes of entering the place, customers got a drink and something to eat. We worked for the customer—not for our hours of business, our staff, a strict menu, or a strict anything. Hospitality is personal.'

A brilliant chef and restaurateur used to begin each day by planning the menu for the day. No one ever became bored with the menu. In fact, the customers never knew what to expect. However, the word spread that whatever he did was delicious, generously proportioned, and exciting.

Another restaurant lets the customer choose the exact amount of steak he or she wants. This is personal and individual service.

Tea and coffee

For most establishments, a drink is just a drink and is served much the same anywhere. But the way in which beverages are served presents an ideal opportunity to excite and enthuse the customer. For example, the Japanese have turned serving tea into a ritual ceremony.

Coffee can be bought everywhere. But one place serves coffee made from beans grown by peasants high up the Andes in Peru. The coffee is brought down by pack mules and shipped especially to the hotel. You cannot get that coffee anywhere else.

Many people are very particular about their coffee and how it is ground, brewed, and presented. Why not offer customers various alternatives? Wise restaurateurs say that coffee should be freshly brewed in front of the customer because nothing quite enhances anticipation as does the look and smell of freshly brewing coffee.

Alcoholic drinks

At some restaurants, customers can taste several wines before making their choice. If they feel uncertain, the wine waiter, who is a recognised judge, recommends one. In several restaurants around the country, an old custom is preserved by the head waiter wearing a tasting cup around his neck to taste every wine before it is poured.

At the bar of one leading hotel, beer can be served in any drinking vessel the customer chooses—a pewter mug, a stein, a chalice, or a ceramic cup. There are dozens of different ways of drinking the same beer.

At another hotel, a first-time customer is given his or her own glass, and the person's name is engraved on it. No one else can use it. A customer can return five years later and find his or her glass waiting.

There are many different ways of doing things when it comes to serving drinks, but the overwhelming majority of places serve drinks in the same way as everyone else! Where is a sense of fun and excitement for the customers? Drinking should be fun.

Turning a failing property around

If a property has slipped into the doldrums, turning that property around requires a change of culture—a whole new attitude from the management and the staff. It means eliminating apathy, ignorance, and arrogance.

On most occasions, it is very difficult to change people who do not under-stand that business is people and that hospitality is 'giving to get'. Turning a property around often requires the removal of staff members who do not have the ability to share the gift of friendship, and replacing them with people who do.

Working in the place has to become an enjoyable experience for the servers as well as for the customers. The staff must be given goals, incentives, and rewards. An establishment should aim to make service a fun thing to do.

It is obvious that every business has to make a profit. But, when sales soar, fixed costs and overheads dwindle rapidly in proportion to turnover. So do not work for budgets, accountants, rosters, and regimented systems. The 'name of the game' is customer numbers, and this means trying at all times to turn the customers into unpaid salespeople to help get those numbers up.

Review the product strategies and the way you do things. Provide excite-ment and interest. But do not be silly and do things that are different simply for the sake of being different. Do what is going to make the people you target say: 'It's been wonderful. Thank you. I'm going to tell my friends!'.

Theory of product development

Hospitality is one of the most traditional and conservative industries in the world. Because of this conservatism, many bright ideas never come to fruition. See the case study 'Bright ideas from students', page 355.

The sort of inertia portrayed in the case study should not be the prevailing culture of hospitality. Entertaining—giving people good food and wine and providing pleasant places to sleep—is fun for hosts and guests alike. And yet, all over the world, there is a dreary sameness about the way things are done. Some owners are wary of innovation; they are frightened of being different. Others worry about how much innovation will cost. But the improvements that are most appreciated by customers are simply improvements in the way that things are done—and these changes cost nothing.

Other property owners are too stubborn to embrace change. They do not listen to their customers and believe that they know best. Too many property owners start out with the assumption that the property is theirs to do what they like with—and they do, irrespective of the customers' preferences and needs.

Improving products and developing exciting new ones for the customers' enjoyment is the zest of hospitality. This does not mean being zany, although being zany is better than being boring! It means management has to think harder about making their places better places for their customers. An hotel

---

CASE STUDY

Bright ideas from students

Marketing students at a well-known hotel school are asked each semester to do an exercise on product development. Their task is to think of new ways of doing the ordinary things of hospitality—such as serving a beer, or serving soup.

Every semester the students overwhelm the lecturers with great new ways of doing things. They come up with ideas that make commercial sense, ideas that would work in the marketplace, ideas that would please the customers, and ideas that would make money. Unfortunately, you will probably never see any of their ideas used by a commercial operator. Why is this?

It is because hospitality is one of the most traditional and conservative industries in the world.

CASE STUDY

'Cheers'

The American sit-com, 'Cheers', was a classic portrayal of the comradeship that should be part of an integrated relationship among customers, the staff, and management.

In that situation, the customers had a sense that the property was 'theirs' as much as the owner's. The staff also had a sense of ownership. The result portrayed over many episodes was that the customers kept coming back, the staff was dedicated, and the owners made a profit.

This was a fictional portrayal, but it conveyed the productive relationships that exist among customers, staff, and owners when each feels they have an interest in the property.

depends on the continuing success of its base products—its room hire, dining-rooms, and bars. If any of these key areas of revenue is not working properly, it affects other products and, ultimately, the overall market position and profit of the establishment.

Product development, either through improvement or modification, is a growth strategy. Its purpose is to retain existing customers, and attract new customers. Product development is a continuing concern. Management has to improve sales if possible, remain competitive, and increase or maintain profit levels by improving the products by adding new experiences for the customers.

Product life-cycles

Every product, including the hotel itself, has a life-cycle that involves a series of stages:

- ◆ development;
- ◆ introduction;
- ◆ growth;
- ◆ maturation;
- ◆ decline; and
- ◆ death or revitalisation.

Each of these is considered below.

Development

Development refers to the conception of the product, followed by research and market analysis, selection of target markets, testing of the product, a feasibility study, and preparation for sale.

Introduction

Introduction refers to exposure of the product to the customers, followed by promotion to provide awareness, and assistance in the selling process.

Growth

Growth occurs if the product is accepted by the customers, thus allowing sales to begin to repay the effort of creating the product.

Maturation

Maturation occurs when the product has reached the peak of its sales performance and is providing good profits. At this time there is usually considerable competition from other organisations.

Decline

Decline occurs as the product becomes somewhat boring and sales begin a steady downwards slide.

Death or revitalisation

At this time, management has must decide whether to let the product die a natural death or whether it should be revitalised in some way.

Depending on the product, these stages are of varying duration. Sometimes they are rather drawn out. In other cases, the stages can be startlingly brief.

Without growth or innovation, any hospitality establishment faces the problem of becoming a tired facility. Innovation, glamour, and glitz always appeal to some people in the hospitality market, and many customers move on when they get the feeling that a place is not as good as it used to be.

Beware of drastic change

Product development can represent a problem for management. Change can have unpredictable outcomes, and disastrous mistakes can occur. Most mistakes occur as a result of management making changes without checking to find out if the changes are what the customers want.

New is not necessarily better. There is no point in changing a winning formula. It can be improved, but should not be changed for the sake of change. Before changes are made their outcomes must be assessed.

For example, to increase bar sales an hotel might decide to extend and redecorate its club bar, and might add two additional barpeople to cope with the supposed increase in sales. The presumption is that there is sufficient demand to warrant the expenditure. However, an examination of all the factors affected by these changes could alter that decision. For example:

◆ How will the bar extensions be accepted by the existing patrons? Many people have their favourite positions at the bar, or have favourite table. These people can quite put out if someone else occupies 'their' area. Will many customers be lost when their 'old haunt' changes from being a cosy, busy bar to a larger, less private, strange environment?

◆ How many new customers will be attracted merely because the bar becomes bigger? Is size enough to get them to change their habits? Perhaps the demand has been assessed on the number of occasions that the bar is filled and cramped. Is that really preventing a number of 'new' customers from drinking there? Many customers like to be part of a crowd.

- What will happen to costs if more staff are put on?
- If the additional customers do not materialise, what will happen to profits?
- How will the staff react to the proposed extension? Are they in favour of it? Perhaps the bar is very popular as it is because of the personalities of the staff, and perhaps they do not want new staff members sharing their workplace.

Having assessed these sorts of factors, it might be that an additional bar would achieve the same objective. Or, it might be better to attract customers to other times of the day by offering 'happy hours' with drinks reduced to half price, or 'feeding times' with free canapés on offer. To get more use from the same bar might make sense and achieve the desired objective of increased sales—without adding to infrastructure costs and without running the risk of losing existing custom.

Assessing the outcome of change

The starting-point for developing or improving a product involves research, including consultation with the customers. Usually this provides ideas for improvement or modification that will help to increase sales, build customer numbers, improve market share, or reduce costs. Sometimes the assessment will reveal that the product or facility should be closed down because it has passed its useful life.

When seeking to improve or change a product there are many strategic options to consider involving promotion of the product, staff changes, price offers, changes in merchandise, product presentation, infrastructure, décor, product quality, efficiency, timing, quantity, systems, specialisation, productivity, expansion, contraction, or diversification. Some assessments need to be made of these factors.

The 'Outcome assessment table' (Figure 29.1, page 359) is a tool that can be used in an attempt to make such an assessment. It is a simple screening process for the ideas and strategic options put forward. Its purpose is to cover the factors that might be affected by the proposed change and to make an attempt to forecast the effects over six months. Research should be used to test the reactions of customers, existing and potential, and to establish solutions that are the least disruptive and promise the best outcome.

In using Figure 29.1 to get some assessment of the likely effects of the proposed change, management should place a tick in the column for 'increase', 'decrease', or 'no change' according to its best estimate of the likely effect. If it is possible to make a dollar assessment of the effect, this should be entered in the last column.

	Increase	Decrease	No change	Outcome ($)
Customer appreciation				
Number of existing customers				
Number of new customers				
Prices				
Sales				
Costs—building				
Costs—resources				
Market share				
Staff goodwill				
Property value				
Profit				

Figure 29.1 Outcome assessment table
Authors' presentation

After careful screening of all the options using a table such as that illustrated in Figure 29.1, the most promising concept is chosen and it becomes the strategy for product development. Goals are then set for the product changes and the strategy is implemented. After six months, all the factors are checked and compared with the forecasts. If the outcomes have not met the objectives, further changes might be required. The process is then repeated.

Expectations of the customers

The key to product development is an assessment of the expectations of customers. Although the provision of lodgings and food is the obvious expectation, customers are likely to be also seeking added value in the form of convenience, escape, companionship, an unusual experience, a special occasion, a popular activity, entertainment, fun, comfort, or sheer indulgence. Other factors include the friendliness of the staff or the popularity of a place (some people preferring to be where the 'crowd' is). All of these factors must be considered when change is contemplated. The key to product development is to build on a successful product base and a sound position in the market. Drastic change should be contemplated only when there is nothing to lose by it.

When property owners are faced with the option of 'death or revitalisation', there is often a tendency to blame the location of the building itself and a decision is made to sell. In these circumstances, the new owners buy an unsatisfactory business, and seldom do better than the previous owners. They try to promote their way out of trouble, but this is rarely the answer.

In contrast, something quite different and better in the way of customer experiences might improve the fortunes of the place. It is not easy. A place that has become run down becomes tainted by its reputation.

Opportunities for product development

Managing an establishment in the hospitality industry is like directing a live theatre performance. It is a long-running show that should keep on getting better and better. If it is a good show, people will come from miles around to enjoy the actors' 'performances'. This means the development of exciting and interesting new products. In most cases this simply involves innovative ways of doing things that most places do.

The best hospitality establishments have a flair for making people relaxed, comfortable, and welcome. For customers who prefer things to be happening, they provide a busy environment with many people coming and going. But they also consider those who prefer quietness, privacy, and solitude, and ensure that there is a place where people can retreat when they need to be away from the crowd.

Hospitality is about providing customers with a sense of occasion—a feeling of being involved in something special. It is the 'extras' that count, and this means the development of ways of doing things that go beyond the expectations of customers. But change for change's sake is not a good idea. And change designed for the organisational needs of the organisation is similarly unlikely to be successful. New systems must be perceived by the customers to be of direct benefit to them. You can go out of business in an organised way. The products must be shaped so that they are special and different for the customers. There is not a right or wrong way to do things—only ways that customers appreciate. Management should set out to capture markets that have a synergy with each other, and should explain the reasons for improvements so that customers appreciate what is being done for them.

Unless an hotel has completely 'lost its soul', management should seldom consider abandoning its core base of customers. Instead, it should concentrate on building on the existing base.

Club Mediterranean

The secret of Club Mediterranean—a company that markets organised holidays around villages built by the company in attractive, beachside locations—is having fun-loving organisers and managers. The organisers are carefully chosen for their friendliness, their love of fun, and their ability to involve people in activities. They are gracious hosts who are the 'heart and soul' of the villages.

Club Med has been successful for many years, but it has changed over the years to meet changes in people's needs. From focus groups and extensive studies of customer behaviour, the owners use targeting to pick their markets. Their products are then carefully developed to satisfy new markets while never losing sight of the basics of their successful operations.

Improve before thinking of change

Management should first consider improvement, rather than wholesale change. It makes sense to do better what a place is already doing—rather than trying to do what someone else is doing, and not doing it as well.

Products can be developed independently of each other. A place can make gradual changes to various products without upsetting regular patrons. This could perhaps begin with a new, glitzy cocktail bar while retaining the old established bar. When the new one gains acceptance, the old one can be renovated. Then management can move on with planned improvements to the dining-rooms, and then other parts of the establishment.

Synergy is the relationship between the place's mission, its positioning, and its distinctive competencies. There are many effective product development strategies to consider that can be added to existing products. For example, an hotel should consider increasing the range and nature of merchandise on offer through shops, bars, and reception areas. There might be scope to develop interesting holiday packages, local tours, discount vouchers for shops, ticketing facilities for theatres, sporting events, casinos, and so on.

If the dining-rooms and the food are features of an establishment, it might consider offering new eating experiences. In this case, it is best to experiment with different dishes. When the customers are vocal in their approval, the dishes can be made into regular items on the menu.

Opportunities exist for capitalising on assets by upgrading some sections of the lodgings into different categories—such as fully serviced, eat-in suites, permanent hire suites or rooms, temporary offices, self-service apartments, and so on. If there is a swimming pool, management could consider adding saunas, massage, swimming lessons, games, and so on.

Cycles, fads, fashions, and trends

Cycles, fads, fashions, and trends sometimes cause management to consider deleting some of the less profitable services being offered. The retraction of services and facilities that customers have come to expect is difficult. However, the same outcome analysis as illustrated in Figure 29.1 (page 359) can be used again—this time to test how many customers might be lost by the change. As with introducing new products, experimentation is important before a final commitment is made to deleting a product. Test marketing saves time and money and avoids the embarrassment of failure.

Fads and fashions are usually different ways of doing the same thing. They are often copied by others and then they become simply 'what everybody does' and lose their point and value. To ignore fads and fashions can be folly, but to follow them slavishly is often economically silly for establishments that are attempting to build an individual positioning image.

Recycling means investigating old ideas that can be reintroduced. In fact, most of today's new concepts are yesterday's old concepts in different clothes. The advantage of copying old ideas that will suit today's markets is that they have a 'track record'—a history of success that can be emulated and examples of failures that can be avoided.

Trends are usually decided by economic and technological developments. When times are good, people travel and spend more, and the opposite occurs when the economy tightens. There are usually early indicators of trends. Many of these indicators seem to be missed by operators who then find themselves reacting to change instead of planning for it.

Hospitality is a person-to-person, customised business, and the volatility of its markets means that situations seldom remain stable. To be successful, management must be thinking all the time about making its place better for the customers. Product development is not just the key to success, it is also the means of survival.

Questions for discussion or revision

1   What is meant by 'giving to get'?
2   According to research, what are the main benefits sought by customers?
3   What are five key strategies that you could employ to turn a failing property around?
4   Your restaurant has been successful for the past ten years and business has remained steady until now. Do you make changes? If so, explain why. Describe the types of changes you would contemplate.

Chapter 30

Forecasting Market Demand

Aims of this chapter

The aims of this chapter are:
- to explain the purpose of forecasting market demand;
- to describe how forecasting can be used; and
- to outline the forecasting methodologies available.

Theory

Owners and managers of hospitality properties generally seem to have an optimistic view of the future of their establishments. Their belief is that promotion, glamour, glitz, and 'hype' will override all other market indicators and return a handsome profit on their investment. This is the classic delusion: 'Build a better mousetrap and the world will beat a path to your door'.

Accurate forecasting, based on a careful assessment of market and economic indicators, is one of the most critical aspects of business planning. The commitment of large sums of money and valuable human resources depends on this forecasting. But it is not always possible to forecast every movement in a regional market, let alone a world market. The Asian region experienced an economic and financial crisis in 1997, and this resulted in a marginal fall in inbound tourism arrivals in 1998 (and tourism receipts in that year were 36.4% of the world's total), but regional economies rebounded, and 1999 saw an increase of 4.7% in the number of arrivals compared with the previous year.[1] Despite the improvement, hotel occupancies remained generally low and profitability was therefore also down. None of these events was foreseen in the mid 1990s when economies were booming.

Forecasting is not an easy task because there is an element of risk in every venture. No one can confidently predict the future. However, the purpose of forecasting market demand is to minimise the risks and leave only totally unpredictable events to chance. Even then, good marketers should always allow for the unpredictable by planning for a fall-back position.

The reasons for forecasting are:

◆ to provide a diagnostic tool for setting corporate objectives for sales, profit, and asset realisation; and

◆ to provide an early-warning system to protect an organisation's assets in investment capital, knowledge, staff, premises, facilities, and equipment.

Market size

The size of the hospitality market is assessed by adding up the total sales of each market category in the industry—such as bed–night sales, beverage sales, and so on. Most governments produce statistics from which the industry can extract information to obtain an historical picture of the market. From this it is possible to predict potential for the forthcoming year, after making allowances for known market factors that could affect the result.

Market expansion occurs as a result of population increases (natural and migration), increased number of tourists, new trends in product usage, or economic changes that increase the amount of discretionary expenditure available to the population. The market recedes when the demand by holiday-makers or businesses decreases. These are termed 'market factors'—changes in consumer behaviour or changes in circumstances that affect market demand and, therefore, affect the market's total sales potential.

The *market demand* for a product is the anticipated number of customers who, based on previous sales and trends, will buy the product in a given location over a specified time. The *market potential* for a product is the anticipated total number of sales of a product (by all sellers in the market) over a specified time, given a defined set of circumstances. By calculating market demand and market potential, a property can estimate its share of the total market or its share of some segments of that market. It can also decide which share it wants in the future.

Sometimes, despite predictions based on market factors, expansion or contraction of demand depends upon how the users and consumers respond to the forces of change. For example, it is fair to say that there has been a world-wide trend towards more people eating away from home, and it can be anticipated that this trend will continue.

Predicting the future is therefore a guessing game. Economists are often wrong in their predictions of overall market factors. Some can say with modest justification that they have been proved less wrong than others in their predictions, but which economist will be right next time is still a gamble. The best that anyone can say is that the demand for hospitality will continue. Four thousand years of history indicates that it will always be a viable business in which to be involved.

Many managers fail to recognise that in a static market any growth in their own market must occur at the expense of other establishments. This means that the property's marketing strategies have to offer a sustainable competitive advantage to keep their existing customer base while attempting to get the customers from rival establishments to break with habit and shift their business to them.

If investors and new business owners are looking for reassurance on return for their capital, they could do no better than to assess the future of a property on the ability of their marketing strategies to perform competitively. A realistic appraisal of the amount of business that can be captured from the targeted customer groups, together with favourable market factors, is a sound basis for forecasting sales. When coupled with the arithmetic of costs and return on capital, investors can be more certain of their outlay.

A market forecast is the realistic anticipation of market demand for a product, provided that the expected circumstances prevail. From the market forecast, a property can make a sales forecast in dollars (or numbers of units to be sold) upon which it prepares a sales budget. Production and expenditure estimates are then set, based on the sales forecast that will direct the operation's performance over the ensuing budgetary period within prescribed financial guidelines.

The forecast should have projections of market factors and influences for, say, three to five years, and projections of internal factors such as occupancy for similar periods. These projections will have descriptive and statistical elements that can be brought into budgets and market planning.

Market factor analysis

Forecasting relies on a combination of some or all of the methods used to examine market factors. When attempting to measure demand and forecast change, management must specify what it wants measured. For example, in forecasting luxury hotel accommodation requirements it is misleading to predict demand merely on the basis of a general increase in travel to the area near the establishment. The travellers might be caravanners, families in cars, or backpackers—all of whom might have limited or no interest in staying at the accommodation property in question.

Forecasting must be measured against demand criteria that predict and segment the following:

◆ number of people by their demographic and psychographic types, and from where they are coming (geographic sources);
◆ number of people by their requirements for products, frequency of purchase, and durations of stay (bed–nights);
◆ number of people by unit sales and their dollar expenditure; and
◆ number of competitors after the same market segments.

Using the above criteria, the history of a market measured over several years is an indication of trends that can be projected into the forthcoming year. However, such projections have to be modified by the information acquired from various other forecasting methods. Havoc can be wreaked with a projection that is based merely on trends, and that fails to consider shifts in market preferences, impending economic change, or government intervention.

If a project is so finely balanced that the profit, interest repayments, and required capital return on the investment cannot withstand a 25% shortfall in the forecast sales, it becomes a gamble, rather than a venture, and it would be unwise to proceed.

Many properties rely heavily on asset growth and the sale of the property to make their investment worthwhile. For example, it has been accepted practice to believe that capital recovery requires seven to ten years for completion. That is a debatable proposition.

Running costs are variable and can be adjusted to match sales. The fixed costs of rent, interest repayments, and capital recovery march on remorselessly despite the sales—often making a mockery of profit projections.

There should not be too much reliance on asset growth because the tangible assets of a hospitality property—such as the real estate (building and land), stock and fittings, and goodwill (numbers of customers, sales and profit)—tend to depreciate in real-value terms (after the inflationary effect is discounted) when there is a declining market.

What it all means from an investment viewpoint is that the viability of a hospitality venture is more dependent upon strategic marketing than is real estate, because the real estate value in most cases relies on the income-earning potential of the business. A high income-earning property that has a burgeoning customer base is worth money. A tired property with waning customer interest is not.

Market research and market analysis

Market research and market analysis are used to find out if there is untapped potential for sales in the current market. There might be people who cannot use the facilities because of cost or distance, and there might be those who do not find the facilities attractive, or have been given no reason to use the facilities. This situation can change when wider markets are opened up by increased transport capacity such as a new airport or better flight schedules.

Market analysis can thus indicate if the total market can be increased, or whether the competition is vulnerable to attack. Market analysis can take the following forms:

◆ surveys of buyers' intentions;
◆ assessment of economic indicators;
◆ assessment of leading indicators;
◆ consideration of impending events;
◆ extension of demand curve;
◆ measurement of trends;
◆ assessment of changing technologies; and
◆ assessment of the property's potential.

Each of these is considered below.

Surveys of buyers' intentions

Market research among known users of hospitality can be an effective way of estimating demand. Their responses can be graded from 'almost certain' to 'most unlikely', and an average of their total responses can be taken.

Economic indicators

An assessment of economic indicators refers to changes in overall economic conditions. These include significant changes to interest rates, wages, taxation (personal and company), investment incentives, availability of credit, tariffs, imposts, exchange rates, and so on.

Leading indicators

Various indicators can give a lead to possible changes in sales—although there is usually a lag time involved. For example, in the building industry, certain factors—such as architectural activity, applications for finance, and the calling of tenders—can indicate the amount of building work that is in the pipeline. In the hospitality industry, travel agencies and tourism offices first notice changes in interest by the travelling public. Financiers, banks, and trade commissioners might note a change in the attitudes of business towards corporate expansion or contraction, and therefore the likelihood of there being an increase or decrease in business travel.

Impending events

Large festivals, sporting events, big development projects, new industries, better transport facilities, and so on can all indicate the likelihood of increased hospitality business.

Extension of demand curve

Statistical demand analysis (or correlation analysis) is a set of procedures designed to discover and rate the market factors affecting demand. These factors include prices, incomes, population, market size, promotion, and product evolution or innovation.

Measurement of trends

Trends spread from state to state, and from country to country. Observable changes to the hospitality industry in other countries can be transferred and possibly win acceptance elsewhere. Assessment of these is made on:

◆ the size of the market affected by certain trends;
◆ the demographics of the market affected by certain trends;
◆ the cities, states, and countries affected by certain trends;
◆ the kinds of outlets used in the trend;
◆ the rate of rise and fall of the trend; and
◆ the needs involved in the trend (including utilitarian, fashion, fun, or psychological needs).

Some trends that are forecasted for the Asia–Pacific region in the twenty-first century include the following:[2]

◆ mass-market tourism—the volume of travel and tourism is expected to increase significantly, with growth from markets such as China and India;
◆ religious tourism—pilgrimages are growing drawcards and, as the 'baby boomers' of the West age, they are also expected to be seeking out religious destinations;
◆ shorter holidays—urban professionals are expected to utilise the convenience of Internet booking, and to increase the frequency of their holidays while making their stays shorter;
◆ student travel—this is expected to increase, especially as students undertake a range of academic pursuits (including field trips and language studies);
◆ women travel—this is expected to expand even more as more Pacific and Asian women gain tertiary qualifications, enter the workforce, and marry later;
◆ telecommuting—some suggest that the age of telecommuting will be a trend that reduces business travel the world over.

Figure 30.1 A good website, such as this one for Fraser Escape Backpackers and Four-wheel Drive Tours in Queensland, Australia, catches the eye and allows easy navigation through its features.

Thanks to David Sterling's IT Solutions for permission to reproduce part of their website

Whether these trends develop or not, it is certain that hospitality will continue to grow and take a greater share of the world's economy.

Changing technologies

Few analysts foresaw the exponential growth of the Internet, with its possibilities for online booking and information to challenge global distribution and marketing systems. In 1997, travel became the second-largest sector in online marketing, obtaining approximately a quarter of the United States market.[3]

The property's potential

Forecasting is relevant to the property's capacity to meet demand on its premises, facilities, staff, and finances. As a result of forecasts, management can plan for change and capitalise on growth opportunities through market development or product development.

A market is seldom as big as everyone expects. Because so much investment is involved—in premises, equipment, and people—it is better to err on the side of caution than optimism. However, the industry prospers on the hopes and enthusiasm of its participants, and this is why hospitality is arguably the world's most exciting industry.

Questions for discussion or revision

1 List the reasons for forecasting.
2 Explain the terms 'market demand', 'market potential', and 'market factors'.
3 Describe the main methodologies that are applied when forecasting demand.

Chapter Notes

Chapter 1 ◆ The Marketing Function

1. *Concise Oxford Dictionary*, 9th edn, p. 656.
2. Baker, K. & Huyton, J. 2001, *Hospitality Management—an Introduction*, Hospitality Press, Melbourne.
3. Gross domestic product (GDP), simply defined, is the sum total of all the production of goods and services—that is, the economic activity of an entity.
4. Davidson, J. & Spearritt, P. 2000, *Holiday Business—Tourism in Australia since 1870*, The Miegunyah Press, Melbourne, p. 351.
5. Estimates of the World Travel and Tourism Council for 1999.
6. For an extended treatment of 'B&Bs', refer to Dickman, S. & Maddock, M., 2000, *The Business of Bed and Breakfast*, Hospitality Press, Melbourne.
7. For an excellent source on statistics, readers can refer to the website of Travel and Tourism Intelligence at <www.t-ti.com>.
8. *New Shorter Oxford Dictionary*, CD version 1.0.03, Oxford University Press, Oxford.
9. Richardson, J. 1993, *Ecotourism and Nature-based Holidays*, Simon & Schuster Australia, Sydney, p. vi.
10. Arthur Andersen 1999, *The Hotel Industry Benchmark Survey*, p. 6.
11. Statistics from Arthur Andersen 1999, *The Hotel Industry Benchmark Survey*, October, p. 7.

Chapter 2 ◆ Hospitality and e-Commerce

1. Hensdill, C. 1996, 'Partnerships in Dining', *Hotels*, February 1996, p. 57.
2. Dickey, C. 1996, 'Niche for the Night', *Newsweek*, 9 December 1996, p. 71.
3. Nykiel, R. 1983, *Marketing in the Hospitality Industry*, CBI Publishing Inc., New York, pp 182–5.
4. Ibid., p. 10.
5. Gill, T. & Satyanarayan, S. 1995, 'Critics See Downside to Thai-style Ecotourism, *Nation*, 12 February, quoted by Dowling, R. K., 'Ecotourism in Southeast Asia: Appropriate Tourism or Environmental Appropriation', paper at the Third International Conference, 'Tourism and Hotel Industry in Indo-China and Southeast Asia', 4 June 1998.
6. Cover story, 'The Future is Now', *Hotel Asia Pacific*, Jan./Feb. 2000, pp 26–9.

7. Robichaux, M., ' "Competitor Intelligence"—a Grapevine to Rivals' Secrets', *Wall Street Journal*, 12 April 1989, p B2, quoted in Robbins, S. & Mukerji, D. 1994, *Managing Organisations*, 2nd edn, Prentice Hall of Australia P/L, Sydney, p. 167.

8. Readers can refer to the National Online Tourism Strategy website at <www.tourism.gov.au>.

9. Author not noted, *Fast Company*, September 2001, quoted at <www.customerservice.com>, May 2001.

10. An Intranet is a net within the Internet.

11. Currently, this service operates only in Germany.

12. *Australian*, 19 June 2001.

13. Gilley, B. & Crispin, S., writing in *Far Eastern Economic Review*, 7 May 2001.

14. Developed by an organisation called Digicash at <www.digicash.com>.

Chapter 3 ◆ The Marketing Mix

1. McCarthy, E., Perreault, W., Quester, P., Wilkinson, J. & Lee, K. 1994, *Basic Marketing—a Managerial Approach*, Richard D. Irwin Inc., Sydney, p. 73.

2. Tarras, J. 1990, 'Accuracy of Project Evaluation Projections, *Hospitality Review*, Spring 1990, pp 53–9.

3. Rushmore, S. 1996, 'Feasibility Studies: Fact or Fiction', *Lodging Hospitality*, October 1996, p. 14.

4. Nykiel, R. 1983, *Marketing in the Hospitality Industry*, CBI Publishing Inc., New York, p. 114.

5. McDonald, M. 1995, *Marketing Plans—How to Prepare Them and How to Use Them*, 3rd edn, Butterworth-Heinemann Ltd, Oxford, pp 3–4.

6. These characteristics are discussed in more detail in Kotler, P., Bowen, J. & Makens, J. 1996, *Marketing for Hospitality and Tourism*, Prentice Hall International Editions, New Jersey, pp 82–4.

7. See also Morrison, A. 1994, *Hospitality and Travel Marketing*, Delmar Publishers Inc., New York, p. 393.

Chapter 4 ◆ Market Analysis

1. This chapter provides an overview of market analysis. Other chapters cover the subject in more detail—especially Chapter 5 'Segmentation by Purchase Motivations', Chapter 7 'Target Marketing', and Chapter 14 'Marketing Audits and the Marketing Information System'.

2. Miller, K. & Layton, R. 2000, *Fundamentals of Marketing* 4th edn, Irwin/McGraw-Hill, Sydney, pp 214 ff.

3. Horwath International, and Smith Travel Research, quoted by Bailey, M. 1998, *The International Hotel Industry—Corporate Strategies and Global Opportunities*, Travel and Tourism Intelligence Research Report, 2nd edn, p. 13.

4. Plummer, A. 1992, 'Projected Growth in Technologies Required by a Teleresort', Pacific Asia Travel Association, PATA Conference 1992, San Francisco, pp 267–8.

5. Details reported in the *Australian*, 7 November 2000.

6. Kotler, P. 1994, *Marketing Management*, Prentice Hall International, New Jersey, p. 156.

7. According to Travel and Tourism Intelligence, quoted in Baker, K. & Huyton, J. 2001, *Hospitality Management—an Introduction*, Hospitality Press, Melbourne.

8. Davidson, J. & Spearritt, P. 2000, *Holiday Business—Tourism in Australia since 1870*, The Miegunyah Press, Melbourne, p. 354.

Chapter 5 ◆ Segmentation by Purchase Motivations

1. 'Cherry Ripe' (pseudonym) 1992, 'Food', *Australian*, 18–19 April.

2. Scoviak-Lerner, M. 1996, 'Market-Driven Design Trends for the Millennium', *Hotels*, May, p. 58.

Chapter 6 ◆ The Customer Mix

1. Bureau of Tourism Research, *Domestic Tourism Monitor 1995–96.*
2. Ibid.
3. Australian Bureau of Statistics, Catalogue number 8653.0—Travel Agency Services, Australia.
4. Davidson, J. & Spearritt, P. 2000, *Holiday Business—Tourism in Australia Since 1870*, The Miegunyah Press, Melbourne, p. 331.
5. The source of these statistics is Bureau of Tourism Research, <www.btr.gov.au>, from whom further information on this matter and other tourism data can be obtained.

Chapter 8 ◆ The Product Mix

1. Baker, K. & Huyton, J. 2001, *Hospitality Management—an Introduction*, Hospitality Press, Melbourne.
2. Dickey, C. 1996, 'Niche for the Night', *Newsweek*, 9 December 1996, p. 71.
3. Hensdill, C. 1996, 'Partnerships in Dining', *Hotels*, February 1996, p. 57.
4. Dickey, C. 1996, 'Niche for the Night', *Newsweek*, 9 December 1996, p. 71.

Chapter 9 ◆ The Service Concept in the e-Commerce Age

1. Berry, L. 1995, *On Great Service—a Framework for Action*, The Free Press, New York, p. 54.
2. Ibid., p. 69.

Chapter 10 ◆ Service Strategies

1. Noted by one of the authors several years ago. Original source no longer available.
2. The '15th Street Fisheries' restaurant of Fort Lauderdale, Florida, USA, has operated since 1979. Michael Hurst has been in the industry for fifty years. According to his website: 'Applying fun and a sense of humor to his business has helped make Hurst one of the country's most successful independent restaurateurs'. Further details can be found at the website at <www.15streetfisheries.com>.
3. Michael Hurst on 'Pizzaz', a training videotape sponsored by SPHC. For more on Hurst, see <www.15streetfisheries.com>.
4. As told to original author Neil Wearne, personal communication.
5. As told to original author Neil Wearne, personal communication.

Chapter 11 ◆ e-Commerce Strategies

1. *Canberra Times*, 17 May 1999.
2. The Travel Compensation Fund (TCF) was constituted by a trust established by the various state and territory governments of Australia (excluding the Northern Territory) in 1986. The TCF monitors the financial resources of licensed travel agents to ensure that they have sufficient financial worth to conduct business, and compensates persons who have suffered a financial loss when a travel agent has failed to account for money received.
3. Acknowledgment to <www.hotelmarketing.com/archive/triedtrue/customerdevcycle_1.htm>.
4. Search Engine Placement Myths, Hotel Marketing.Com, at <www.hotelmarketing.com/archive>.
5. <www.hotelmarketing.com/archive/cutpaste>, May 2001.
6. *Australian,* 19 June 2001.

Chapter 12 Marketing Management

1. Blanchard, K. & Lorber, R. 1993, *The One Minute Manager*, Berkley Publishing Group.

Chapter 13 ◆ The Planning Discipline

1. Nykiel, R. 1983, *Marketing in the Hospitality Industry*, Van Nostrand Reinhold, New York, pp 175 ff.

Chapter 14 ◆ Marketing Audits and Marketing Information Systems

1. The case study is based on real persons; the name has been changed.
2. Hotel manager's comment to one of the authors on the importance of timely information.

Chapter 16 ◆ Sustainable Competitive Advantage

1. de Bono, E. 1992, *Sur/petition—Creating Value Monopolies When Everyone Else is Merely Competing*, out of print.
2. Ries, A. & Trout, J. 1997, *Marketing Warfare*, McGraw-Hill Professional Publishing, New York.
3. de Bono, Edward, <www.sixhats.com/edsurpet.htm>, accessed 26 September 2001.
4. The Latin word is *competere*. It means 'striving together', or 'seeking together', or 'choosing to run in one race together'. Whichever meaning is preferred, the essential point for our purposes (and for de Bono) is that the competitors *choose* to compete in the one race, whereas de Bono advocates a more 'lateral' approach that seeks a distinctive difference.
5. Note de Bono's use of the term 'integrated value' in the quotation provided above.
6. Source: <www.nykline.co.jp>, accessed 26 September 2001.
7. Koldowski, J. 2000, 'Beyond 2000: Pacific Asia Tourism Forecast', *PATA Compass*, May–June 2000, p. 29.
8. Walker, J. 1996, *Introduction to Hospitality*, Prentice Hall, New Jersey, p. 34.
9. Robbins, S. & Mukerji, D. 1994, *Managing Organisations—New Challenges and Perspectives*, 2nd edn, Prentice Hall of Australia, Sydney, p. 167.
10. Personal communication with original author, Neil Wearne. For more on Hurst, see <www.15streetfisheries.com>.

Chapter 17 ◆ Positioning

1. And there is even the 'seven-star' style of the 202 luxury suites of the Burj Al Arab (the Arab Tower) Hotel in Dubai, opened in 1997.

Chapter 18 ◆ Local Hotel Strategies

1. Samuel Johnson 1776, *On the Scots*, p. 452, 22 March 1776.
2. The story was originally noted by one of the authors in the TAFE 'Open Learning Marketing and Promotion Course for Liquor Licensees'. Precise reference now unavailable.

Chapter 19 ◆ Strategic Solutions

1. Stoner, J. 1995, *Management*, 6th edn, Prentice Hall Inc., New Jersey, p. 242.

Chapter 20 ◆ Growth Strategies

1. Lewis, R. 1989, in Hart, C. & Troy, D. (eds) *Strategic Hotel/Motel Marketing*, Educational Institute of the American Hotel & Motel Association, Michigan, p. 212.
2. Source: <www.centra.com/aboutus>, accessed September 2001.

Chapter 21 ◆ Pricing Strategies

1. An extended discussion of pricing procedures is in Baker, K. 2000, *Project Evaluation and Feasibility Analysis*, Hospitality Press, Melbourne, ch. 10.
2. Coltman, M. 1998, *Hospitality Management Accounting*, Van Nostrand Reinhold, New York, p. 278.

Chapter 22 ◆ Promotion Strategies

1. Professor Peter Drucker is a noted authority on corporate management and author of *Management Challenges for the 21st Century*, Harperbusiness, New York.

Chapter 23 ◆ Inreach and Outreach Sales Tactics

1. Penoyer, F. 1997, *Teleselling Techniques that Close the Sale*, American Management Association, New York, p. 18.

Chapter 28 ◆ Direct Marketing Strategies

1. Penoyer, F. 1997, *Teleselling Techniques that Close the Sale*, American Management Association, New York, p. 12.
2. Noted at <www.hotelmarketing.com>, June 2001.
3. Quoted in the *Australian*, 9 June 2001.
4. Lewis Carroll, *The Hunting of the Snark*, Fit 1. The Landing.

Chapter 29 ◆ Product Development Strategies

1. Personal communication with original author, Neil Wearne. For more on Hurst, see <www.15streetfisheries.com>.
2. Personal communication with original author, Neil Wearne. For more on Hurst, see <www.15streetfisheries.com>.
3. Personal communication with original author, Neil Wearne.

Chapter 30 ◆ Forecasting Market Demand

1. Koldowski, J. 2000, 'Beyond 2000: Pacific Asia Tourism Forecast', *PATA Compass*, May–June 2000, pp 22–4.
2. Muqbil, I. 2000, '100 Points on the Horizon—Issues that will Change the Face of Travel and Tourism', *PATA Compass*, Hong Kong, May/June, pp 26 ff.
3. Forrester Research, quoted in Travel and Tourism Intelligence (1998), *The International Hotel Industry*, p. 152.

Index